Gender, Crime

Lizzie Seal

Gender, Crime and Justice

palgrave
macmillan

Lizzie Seal
School of Law, Politics and Sociology
University of Sussex
Brighton, UK

ISBN 978-3-030-87487-2   ISBN 978-3-030-87488-9   (eBook)
https://doi org/10.1007/978-3-030-87488-9

This Palgrave Macmillan imprint is published by the registered company Springer Nature Switzerland
AG
The registered company address is: Gewerbestrasse 11, 6330 Cham, Switzerland

For my mother, Susan Jean Seal 1948–2021

Contents

1

Introduction

This book looks at crime and punishment through the lens of gender. Crime and punishment are incredibly gendered facets of social life. Two enduring facts illustrate this: most recorded crime is committed by men and most people in prison and under other forms of criminal justice supervision are men. In England and Wales in 2019, 74% prosecutions were of men and 26% were of women (Ministry of Justice, 2020). For violent crime, the differences are especially stark. In 2017, men in Canada were nearly four times more likely to be accused of a violent crime than women and 95% of people accused of sexual assault were men (Savage, 2019). Women are only 7% of the prison population worldwide (Walmsley, 2017). The significance of these glaring gender disparities pertains to criminology. However, these disparities are not the only reason to examine crime, punishment and justice through a gendered lens. Gender differences in the commission of crime and the application of punishment, and differences in how deviance and transgression are understood in relation to femininity and masculinity, are crucial to how gender is socially constructed and reproduced. Before exploring the significance of gender to criminology further, it is necessary to consider what gender actually is.

© The Author(s), under exclusive license to Springer Nature
Switzerland AG 2022
L. Seal, *Gender, Crime and Justice*,
https://doi.org/10.1007/978-3-030-87488-9_1

What Is Gender?

Gender is both a form of identity and a social practice. It is created in the policies and practices of social institutions, through social and intimate interactions between people and by representations, such as in the media (Yuval-Davis, 2006). Femininity and masculinity are constructed in relation to each other (Connell, 1999). To say that gender is constructed is not to say that understandings of femininity or masculinity have been created and then fixed. It is to acknowledge that they are subject to ongoing processes of negotiation and recreation (Ferree et al., 1999; Messerschmidt, 2013). Gender is made actively—it is something that people do, accomplish and perform (Butler, 1990; Messerschmidt, 2013; West & Zimmerman, 1987). Gender identity is never 'finished', rather it is a continuous project (Connell, 1999).

The active creation of gender is not free or unconstrained as it takes place in the context of well-established and unequal power relations (Messerschmidt, 2013; West & Zimmerman, 1987). There are ideal, dominant versions of femininity and masculinity that influence how gender is enacted and regulated by institutions, in social interactions, in representations and in individuals' own imaginations (Connell, 1987). These ideal versions are not fixed or universally agreed upon but have a profound effect on people's lives (Scott, 1988). The expectation that femininity entails mothering and that women should do most of the caring for small children shapes the kinds of provision for childcare offered by governments and employers, and their policies of parental leave. It influences the arrangements within families around who does paid work and childcare and how much. It is perpetuated in cultural portrayals of mothering and affects how women themselves feel about motherhood. This normative expectation can be subverted, rejected or simply unmet, but its institutionalised, intersubjective and representational effects are real and frequently constraining.

Gender is, however, not only a constraint. Its dynamic nature means it is also a resource, something that can be deployed strategically for a particular end (Miller, 2002). Neuhouser (2008) explores how women community activists in Brazil strategically deployed a mothering identity to campaign for material improvements in housing, water, electricity, healthcare and traffic lights. They argued these improvements were needed to adequately care for their families. In Miller's (1998) research on gender differences in street robberies, she found that men used the threat of physical violence to intimidate victims, whereas women feigned sexual interest in male victims to make them let their guard down.

Idealised versions of femininity and masculinity, and of women and men, are not descriptions of actual people (Scott, 1999). They are forms of regulation that operate in all areas of life, from the foreign policymaking of governments to the clothing worn by individuals. Although femininity and masculinity are relational, in that one cannot exist without the other, the distinction between them is not static. Gender is embodied, but it is not embodied essentially in the sense that only women are feminine and only men are masculine, or that individuals consistently embody either femininity or masculinity. Sexed differences—women and men inhabiting bodies with or without certain specific characteristics—are also complex and are not separable from gender (Butler, 2004). How women and men are defined and recognised as two separate categories is socially, historically and politically produced, rather than 'natural' or biological (Scott, 1999). Gender relates to bodies and what they do, but cannot be reduced to particular bodily functions or attributes (Connell, 1999).

Gender is complex and cannot be conceptualised solely through reference to the binary of femininity and masculinity. This binary division is frequently naturalised but has not been stable across all times and places, and does not encompass all gender identities. Transgender and gender non-conforming incorporate a range of identities and lived experiences, including non-binary identities (Hines, 2010; Monro, 2019). Non-binary and gender non-conforming people may have no gender, fluid gender or a stable gender identity that is not feminine or masculine (Richards et al., 2017). Gender variance exists across societies and cultures; in India and South Asia, the Pacific Islands and among certain Indigenous societies in North and Central America there are three genders (Mirandé, 2016). Even with regard to binary gender, the meanings attached to what a woman is and what a man is—what they look like, how they behave and what they should think or feel—vary greatly, not just across historical periods and cultures, but also within societies and between individuals.

Making Gender Through Crime and Punishment

Gender is highly relevant to understanding crime and punishment, but exactly how it becomes significant requires explanation and analysis. Committing crime, particularly violent crime, is more culturally consistent with masculinity than it is with femininity (Seal, 2010). Masculinity is closely associated with risk-taking and with physical strength and prowess, while femininity is associated with gentleness and conformity. Men who engage in violent behaviour may sometimes do so to affirm their manliness through gaining respect and saving face in situations where they are challenged. In this sense, violence is a way of accomplishing masculinity (Messerschmidt, 2013). On the other hand, for women to accomplish femininity, they must refrain from violence to avoid crossing appropriate boundaries of feminine behaviour.

There are limitations to interpreting crime and other forms of behaviour as motivated by fulfilling norms of gender (Miller, 2002). The spur of the moment and reactive nature of much violence indicates that it is not enacted straightforwardly to 'accomplish' a particular identity. Violent crime does not actually constitute normative behaviour for men, and why some men seek to demonstrate masculinity through violence and others do not remains unexplained (Gadd, 2002). Women's violence is difficult, if not impossible, to comprehend through an interpretation of behaviour as gender accomplishment. Violence contravenes dominant idealised femininity, which connotes peacefulness and nurturance (Miller, 2002). Interpreting crimes as a route to accomplishing normative gender identities also entails circular reasoning—violence is masculine so men commit violence to achieve masculinity (Hood-Williams, 2001). This interpretation overlooks the diverse range of femininities and masculinities, and while some are more culturally dominant or approved, not everyone enacts or identifies with these versions.

Gender performance is only partly intentional (Butler, 1990). Much of the time, individuals do not reflect on the gendered implications of their appearance, interactions and behaviour. Even if they do, they do not necessarily strive to meet normative expectations. In this sense, gender identity does not offer much explanation for why individuals do or do not commit certain crimes at all. However, gender identity involves work at the institutional, intersubjective and representational levels and this has relevance to crime and punishment.

Gender is structural and political, which shapes how it is lived. Gendered actions and inactions take place within situated and structural constraints and possibilities (Miller, 2002). Massive financial corruption or mismanagement can only be perpetrated by people with the necessary knowledge, opportunity and access—which is disproportionately upper middle-class white men (Steffensmeier et al., 2013). Understanding how these crimes and harms are gendered is not only a matter of who has the opportunity to perpetrate them but also requires attention to the context of masculinised working cultures, and gendered power and privilege under capitalism (Griffin, 2013).

Gendered social position, power and privilege intertwine with processes of criminalisation. In the example of largescale financial mismanagement and corruption, the perpetrators are frequently not criminalised. This can be because there is inadequate compliance by companies with ethics standards, lack of enforcement by the authorities or because forms of financial mismanagement that are extremely harmful are not necessarily illegal (Hillyard & Tombs, 2007; O'Brien & Dixon, 2013). Occupying a privileged and powerful position—such as upper middle class white man—insulates individuals against criminalisation and punishment.

Gendered social marginalisation makes people vulnerable to criminalisation. In the UK, penalties for television licence evasion (the licence is mandatory with ownership of a television, computer or smartphone) disproportionately affect poor women. Enquiry Officers call during the day, when women are more likely to be at home due to their domestic routines. Initially, they face a fine for not having paid the licence, which is in itself a result of poverty. Defaulting on the fine can lead to a short prison sentence. In 2019, women accounted for 74% of convictions for television licence evasion in England and Wales (Ministry of Justice, 2020). It is numerically the most common crime of which women are convicted in the UK. This example demonstrates the gendered effects of what Pantazis and Gordon (1997) termed 'the crim-inalisation of poverty', and that levels of criminalisation often do not correlate to levels of harmfulness.

Issues of structural privilege and disadvantage relate to the different ways people are subject to the law and social control. Cultural representations of gender intervene and affect the kinds of controls exerted over different social groups. This is where it is useful to return to the significance of normative conceptions of gender. In late nineteenth-century England, men's violence against women was prosecuted more frequently and punishments became more severe. This instantiated a respectable working class masculinity against which such violence was unacceptable (Weiner, 2005). The Magdalene laundries of mid twentieth-century Ireland were confining institutions specifically for women. They were based on interpretations of young women's sexuality as troublesome and the need to uphold the purity of Irish womanhood (Seal & O'Neill, 2019).

How individuals' behaviour is understood is filtered through the lens of gender and involves the assignation of gendered attributes. The same behaviour from women and men can be interpreted differently through gendered understandings (Lorber, 1994). Women may not intend any particular gendered performance in using violence but, in the criminal justice system and in the media, are likely to be portrayed as violating norms of femininity and as therefore deviant (Seal, 2010). How gender is understood, what is perceived as a good or approved performance of femininity or of masculinity in different situations, is crucial to making gender. The categorisation of gendered attributes as feminine or masculine cements the gender binary, which is institutionally reproduced. When it comes to the actions of the police, what happens in the courts and how punishment is organised, gendered performance is both enacted and regulated. This has significant implications, from how the police treat suspects and victims, to sentencing in court, to the kinds of regimes found in prisons. Prisons are a paradigmatic example of the institutionalised gender binary.

Gendering Criminology

Feminist criminologists were the first to pay explicit attention to the relevance of gender to crime and punishment. A body of research developed in the 1970s and 80s that argued 'malestream' criminology had neglected women, both as offenders and victims, while ignoring the relevance of gender to criminological questions (Gelsthorpe & Morris, 1988; Klein, 1973; Smart, 1976) (Anderson, 1976; Chesney-Lind, 1986) Concepts such as respectability, 'double deviance' and 'regimes of femininity' enabled feminist criminologists to highlight the significance of gender regulation in the law and the criminal justice system. Kruttschnitt (1982) found that women who were perceived as disreputable received harsher sentences from the courts. Heidensohn (1985) coined 'double deviance' to encapsulate how women who commit crime are judged to have violated both the law and idealised standards of gender. Carlen (1983) used the concept of 'regimes of femininity' to elucidate how women's prisons attempted to reform women by training them in gender normative activities, such as cooking and sewing, and valued traditionally feminine behaviour, such as passivity, as evidence of rehabilitation. Women's experiences as victim/survivors of men's violence, coupled with analyses of gendered power differences, developed as a major strand of feminist criminological research, closely related to feminist praxis (Dobash & Dobash, 1979; Klein, 1981).

Following the emergence of men's studies in the 1980s, criminologists in the 1990s turned their attention to men as gendered beings and explored the significance of masculinity to crime and punishment (Kersten, 1993; Stanko & Newburn, 1994; Tomsen, 1996). Messerschmidt (1993) employed Connell's (1987) concept of 'hegemonic masculinity' to explore issues of men, masculinity and crime. Hegemonic masculinity is the most dominant form of masculinity, against which femininity and other forms of masculinity are subordinate or opposed. What constitutes hegemonic masculinity is not fixed, but in Western societies has entailed whiteness, heterosexuality, being in paid employment—especially professional or managerial level occupations—and subordinating women, girls and LGBTQ people. Connell (1987) described this form of masculinity as 'hegemonic' to encapsulate how it secured power through cultural norms.

Criminologists have argued hegemonic masculinity can influence criminal and other forms of harmful behaviour. This can be valuing and striving for success in a competitive business or professional environment (Levi, 1994; Messerschmidt, 2013), or crime as a solution to subordinate masculinity, where a measure of success or status is attained through illegal means, such as acquisitive crime to fulfil the traditional 'bread-winner' role (Messerschmidt, 1993). Criminologists have also examined the significance of cultural ideals of masculinity in the 'ultramasculine' world of men's prisons (Bandyopadhyay, 2006; Newton, 1994; Sabo et al., 2001).

It is no longer the case that either women or gender as a social identity are ignored by criminologists (Cook, 2016; Kruttschnitt, 2016). Reducing and eliminating gender-based violence against women is a flourishing area of research, as well as of national and international policymaking (Buzawa & Buzawa, 2017; Westmarland, 2015). Knowledge of men's gendered victimisation is a less well developed but growing area (Hester, 2013; Lombard, 2013), and there is a well-established literature on the gendered victimisation of LGBTQ people (Hester et al., 2010; Perry & Dyck, 2014).

Criminologists examine the ways gender structures how women and men live their lives and how this leads them to commit different types of crimes, or to be criminalised in different ways. The gendered pathways approach entails assessing how the routes into crime are influenced by gendered experiences such as relationships, experiences of abuse and limited access to employment and housing (Belknap & Holsinger, 2006; Russell et al., 2020; Wattanaporn & Holtfreter, 2014). Feminist criminologists have emphasised the links between the criminalisation and prior victimisation of women and girls, and such links are also relevant to men and boys (DeHart & Lynch, 2013). To gain a nuanced understanding of gendered pathways to crime, it is necessary to incorporate attention to how individuals exercise agency and their experience of structural constraints (Daly, 1998).

Research employing biographical methods and narrative analysis has explored how women and men make sense of their experiences of lawbreaking, victimisation and punishment in relation to lived experiences of gender, and their understandings of gender identity. Carlen's

(1985) collection of four autobiographical accounts by women who had spent time in prison pioneered this approach. O'Neill's (2001) ethnographic life history work explores women's involvement in sex work through listening to their narratives about their lives and working lives. Goodey (2000) advocates situating individual biographical accounts of men's criminal lives in their socio-historical context in order to understand the significance of masculinity. Psychosocial criminology employs psychoanalytic interpretations of life histories to augment understanding of gendered masculine subjectivity (Gadd, 2002). The stories that women and men tell about themselves offer ways for them to relate gendered experiences of lawbreaking and help to create gender identity, as well as providing insight into why individuals act in the way do (Fleetwood, 2015; Presser, 2012).

Researching women and men as gendered beings with gendered experiences, and analysing gender regulation through constructions of femininity and masculinity, are accepted and well established within criminology. So far, criminologists have paid comparatively little attention to trans and non-binary gender identities, particularly beyond the issues of victimisation through violence and experiences of imprisonment—although this is changing (see Colliver et al., 2019; Jones, 2020). As Buist and Lenning (2015) highlight, gender expression is heavily regulated and frequently criminalised. Beyond empirical work, it is necessary to consider the conceptual and theoretical importance of gender nonconformity to the ways criminologists understand gender regulation. Ball (2016) recommends utilising the disruptive and deconstructive aspects of queer theory in order to do so.

Although criminology as a discipline no longer neglects gender, there are influential, widely cited critical theoretical works from the past two decades that do not include gendered analysis. Heidensohn (2012) mentions as examples 'the culture of control' (Garland, 2001), the insecurity of late modernity (Young, 2007) and the relationship between neoliberalism and punishment (Wacquant, 2009). A gender lens can be applied in order to modify and further develop these arguments (Gelsthorpe, 2004; Kruttschnitt et al., 2013; Naegler & Salman, 2016; Roberts, 2014), but their neglect of gender indicates that there is still a criminological 'malestream'.

What Is Intersectionality?

Gender is the predominant focus of this book, but gender is always modified by other aspects of social identity such as race, class, age, dis/ability and citizenship. Everyone has multiple social identities that affect and interact with their social position and their lived experiences (Davis, 2008; Nash, 2008; Phoenix & Pattynama, 2006). To know someone's gender identity by itself tells us relatively little as one identity category is always permeated by others (Cho et al., 2013). Intersectionality is an approach that captures this multiplicity and enables analysis of its relevance to the social world (Collins & Bilge, 2016). The term was devised by critical race theorist and feminist Crenshaw (1989) as a metaphor for the ways an analytical focus on gender or race alone detrimentally affected Black women. In relation to employment law, she highlighted how Black men were able to challenge discrimination based on race and white women were able to challenge discrimination based on gender, but Black women were not able to mobilise either argument. Black women, who occupied the point at which gender and race intersected, did not have their experiences of discrimination recognised by the law. Furthermore, forms of identity politics that treated race and gender as mutually exclusive could not adequately account for this lack of recognition—or seek to remedy it.

Although Crenshaw (1989) invented the term 'intersectionality', her analysis built on arguments that were historically well established within Black feminism in the United States, especially the point that white feminists frequently neglected race and male anti-racists frequently neglected gender (Carastathis, 2014; Cooper, 2016). Feminists such as hooks (1981), Davis (1981) and Collins (1986) had argued for the need to analyse the interactions between race, class and gender, contending that failure to do so disadvantaged Black women as well as erasing the history of their intellectual work and political activism.

In Britain, Anthias and Yuval-Davis (1992) criticised the notion of 'triple oppression'—the perception that prejudice based on race, gender and class added together to entrench inequality. Instead, they argued that oppression along one axis of identity, such as gender, intermeshed with other social divisions, such as race and class. This is a crucial analytical contribution of intersectionality. It recognises that one aspect of identity is relationally shaped by others and helps to account for difference (Collins & Bilge, 2016; Prins, 2006; Yuval-Davis, 2006). For example, the intersection of gender and age means that the femininity of women in their twenties is constructed very differently from the femininity of women in their sixties. Femininity and age are deeply enmeshed and cannot be pulled apart.

Intersectionality involves attention to power relations: to dominance and oppression, to opportunity and constraint. It also recognises the complexity of these relations, which can be conceptualised at the institutional, intersubjective and representational levels (Anthias, 2013; Yuval-Davis, 2006). Identities and social positioning are fluid rather than fixed (Cho et al., 2013). This does not mean that people have free choice or total control over their lives, or simply shift identity at will. They are constrained by their social position and sedimented power relations (Collins, 2019). However, identities, social positioning and power relations change over time due to a range of factors such as government policies, employment, relationships and shifting cultural mores.

Identities, social positioning and power relations are also fluid in the context of particular interactions and social settings (Cho et al., 2013; Yuval-Davis, 2006). Individuals may have more or less power, more or less status or influence, in different areas of life, for example, their status within their family and their status at work might be very different. They may embody aspects of identity usually associated with privilege, such as masculinity, while also embodying aspects associated with disadvantage such as disability, with the intersections between these being crucial to understand (Coston & Kimmel, 2012). Intersectionality highlights how certain strands of identity can be more salient in one situation than they are in another (Anthias, 2013).

Black feminists developed intersectionality as a way to better analyse the life experiences and subordination of Black women and other women of colour, and as a basis for activism to challenge this subordination (Cho et al., 2013; Collins & Bilge, 2016). The success of intersectionality as a perspective and as a way of doing politics means that use of the term has extended beyond its origins and intersectionality sometimes becomes a depoliticised 'buzzword', employed even where issues of race and power are neglected (Collins, 2019; Davis, 2008). Given intersectionality's roots in Black feminism and critical race theory, this depoliticisation has been criticised as deeply problematic (Bilge, 2014).

There is no set way to deploy intersectionality, rather it is done best in relation to specific contexts (Bilge, 2014). Carbado (2013) argues that, as a perspective, intersectionality does not inherently prioritise one social category or particular intersection of categories as its focus. There is no reason why a perspective originally developed by and about Black women cannot have a wider application, although its roots in Black feminism and critical race theory remain imperative. An intersectional approach can examine intersections of privilege, as well as of subordination. However, in order to carry out useful intersectional analysis, attention to power differences is needed. This is important as dominant or privileged identities are frequently less visible than subordinated ones; for example, whiteness is naturalised by its invisibility and this is a crucial aspect of its dominance in the racial order (Carbado, 2013).

Intersectionality is not only an academic approach but also a form of 'critical praxis', which aims to challenge inequalities in daily life and transform power relations. Praxis is the linking of scholarship and activism in ways that inform each other (Cho et al., 2013; Collins & Bilge, 2016). Activism and organising for change based on intersectionality involves building alliances across different groups and entails considering which groups need to be included to bring change about (Collins, 2019). Bringing about transformation that reduces inequalities, challenges power differentials and promotes social justice is consistent with long-standing aims of feminist and anti-racist criminology (Chesney-Lind & Morash, 2013; Daly, 2005).

Intersectional Criminology

Prior to the explicit adoption of 'intersectionality', criminologists, particularly in the United States, had adopted a 'class-race-gender' approach in order to analyse multiple, overlapping inequalities (Daly, 1993; Schwartz & Milovanovic, 1999). Criminologists have increasingly embraced intersectionality as an integrative analysis of gender, race and class, and used it to examine the complex relationships between hierarchies, crime and justice (Barak et al., 2010; Burgess-Proctor, 2006). Sokoloff and Burgess-Proctor (2011) argue that feminist criminology needs to be intersectional. British feminist criminology in particular has paid more attention to intersections of gender and class than it has to intersections of gender and race, and a consciously intersectional approach is a way to change this (Parmar, 2017). Carlen (1990) critiqued feminist criminology's inability to adequately explain that women's lawbreaking is mainly minor, that women in prison are disproportionately women of colour, and disproportionately poor. An intersectional approach is a means to grapple with these multiple elements of women's imprisonment.

Intersectionality's attention to multiple dimensions of social disadvantage and privilege is indispensable for the study of crime and punishment (Trahan, 2011). Bernard (2013) employs intersectionality along with 'doing gender' to analyse the life story of a Black Jamaican woman incarcerated for drug related crimes, and how doing identity involved navigating multiple power structures and interlocking oppression. Historically, criminology's focus has largely been on the oppressed and subordinate—those sanctioned by the state and those who are victims of crimes—and intersectional analysis enables the marginalised to be centred (Henne & Troshynski, 2013; Sokoloff & Burgess-Proctor, 2011). Intersectionality is also applicable to studying crimes of the powerful as this too involves attention to power, privilege and the perpetration of oppression.

An intersectional approach can challenge the default 'whitemaleness' of criminological theorising, through recognition of plurality and rejection of essentialist notions of identity (Potter, 2015). The deep roots of state punishment in racism and colonialism, and the role of social control and punishment in upholding national boundaries and creating exclusionary citizenship mean that such issues must be centred along with gender (Parmar, 2017). In her research on British Asian men's interactions with the police, Parmar (2017) found that racialisation was related to intersections of citizenship, belonging and nationality. Irvine (2014) discovered trans people of colour in New Orleans were significantly more likely than white cis and trans people to experience negative treatment from the police. She argues feminist criminology must include trans and non-conforming gender identities in its understanding of gender and also be committed to intersectional perspectives that incorporate race.

The legacy of Western colonialism is a relatively neglected area of feminist criminological analysis, especially in British Criminology—an oversight given Britain's role as the dominant colonial power in the late nineteenth and early twentieth-centuries. This neglect impoverishes feminist criminology as gendered, racialised and classed identities and social positioning reflect histories of colonial domination. Choak (2020) calls for a Black and Postcolonial Feminist Criminology that opposes the 'criminological amnesia' about the discipline's roots in colonialism and which includes attention to the full panoply of intersectional identities in its work. Feminist criminology must analyse the various ways colonialism continues to shape approaches to crime and punishment in the present.

Recent debates have addressed whether certain feminist perspectives and approaches to crime and punishment, and their influence on policy and practice, have ultimately been harmful, especially when they do not incorporate analysis of the interweaving of racism and state power. These debates are not new but have gained strength in the context of abolitionist and intersectional critiques of mainstream feminism (Phipps, 2016, 2020). Carceral feminism refers to perspectives, forms of activism, policies and practices that seek to achieve gender justice through law enforcement, militarism and criminal justice-based solutions. Examples include criminalisation of the perpetrators of domestic violence and abuse through policies related to arrest and sentencing to state punishment (Kim, 2018), and anti-trafficking measures that combine carceral politics with militarisation (Bernstein, 2010).

Carceral approaches perceive state and legal systems as neutral, which neglects the violence that state punishment perpetrates and the ways that the criminal justice system enacts repression (Whalley & Hackett, 2017). Belief in the potential of the criminal justice, immigration control or security systems to protect women pursues a colonial logic of women as victims in need of protection, which primarily benefits white cis women at the expense of racialised women and men (Bernstein, 2012). Carceral feminism has been implicated in the expansion of racialised state-based control, including through mass incarceration in the United States (Brady & Sarah, 2017). This expansion has disadvantaged women, particularly women of colour, as carceral anti-domestic violence, anti-sex work and anti-trafficking policies and practices have had the effect of criminalising the people they were supposedly designed to protect (Whalley & Hackett, 2017).

An intersectional approach to feminism can recognise the importance of interlocking systems of power, and the deep connections between state-based control, colonialism and racism (Saleh-Hanna, 2015). Feminism has a history both of challenging institutionalised state power and of complicity with imperial power structures. In feminist criminology, there are anti-carceral traditions derived from opposition to women's imprisonment (Carlton, 2018) and critiques of the masculinist power of the law (Smart, 2002), but there are also more pro-carceral traditions that advocate policing and punishment to limit violence against women. Now that criminology has awakened from its 'androcentric slumber' (Cook, 2016) it is crucial to interrogate the impact of the politics of gender in criminology, and the ways power can operate through such politics.

Overview and Structure

Gender, Crime and Justice takes an intersectional and inclusive approach to exploring the significance of gender to a range of criminological topics. It understands gender as constructed, multiple and not necessarily binary, but also as a diverse lived experience. It aims to examine the current state of the field in relation to gender, crime and punishment through reference to global research. Informed by critiques of carceral feminism, the book is distinguished by its intention to take a critical perspective towards gendered state-based interventions and punishments, which incorporates attention to the importance of racism and colonialism to their development.

Another distinguishing feature of Gender, Crime and Justice is its use of films, television series and documentaries to further illustrate the discussion of the topics. This approach is informed by Rafter and Brown's (2011) popular criminology, a perspective which pays attention to how popular cultural forms, such as films and television programmes, represent and analyse crime and punishment. Popular criminology complements and extends academic criminology. A far greater number of people engage with popular criminology than academic criminology, making it arguably of greater social significance. Sources such as films raise questions of justice and enable viewers to imagine alternatives beyond their immediate reality. Sources of popular criminology can offer critiques of inequality and injustice, but they can also reinforce the status quo and perpetuate harmful stereotypes (Kohm & Greenhill, 2011). Frequently, popular sources have multiple messages, some of which have liberatory potential and some of which are conservative (O'Neill & Seal, 2012).

The book also draws on Seal and O'Neill's (2019) imaginative criminology, which argues analysis of fictional and popular sources extends our criminological imagination. Cultural representations of gender, crime and punishment—and associated questions of justice—are part of most people's everyday lived experience of these phenomena. We can use films, television series and documentaries to think through and about these issues, while retaining a critical perspective on the portrayals they construct.

Chapter 2 takes an intersectional feminist perspective towards interpersonal violence, namely domestic violence and abuse, and homicide. Drawing on Collins (1998, 2017), it analyses violence as something which binds systems of domination together. Chapter 3 continues this analysis and applies it to sexual violence. Chapter 4 examines the significance of gendered space and moral geographies to sex work and the night-time economy and Chapter 5 assesses the gendered aspects of street crime, gangs and drugs in the context of the street as both a space and a culture. Chapter 6 brings attention to gendering the crimes of powerful, focusing in particular on corporate crime, green crime and genocide. The book turns to the criminal justice system with Chapter 7, which examines gendered issues of control and authority in relation to policing and the courts. Chapter 8 analyses punishment as a form of gendered social control, addressing imprisonment and community penalties. Chapter 9 extends the analysis to the 'extreme' punishments of immigration detention, whole life sentences and the death penalty. This chapter includes a discussion of anti-carceral feminism and queer abolitionism, which encourage us to imagine hopeful futures. Chapter 10 concludes the book with reflections on how research on gender, crime and justice can be taken forward.

References

Anderson, E. A. (1976). The "Chivalrous" treatment of the female offender in the arms of the criminal justice system: A review of the literature. *Social Problems, 23*(3), 350–357.

Anthias, F. (2013). Intersectional what? Social divisions, intersectionality and levels of analysis. *Ethnicities, 13*(1), 3–19.

Ball, M. (2016). *Criminology and queer theory: Dangerous bedfellows?* Springer.

Bandyopadhyay, M. (2006). Competing masculinities in a prison. *Men and Masculinities, 9*(2), 186–203.

Barak, G., Leighton, P., & Flavin, J. (2010). *Class, race, gender, and crime: The social realities of justice in America.* Rowman and Littlefield.

Belknap, J., & Holsinger, K. (2006). The gendered nature of risk factors for delinquency. *Feminist Criminology, 1*(1), 48–71.

Bernard, A. (2013). The intersectional alternative: explaining female criminality. *Feminist Criminology, 8*(1), 3–19.

Bernstein, E. (2010). Militarized humanitarianism meets carceral feminism: The politics of sex, rights, and freedom in contemporary antitrafficking campaigns. *Signs: Journal of Women in Culture and Society, 36*(1), 45–71.

Bernstein, E. (2012). Carceral politics as gender justice? The "traffic in women" and neoliberal circuits of crime, sex, and rights. *Theory and Society, 41*(3), 233–259.

Bilge, S. (2014). Intersectionality undone: Saving intersectionality from feminist intersectionality studies. *Du Bois Review: Social Science Research on Race, 10*(2), 405–424.

Brady, T. H., & Sarah, K. T. (2017). Feminism and the carceral state: Gender-responsive justice, community accountability, and the epistemology of antiviolence. *Feminist Philosophy Quarterly, 3*(1).

Buist, C., & Lenning, E. (2015). *Queer criminology.* Routledge.

Burgess-Proctor, A. (2006). Intersections of race, class, gender, and crime: Future directions for feminist criminology. *Feminist Criminology, 1*(1), 27–47.

Butler, J. (1990). *Gender trouble*. Routledge.

Butler, J. (2004). *Undoing gender*. Routledge.

Buzawa, E. S., & Buzawa, C. G. (2017). *Global responses to domestic violence*. Springer.

Carastathis, A. (2014). The concept of intersectionality in feminist theory. *Philosophy Compass, 9*(5), 304–314.

Carbado, D. W. (2013). Colorblind intersectionality. *Signs: Journal of Women in Culture and Society, 38*(4), 811–845.

Carlen, P. (1983). *Women's imprisonment: A study in social control*. Routledge & Kegan Paul London.

Carlen, P. (1985). *Criminal women: Autobiographical accounts*. Polity Press.

Carlen, P. (1990). Women, crime, feminism, and realism. *Social Justice, 17*(4)(42), 106–123.

Carlton, B. (2018). Penal reform, anti-carceral feminist campaigns and the politics of change in women's prisons, Victoria, Australia. *Punishment & Society, 20*(3), 283–307.

Chesney-Lind, M. (1986). "Women and Crime": The female offender. *Signs, 12*(1), 78–96.

Chesney-Lind, M., & Morash, M. (2013). Transformative feminist criminology: A critical re-thinking of a discipline. *Critical Criminology, 21*(3), 287–304.

Cho, S., Crenshaw, K. W., & L. McCall (2013). Toward a field of intersectionality studies: Theory, applications, and praxis. *Signs: Journal of Women in Culture and Society, 38*(4), 785–810.

Choak, C. (2020). British criminological amnesia: Making the case for a Black and postcolonial feminist criminology. *Decolonization of Criminology and Justice, 2*(1), 37–58.

Collins, P. H. (1986). Learning from the outsider within: The sociological significance of Black feminist thought. *Social Problems, 33*(6), s14–s32.

Collins, P. H. (1998). The tie that binds: Race, gender and US violence. *Ethnic and Racial Studies, 21*(5), 917–938.

Collins, P. H. (2017). On violence, intersectionality and transversal politics. *Ethnic and Racial Studies, 40*(9), 1460–1473.

Collins, P. H. (2019). The difference that power makes: Intersectionality and participatory democracy. *The palgrave handbook of intersectionality in public policy* (pp. 167–192). New York, Springer.

Collins, P. H., & Bilge, S. (2016). *Intersectionality*. Polity Press.

Colliver, B., Coyle, A., & Silvestri, M. (2019). *The 'online othering' of transgender people in relation to 'gender neutral toilets'* (pp. 215–237). Springer.

Connell, R. (1987). *Gender and power*. Blackwell.

Connell, R. W. (1999). Making gendered people. In M. Ferree, J. Lorber, & B. B. Hess (Eds.), *Revisioning gender* (pp. 449–471). Sage.

Cook, K. J. (2016). Has criminology awakened from its "Androcentric Slumber"? *Feminist Criminology, 11*(4), 334–353.

Cooper, B. (2016). Intersectionality. In L. a. H. Disch, M. (Eds.), *The Oxford handbook of feminist theory* (pp. 385–406). Oxford University Press.

Coston, B. M., & Kimmel, M. (2012). Seeing privilege where it isn't: Marginalized masculinities and the intersectionality of privilege. *Journal of Social Issues, 68*(1), 97–111.

Crenshaw, K. (1989). Demarginalizing the intersection of race and sex: A Black feminist critique of antidiscrimination doctrine, feminist theory and antiracist politics. *University of Chicago Legal Forum, 1989*, 139.

Daly, K. (1993). Class-race-gender: Sloganeering in search of meaning. *Social Justice, 20*(1/2) (51–52), 56–71.

Daly, K. (1998). Gender, crime, and criminology. *The handbook of crime and punishment* (85–108).

Daly, K. (2005). *Seeking justice in the 21st century: The contested politics of race and gender*. Griffith University.

Davis, A. Y. (1981). *Women, race and class*. Random House.

Davis, K. (2008). Intersectionality as buzzword: A sociology of science perspective on what makes a feminist theory successful. *Feminist Theory, 9*(1), 67–85.

DeHart, D., & Lynch, S. M. (2013). *Gendered pathways to crime: The relationship between victimization and offending* (pp. 138–156). Routledge.

Dobash, R. E., & Dobash, R. (1979). *Violence against wives: A case against patriarchy*. Free Press.

Ferree, M., Lorber, J., Hess, & Beth B. (1999). Introduction.In M. Ferree, J. Lorber, & B. B. Hess. *Revisioning gender* (pp. xi–xxxvi). Sage.

Fleetwood, J. (2015). A narrative approach to women's lawbreaking. *Feminist Criminology, 10*(4), 368–388.

Gadd, D. (2002). Masculinities and violence against female partners. *Social & Legal Studies, 11*(1), 61–80.

Garland, D. (2001). *The culture of control*. Oxford University Press.

Gelsthorpe, L. (2004). Back to basics in crime control: Weaving in women. *Critical Review of International Social and Political Philosophy, 7*(2), 76–103.

Gelsthorpe, L. & Morris, A. (1988). Feminism and criminology in Britain. *The British Journal of Criminology, 28*(2), 93–110.

Goodey, J. O. (2000). Biographical lessons for criminology. *Theoretical Criminology, 4*(4), 473–498.

Griffin, P. (2013). Gendering global finance: Crisis, masculinity, and responsibility. *Men and Masculinities, 16*(1), 9–34.

Heidensohn, F. (1985). *Women and crime*. Macmillan.

Heidensohn, F. (2012). The future of feminist criminology. *Crime, Media, Culture, 8*(2), 123–134.

Henne, K., & Troshynski, E. (2013). Mapping the margins of intersectionality: Criminological possibilities in a transnational world. *Theoretical Criminology, 17*(4), 455–473.

Hester M. (2013). Who does what to whom? Gender and domestic violence perpetrators in English police records. *European Journal of Criminology, 10*(5), 623–637.

Hester, M., Donovan, C., & Fahmy, E. (2010). Feminist epistemology and the politics of method: Surveying same sex domestic violence. *International Journal of Social Research Methodology, 13*(3), 251–263.

Hillyard, P., & Tombs, S. (2007). From 'crime' to social harm? *Crime, Law and Social Change, 48*(1), 9–25.

Hines, S. (2010). Introduction. In Hines, S. & T. Sanger. *Transgender identities: Towards a social analysis of gender diversity* (pp. 1–22). Taylor & Francis.

Hood-Williams, J. (2001). Gender, masculinities and crime: From structures to psyches. *Theoretical Criminology, 5*(1), 37–60.

hooks, b. (1981). *Ain't I a woman: Black women and feminism*. South End Press.

Irvine, A. (2014). You can't run from the police: Developing a feminist criminology that incorporates Black transgender women symposium: Locking up females, failing to protect them, and punishing their children & families: A symposium honoring the work of professor Myrna S. Raeder. *Southwestern Law Review, 44*, 553.

Jones, A. (2020). Where the trans men and enbies at?: Cissexism, sexual threat, and the study of sex work. *Sociology Compass, 14*(2), e12750.

Kersten, J. (1993). Crime and masculinities in Australia, Germany and Japan. *International Sociology, 8*(4), 461–478.

Kim, M. E. (2018). From carceral feminism to transformative justice: Women-of-color feminism and alternatives to incarceration. *Journal of Ethnic & Cultural Diversity in Social Work, 27*(3), 219–233.

Klein, D. (1973). The etiology of female crime: A review of the literature. *Issues Criminology, 8*(2), 3–30.

Klein, D. (1981). Violence against women: Some considerations regarding its causes and its elimination. *Crime & Delinquency, 27*(1), 64–80.

Kohm, S. A., & Greenhill, P. (2011). Pedophile crime films as popular criminology: A problem of justice? *Theoretical Criminology, 15*(2), 195–215.

Kruttschnitt, C. (1982). Respectable women and the law. *The Sociological Quarterly, 23*(2), 221–234.

Kruttschnitt, C. (2016). The politics, and place, of gender in research on crime. *Criminology, 54*(1), 8–29.

Kruttschnitt, C., Slotboom, A.-M., Dirkzwager, A., & Bijleveld, C. (2013). Bringing women's carceral experiences into the "New Punitiveness" Fray. *Justice Quarterly, 30*(1), 18–43.

Levi, M. (1994). Masculinities and white-collar crime. In E. A. Stanko & N. Tim. *Just oys doing business* (pp. 234–252). Routledge.

Lombard, N. (2013). 'What about the men?' Understanding men's experiences. In N. Lombard & M. Lesley (Eds.), *Violence against women: Current theory and practice in domestic abuse, sexual violence, and exploitation* (56: pp. 177–194). Jessica Kingsley.

Lorber, J. (1994). *Paradoxes of gender*. Yale University Press.

Messerschmidt, J. W. (1993). *Masculinities and crime: Critique and reconceptualization of theory*. Rowman & Littlefield Publishers.

Messerschmidt, J. W. (2013). *Crime as structured action: Doing masculinities, race, class, sexuality, and crime*. Rowman & Littlefield.

Miller, J. (1998). Up it up: gender and the accomplishment of street robbery. *Criminology, 36*(1), 37–66.

Miller, J. (2002). The strengths and limits of 'doing gender' for understanding street crime. *Theoretical Criminology, 6*(4), 433–460.

Ministry of Justice. (2020). *Statistics on women and the criminal justice system 2017*. Ministry of Justice.

Mirandé, A. (2016). Hombres Mujeres: An indigenous third gender. *Men and Masculinities, 19*(4), 384–409.

Monro, S. (2019). Non-binary and genderqueer: An overview of the field. *International Journal of Transgenderism, 20*(2–3), 126–131.

Naegler, L., & Salman, S. (2016). Cultural criminology and gender consciousness: Moving feminist theory from margin to center. *Feminist Criminology, 11*(4), 354–374.

Nash, J. C. (2008). Re-thinking intersectionality. *Feminist Review, 89*(1), 1–15.

Neuhouser, K. (2008). I am the man and woman in this house: Brazilian jeito and the strategic framing of motherhood in a poor, urban community. In J. Reger, D. J. Myers, & R. L. Einwohner (Eds.), *Identity work in social movements* (pp. 141–166). Minneapolis, University of Minnesota.

Newton, C. (1994). Gender theory and prison sociology: Using theories of masculinities to interpret the sociology of prisons for men. *The Howard Journal of Criminal Justice, 33*(3), 193–202.

O'Brien, J., & Dixon, O. (2013). Deferred prosecutions in the corporate sector: Lessons from LIBOR. *Seattle University, 37*, 475.

O'Neill, M. (2001). *Prostitution and feminism: Towards a politics of feeling.* Polity Press.

O'Neill, M., & Seal, L. (2012). *Transgressive imaginations: Crime, deviance and culture.* Palgrave.

Pantazis, C., & Gordon, D. (1997). Television licence evasion and the criminalisation of female poverty. *The Howard Journal of Criminal Justice, 36*(2), 170–186.

Parmar, A. (2017). Intersectionality, British criminology and race: Are we there yet? *Theoretical Criminology, 21*(1), 35–45.

Perry, B., & Dyck, D. R. (2014). "I don't know where it is safe": Trans women's experiences of violence. *Critical Criminology, 22*(1), 49–63.

Phipps, A. (2016). Whose personal is more political? Experience in contemporary feminist politics. *Feminist Theory, 17*(3), 303–321.

Phipps, A. (2020). *Me, not you: The trouble with mainstream feminism.* Manchester University Press.

Phoenix, A., & Pattynama, P. (2006). Intersectionality. *European Journal of Women's Studies, 13*(3), 187–192.

Potter, H. (2015). *Intersectionality and criminology: Disrupting and revolutionizing studies of crime.* Routledge.

Presser, L. (2012). Getting on top through mass murder: Narrative, metaphor, and violence. *Crime, Media, Culture, 8*(1), 3–21.

Prins, B. (2006). Narrative accounts of origins: A blind spot in the intersectional approach? *European Journal of Women's Studies, 13*(3), 277–290.

Rafter, N., & Brown, M. (2011). *Criminology goes to the movies.* New York University Press.

Richards, C., Bouman, W. P., & Barker, M. (2017). *Non-binary genders.*

Roberts, D. (2014). Complicating the triangle of race, class and state: The insights of black feminists. *Ethnic and Racial Studies, 37*(10), 1776–1782.

Russell, T., Jeffries, S., Hayes, H., Thipphayamongkoludom, Y., & Chuenurah, C. (2020). A gender-comparative exploration of women's and men's pathways to prison in Thailand. *Australian & New Zealand Journal of Criminology, 53*(4), 536–562.

Sabo, D. F., Kupers, T. A., & London, W. J. (2001). *Prison masculinities.* Temple University Press.

Saleh-Hanna, V. (2015). Black feminist hauntology. Rememory the ghosts of abolition? *Champ pénal/Penal Field* 12.

Savage, L. (2019). *Female offenders in Canada, 2017*. Canadian Centre for Justice Statistics.

Schwartz, M. D., & Milovanovic, D. (1999). *Race, gender, and class in criminology: The intersections.* Taylor & Francis.

Scott, J. W. (1988). *Gender: A useful category of historical analysis.* Columbia University Press.

Scott, J. W. (1999). Some reflections on gender and politics. In M. Ferree, J. Lorber & B. B. Hess (Eds.),*Revisioning gender* (pp. 70–96). Sage.

Seal, L. (2010). *Women, murder and femininity: Gender representations of women who kill*. Palgrave.

Seal, L., & O'Neill, M. (2019). *Imaginative criminology: Of spaces past*. Bristol, Bristol University Press.

Smart, C. (1976). *Women, crime and criminology: A feminist critique*. Routledge and Kegan Paul.

Smart, C. (2002). *Feminism and the power of law*. Routledge.

Sokoloff, N. J., & Burgess-Proctor, A. (2011). Remembering criminology's 'Forgotten Theme': Seeking justice in us crime policy using an intersectional approach.In M. Bosworth & H. Caroline. *What is criminology?* (pp. 235–248). Oxford University Press.

Stanko, E. A., & Newburn, T. (1994). *Just boys doing business? Men, masculinities and crime*. Routledge.

Steffensmeier, D. J., Schwartz, J., & Roche, M. (2013). Gender and twenty-first-century corporate crime: Female involvement and the gender gap in Enron-Era Corporate Frauds. *American Sociological Review, 78*(3), 448–476.

Tomsen, S. (1996). Ruling men? Some comments on masculinity and juvenile justice. *Australian & New Zealand Journal of Criminology, 29*(2), 191–194.

Trahan, A. (2011). Qualitative research and intersectionality. *Critical Criminology, 19*(1), 1–14.

Wacquant, L. (2009). *Punishing the poor: The neoliberal government of social insecurity*. Duke University Press.

Walmsley, R. (2017). *World female imprisonment list*. Institute for Crime and Justice Policy Research.

Wattanaporn, K. A., & Holtfreter, K. (2014). The impact of feminist pathways research on gender-responsive policy and practice. *Feminist Criminology, 9*(3), 191–207.

Weiner, M. J. (2005). *Men of blood: Violence, manliness and criminal justice in Victorian England*. Cambridge University Press.

West, C., & Zimmerman, D. H. (1987). Doing gender. *Gender & Society, 1*(2), 125–151.

Westmarland, N. (2015). *Violence against women: Criminological perspectives on men's violences*. Routledge.

Whalley, E., & Hackett, C. (2017). Carceral feminisms: The abolitionist project and undoing dominant feminisms. *Contemporary Justice Review, 20*(4), 456–473.

Young, J. (2007). *The vertigo of late modernity*. Sage.

Yuval-Davis, N. (2006). Intersectionality and feminist politics. *European Journal of Women's Studies, 13*(3), 193–209.

Yuval-Davis, N., & Anthias, F. (1992). *Racialized boundaries: Race, nation, gender, colour, and class and the anti-racist struggle*. Routledge.

2

Interpersonal Violence

Violence takes many forms. It can be the infliction of physical pain and injury by one person towards another, but it also encompasses other harms—the violence of living in poverty or of being subjected to hate speech, for example. This chapter focuses on interpersonal violence between individuals, excluding sexual violence, which is discussed in Chapter 3. Interpersonal violence is not separate from other forms of violence. It is interrelated with state violence, which includes violence associated with law enforcement and immigration restriction, and structural violence, which refers to the harms of social inequality and the maldistribution of resources.

Violence is central to securing political domination and to the maintenance of social hierarchies of race, gender, sexuality, class and nation (Collins, 2017). While acts of violence can be largescale and spectacular, violence is frequently embedded in the routine and everyday. Collins (1998, 2017) analyses how different types of violence sustain social hierarchies in ways that are mutually supporting and constitutive. Racial dominance in the United States relies on spectacular, public violent events such as lynching and police brutality. It also relies on the routine violence of racist speech and the structural violence of discrimination

L. Seal, *Gender, Crime and Justice*, https://doi.org/10.1007/978-3-030-87488-9_2

in housing and employment. Collins (1998, 2017) argues that violence binds different aspects of hierarchy and domination together, making it an incisive entry point for thinking intersectionally. The perpetration and experience of violence makes intersecting power relations visible. White women might experience domestic violence and abuse from a male partner that sustains their subordination in the gender hierarchy. They might also use racist speech and benefit from structural advantages of whiteness in employment, housing and education that secure and reinforce their domination in the racial hierarchy.

Domestic Violence and Abuse: An Intersectional Perspective

State intervention into intimate violence, primarily by men against women, has historical precedents, particularly from the nineteenth century onwards (Clark, 2000; Ramsey, 2011; Syrett, 2021). The feminist understanding of men's use of violence against women as a means to secure and perpetuate dominance also emerged in the nineteenth century (Hamilton, 2001). The women's movement against violence against women in the form of establishing refuges and seeking greater state intervention dates from the 1970s.

The concept of gender-based violence to encapsulate violence against women and girls is well established and widely accepted. In intimate relationships, it refers to physical, sexual, emotional, psychological and financial abuse, as well as threatening and controlling behaviours. It reflects longstanding feminist analysis of intimate violence by men against women as an abuse of power and a form of gendered inequality and of social control, the perpetuation of which secures and reinforces men's superior position in the gender hierarchy (Dobash & Dobash, 1979). The concept of coercive control recognises abuse in relationships as patterned over time rather than as discrete events. Physical violence is an aspect of exerting control and is frequently perpetrated by abusers. However, abusers can be controlling without resorting to physical violence. Controlling behaviour includes, among other things, socially isolating the victim, preventing them from making decisions and telling them how to dress (Stark, 2013).

Domestic violence and abuse is portrayed in major films and television dramas, particularly since the early 1990s, when *Sleeping with the Enemy* (1991) and Tina Turner biopic *What's Love Got to Do with It* (1993) were globally successful. Shoos (2017) argues the ideological work of these films is problematic; they portray domestic violence as something done by a few monstrous, abnormal men and as something female victim/survivors can overcome through individual empowerment to defeat or leave their abusers. Wider structural inequalities and the need for collective action remain unaddressed. Shoos (2017) highlights the 1944 film *Gaslight* as one that offers a more nuanced and expansive representation of domestic violence and abuse, which resonates with contemporary attention to coercive control. Adapted from the play *Gas Light* (Hamilton, 1939), the origin for the term 'gaslighting', the plot concerns a woman whose husband isolates her and attempts to convince her she is losing her mind—one such tactic being the intermittent dimming and brightening of the gas lights. The film takes a dramatic turn but represents the psychological aspects of abuse and the inducement of fear through control.

More recently, Hollywood films have deployed metaphor and allegory to show both the dynamics of psychological abuse and coercive control and their effects on victim/survivors. In *Colossal* (2017), protagonist Gloria's new boyfriend Oscar appears to be a regular nice guy who wants to help her get her life back on track, before he starts ordering her around and belittling her in front of others. He is able to manipulate her further via the monsters terrorising Seoul to which he and Gloria are psychically connected, and which stand for their abusive behaviour and alcoholism, respectively. He threatens to destroy the city if she leaves him. In *The Invisible Man* (2020), Cecilia's emotionally, physically and sexually abusive boyfriend fakes his own death and wears an invisibility suit to continue his mistreatment of her. His invisibility means he can abuse her in the presence of others while she appears to be delusional and is disbelieved by her friends and family. Via the abuser's invisibility, the film allegorises the insidiousness of emotional abuse and coercive control. Horror film and Steven King adaptation *Gerald's Game* (2017) portrays the trauma of domestic violence and abuse through the memories of heroine Jessie while she is handcuffed to a bed and cannot escape.

Gender-based violence is understood to be common and a widespread risk for women and girls. This concept informs policies related to domestic violence and abuse in many jurisdictions around the world and is employed by international bodies such as the United Nations and World Health Organization. The WHO (2021) highlights that globally one in three women experiences gender-based violence in their lifetime, frequently from a male intimate partner, and defines it as 'a major public health and clinical problem'. The United Nations (2021) defines gender-based violence as a 'widespread, persistent and devastating human rights abuse'.

Men are much more frequently the perpetrators of domestic violence and abuse than women and are far less likely to be victim/survivors than women and gender non-conforming people. Intimate violence is deeply gendered. However, analysis based on gender alone misses the importance of the intersection of gender with other aspects of social positioning. Such intersections affect the rates at which individuals from different social groups experience DVA, the effect it has on their lives and the solutions available to them. Although DVA takes place in 'private' relationships, the nature of the state's response or lack of response is significant, dissolving the binary between private and public violence. All women are not equally at risk of experiencing DVA and differences in status and access to resources between those who do shape its impact (Josephson, 2002; Nixon & Humphreys, 2010). Returning to Collins's (1998, 2017) insight that violence binds different social hierarchies together, it is necessary to examine how intimate partner violence is not caused by gendered subordination alone but is also attributable to hierarchies of race, class, sexuality, citizenship status, dis/ability and age. Focusing exclusively on gender obscures these differences and can lead to policies and interventions that are unsuitable, or even harmful, for victims and survivors (George & Stith, 2014; Nixon & Humphreys, 2010).

In a foundational article, Crenshaw (1991) theorises the importance of intersectionality with regard to women of colour's experiences of intimate violence in the United States. She argues these experiences result from intersections of racism and sexism, making them different from the experiences of white women and requiring analysis of structural positioning that incorporates race and racism. Black women in the United States are at a disproportionate risk of domestic violence and abuse and are more likely to be killed by a partner than women from other groups—twice as likely as white women (Richie & Eife, 2021). Black women are at a higher risk of death by homicide than white men (Threadcraft & Miller, 2017). They are also at risk from experiencing racism in shelters, being overlooked in the health system and disbelieved in the criminal justice system—and being punished by the criminal justice system (Waller et al., 2021).

Domestic violence shelters are less likely to be located in communities of colour, meaning victim/survivors of colour need to travel further and potentially leave behind other sources of support to access shelters (Josephson, 2002). Leaving the community can also mean greater exposure to racism (Sokoloff, 2008). Communities of colour, and Black communities in particular, face higher levels of state violence than white communities (Creek & Dunn, 2011). Richie and Eife (2021) deploy the concept of the violence matrix to illustrate how Black women who experience gender-based violence also disproportionately experience the violence of racist criminalisation, police brutality and incarceration.

Film and television (as well as news media) consider DVA through the portrayal of white women victim/survivors primarily. The forgoing discussion of recent representations of emotional and psychological abuse in recent films is illustrative—all three have white protagonists. Shoos (2017) analyses the significance of gender, race and class in *What's Love Got to Do with It* (1993), which dramatises Ike Turner's abuse of Tina Turner and her survival of this abuse before achieving superstardom. During a scene in a diner in which Ike shoves cake into Tina's face before knocking her to the floor, the camera briefly focuses on the distressed reaction of a white woman and her children. Shoos (2017) highlights how this scene could be interpreted as showing how Tina Turner as a working class Southern Black woman had to endure white people's Othering gaze. However, the scene could also invite an Othering reaction from white audiences, which disavows intimate violence and sees it as something perpetrated by Black men.

The Color Purple (1985) tells the story of Celie, a Black woman in early twentieth-century Georgia, from girlhood to middle age. She is sexually and physically abused by her stepfather and then by her husband. Adapted from a novel by Alice Walker, the film shows how Black women experienced gender-based intimate violence but also the structural violence of racism. The character of Sofia is imprisoned for retaliating when the town mayor—a white man—hits her. Upon release, she has to serve as maid to the mayor's wife. *The Color Purple* portrays the disproportionate punishment of Black women and their social control through domestic labour. Bailey (2009) notes that it was significant as a Hollywood film that did not rely on stereotypical portrayals of Black women, but instead represented multidimensional characters. The portrayal of Celie is not simply one of victimhood. At the end of the film, we find Celie thriving, running a tailor's shop and finally being reunited with her children.

Indigenous women in Australia, New Zealand, Canada and the United States face higher rates of intimate partner violence than non-Indigenous women. In Australia, Indigenous women are twelve times more likely to be physically assaulted than other women (Nixon & Humphreys, 2010). The violence matrix for Indigenous women includes violation and traumatisation via settler colonialism, including policies that entrench poverty, child removal and a disproportionate risk of exposure to the criminal justice system and incarceration. Colonialism is not simply a legacy of the past for Indigenous people. Neocolonialism entails ongoing social inequality and structural violence, particularly as a consequence of the loss of land (Blagg & Anthony, 2019; Smye et al., 2021). For Indigenous women, leaving an abusive relationship might mean leaving kinship ties that sustain financial, emotional and spiritual support (Smye et al., 2021). Documentary *Not Just Numbers* (2019) is about the Tangentyere Women's Family Safety Group in Alice Springs, a group of Indigenous women activists who work to end family violence within their community. Filmmaker and group member Shirleen Campbell argues solutions to intimate violence need to be community-based rather than top-down, which often creates more problems (McLaughlin, 2019).

Citizenship status affects the nature of intimate partner violence that women experience and the options available to them. Abusers can exploit undocumented or irregular status with the threat of informing on women to the authorities (Sokoloff, 2008). Even if women have legal status, moving to a new country creates vulnerabilities to abuse. Chiu (2017) found women who immigrated to Hong Kong from mainland China in order to marry experienced domestic violence and abuse in the context of fewer welfare rights, such as entitlement to housing, and greater financial need to stay with abusive partners. Abusive partners employed measures of coercive control such as trapping women at home or preventing them from finding paid work. Women were socially isolated and did not have support networks in Hong Kong. They did not know where or how to access domestic abuse services. Women who migrate in search of a better life may not want to leave an abusive relationship if doing so means being compelled to leave the country (Parson, 2010).

Anitha (2019) defines economic abuse as financial control and exploitation, but also as control of reproductive labour. She interviewed South Asian women in transnational marriages living in the UK and India who experienced economic abuse from their husbands and members of their husband's family. This abuse included control of bank accounts by their husband or father-in-law and sale of their possessions without permission. Abuse via exploitation of reproductive labour involved being forced to perform domestic labour and denied food. This was usually perpetrated by their husband's female relatives. In the UK, some women were coerced into paid work. These forms of abuse are not necessarily only experienced by migrant women, but they are more vulnerable to them.

Disabled women are also at heightened risk of financial abuse (Nixon & Humphreys, 2010). They experience specific types of abusive treatment that are not always recognised, such as withheld medication, neglect of personal care and prevention of use of mobility devices (Cramer & Plummer, 2009). Disabled women are at risk of domestic abuse from a wider range of people than intimate partners, such as personal support and healthcare workers. This wider range of potential perpetrators is also a threat to older women. For older women, the experience of intimate partner violence can however be obscured by perceptions of 'elder abuse' that are not gendered and by the ageist assumption that older women do not experience gender-based violence. Services may be inadequate for older victims/survivors due to access barriers related to mobility and health status (Crockett et al., 2018).

Perceptions of domestic violence and abuse are shaped by heteronormativity. The 'public story' of domestic abuse imagines a female victim/survivor and male protagonist in a cis heterosexual relationship (Donovan & Hester, 2015). However, rates of DVA are higher among LGBTQ people and the heterosexist 'public story' can render the victimisation of queer people invisible (Messinger, 2017; Scheer & Poteat, 2021). Domestic violence and abuse in LGBTQ relationships is not necessarily the same as in cis heterosexual relationships and can therefore be difficult to recognise or to make public (Donovan & Barnes, 2020; Messinger, 2017). Awareness raising short film *Red Flags* (2016) depicts two relationships—one gay, one lesbian—in which one partner is abusive and the particular tactics they use. Another short film, *Smoke* (2015), portrays an abusive lesbian relationship and shows Mollie's fear of her girlfriend Ashley while also examining some of the reasons for Ashley's behaviour. Donovan and Hester (2015) argue power and control are significant in abusive LGBTQ relationships but are not necessarily exercised in relation to gender. They emphasise the work of discourses of love in relationships, with the exploitation of feelings and practices of love being associated with abuse. Coercive control is found in LGBTQ as well as heterosexual relationships (Frankland & Brown, 2014; Stark & Hester, 2019).

Abuse and control in LGBTQ relationships can be specifically related to sexuality or gender identity, such as the threat of outing (Messinger & Roark, 2019). Rogers's (2019) analysis of trans people's narratives of domestic abuse and violence revealed experiences of coercive control, but also transphobia, as a constituent part of the abuse. Transphobia was perpetrated in relationships through emotional abuse related to misgendering, disparaging victim/survivors' bodies and to pathologising their trans and/or gender non-conforming identities (Rogers, 2019). There are fewer services available for victims/survivors of domestic violence and abuse in LGBTQ relationships than for women in cis heterosexual relationships. Services may not welcome LGBTQ people or may be unsuitable to their needs due to using a gender-based framework that assumes a male perpetrator and female victim/survivor. Few DVA intervention and treatment programmes exist that were specifically created for LGBTQ populations (Messinger & Roark, 2019; Subirana-Malaret et al., 2019).

Due to the structural effects of homophobia and transphobia, LGBTQ people disproportionately face inequalities in employment and housing, which expose them to the risk of intimate partner violence (Brubaker, 2020). Trans people, and trans people of colour in particular, experience high levels of precarity through unemployment and homelessness, as well as violence from police and in prisons (Hsu, 2019). This structural and state violence compounds and exacerbates experiences of intimate partner violence, binding different hierarchies together. Participatory documentary *Transagenda* (2015) explores two homeless trans activists' experiences of police violence and transphobia as they carry out a photography project in Minneapolis. Ristock et al. (2019) argue that for LGBTQ people intimate partner violence is not separate from family, structural and state violence but interrelated. Their study with Indigenous LBGTQ and Two Spirit people in Canada explores these interrelationships as well as the violence of colonialism. Colonialism imposed shared historical trauma on Indigenous people. Two Spirit participants felt their status was obliterated by the imposition of norms of gender and sexuality during colonisation. Their experience was distinct from non-Indigenous LBGTQ people in that previously existing social and cultural power had been taken from them.

Women as Perpetrators of Domestic Violence and Abuse

Early research into women as perpetrators of domestic violence and abuse against other women challenged the invisibility of women's violence in relationships in feminist scholarship and activism (Renzetti, 1992; Ristock, 2002). Ristock (2002) outlines two areas of feminist discomfort: that focusing on women as abusers shifts attention away from men and that it risks stigmatising lesbian women, feeding backlash against feminism. Smollin (2016) analyses the portrayal of domestic violence and abuse in lesbian relationships in television shows *Sex and the City* (1998–2004), *The L Word* (2004–2009) and *The O.C.* (2004–2007). She identifies two consistent themes, one of 'the failed woman', where lesbian women's violence is linked to masculinity and aggression and one of women of colour and lower-class women as more likely to be violent and therefore to pose a threat to the dominant order. The main characters in all three shows are white and affluent, whereas the abusive women characters depart from these 'ideal' characteristics.

Women perpetrate domestic violence and abuse in cis heterosexual relationships at far lower rates than men. Hester's (2013) analysis of domestic violence cases in northeast England found women were sole perpetrators in 8.4% of cases reported to the police, and dual perpetrators (with men) in 11.8% of cases. Men were more likely to use physical violence, threats and harassment than women. Women mainly used verbal abuse and their use of physical violence was less severe than men's. Men were also more likely to have two or more incidents reported against them. Women did not exert ongoing control or manipulate fear in relationships in the same way that men did and were less likely than men to initiate violent incidents (Hester, 2012, 2013). A consistent finding is that women's physical violence in cis heterosexual relationships is usually in self-defence, defence of their children or in retaliation to men's violence (Bair-Merritt et al., 2010; Larance et al., 2019).

Women who employ physical violence in self-defence or retaliation do not fit gendered images of victimhood, particularly if they are not white middle-class women. Their own experiences of violence and abuse may consequently not be recognised (Creek & Dunn, 2011; Larance et al., 2019). Perpetrator intervention programmes for women do exist, although as Larance et al. (2019) argue, to be effective these programmes need to appreciate the context of women's use of intimate partner violence and facilitate access to wider community support. Not all violence from women towards male partners is self-defence or in retaliation. McCarrick et al.'s (2016) study of a small number of English male victim/survivors of women's DVA found they experienced disbelief when they reported the violence and did not have a public story to insert themselves into as there is no concept of the 'battered man'. Documentary *Abused by my Girlfriend* (2019) explores the severe abuse Alex Skeel experienced from his girlfriend Jordan Worth, who became the first woman in Britain to be convicted of coercive and controlling behaviour.

Responses to DVA and Carceral Feminism

How best to respond to domestic violence and abuse is subject to debate in among feminists. Legislation and policy in different jurisdictions has criminalised domestic violence and abuse, for example, through pro and mandatory arrest policies. Kim (2018, 2020) outlines how by the early 1980s carceral strategies became central to feminist anti-violence movements in the United States. These strategies were inspired by the Duluth model of intervention in Minnesota, which was developed in the 1970s. This model conceptualises DVA as multidimensional and based on power and control. It entailed cooperation between shelters for abused women and the police, as well as mandatory arrest of the primary aggressor in incidents of domestic violence and abuse. Feminist groups across the United States replicated the Duluth model and worked with the police and criminal justice system, hybridising civil and state approaches.

As this hybridisation took place, feminist forces were subordinated to law enforcement and the criminal justice system and anti-violence movements were depoliticised (Kim, 2018, 2020). Grassroots victim advocacy became professionalised with the consequence that personnel working in domestic violence advocacy no longer necessarily identified as feminist or saw their work as intended to effect social change (Nichols, 2013). State funding of DVA services increased professionalisation and cooperation with the criminal justice system (Mehrotra et al., 2016). As criminal justice policymaking and practice became increasingly punitive in the 1980s and 90s, gender-based violence as a social problem was narrowly defined as a crime rather than as a manifestation of patriarchal violence interlinked with state and structural violence (Kim, 2018, 2020). Kim (2020) describes this process as one of 'carceral creep'. Mehrotra et al. (2016) argue professionalisation, neoliberalism and criminalisation braided together in American approaches to domestic violence and abuse. Beth E. Richie's televised lecture 'Race, Gender and Carceral Feminism' (2015) critiques carceral feminism and examines how it negatively impacts on Black women.

Day and Gill (2020) analyse how the braiding of the support for domestic violence victims/survivors with the criminal justice system in England and Wales creates positive outcomes for some and damages others. They note that the police is the only agency open 24 hours per day, seven days a week that also has the authority to remove and detain perpetrators. The police can potentially prevent serious injury or death. Independent Domestic Violence Advisors based at police stations help victims/survivors with safety management, for instance by providing assistance to find new housing. However, the braiding of support with enforcement has negative effects for women who are seeking asylum or who are irregular migrants. They frequently avoid contacting the police for fear of referral to the border agency. Some victim/survivors who do contact the police are arrested and incarcerated in Immigration Removal Centres.

Mandatory and pro-arrest policies have had the unintended consequence of leading to the greater arrests of women when domestic violence incidents are reported to the police (Burman & Brooks-Hay, 2018; Day & Gill, 2020). Hester (2012, 2013) found when the police identified a woman as the primary aggressor in an incident, they were more likely to arrest her than they were a man in the same circumstances. Feminist criminologists have highlighted Black women in the United States and Indigenous women in Australia have especially borne the brunt of the consequences of mandatory and pro-arrest policies and that this means they are less likely than white women to seek protection or remedy via the criminal justice system. Doing so risks criminalisation and exposure to further violence from the police or in the criminal justice system, and the involvement of child welfare services (Blagg & Anthony, 2019; Richie & Eife, 2021). Durfee (2021) researched how protection orders, which legally require the abuser to stop harming the victim/survivor, can fuel the 'abuse to prison pipeline' for women. They examined cross-filings for protection orders, where both parties file for an order. They found men were more likely to be involved in cross-filings and possibly used them as a resource to further abuse of their partner. The consequences for women victim/survivors were greater risk of arrest and less eligibility for support services.

Case studies:

In 2012, Marissa Alexander, a Black woman, was sentenced to 20 years in prison in Florida for aggravated assault with a lethal weapon. She fired a warning shot towards her abusive husband, against whom she had a restraining order, after he physically attacked and threatened to kill her. Her conviction was overturned in 2014 and in 2015 Alexander accepted a plea deal which enabled her release from prison after three months to serve probation under house detention for a further two years. She was fully freed in 2017. The Free Marissa Now Mobilization Campaign was established in 2013 to raise money for her defence fund, but also to highlight the wider issues of the gender-based violence experienced by Black women and women of colour, and the criminalisation of victim/survivors. Organisation Survived and Punished continues the campaign against the criminalisation of survivors and Marissa Alexander is an advocate and campaigner.

Tamica Mullaley, a First Nations woman from Western Australia, was violently attacked in the street by her abusive partner Mervyn Bell in 2013. When the police arrived an argument developed with Mullaley as she did not want to respond to their questions, and they arrested her for assaulting an officer. Bell subsequently kidnapped and murdered Mullaley's baby son, Charlie. Mullaley's attempt to get an inquest into the role of the police in Charlie's death was unsuccessful. The second episode of documentary series *See What You Made Me Do* tells Tamica Mullaley's story and exposes the disproportionate violence experienced by Indigenous women and police failure. Watego et al. (2021) argue Mullaley's story raises a problem with the series, which calls for the criminalisation of coercive control to protect the victim/survivors of DVA. Indigenous women face violence and coercive control from the state—not only the police, but also other state agencies, making carceral solutions harmful.

The assumption that the state knows best in terms of tackling gender-based violence reflects a 'colonial gaze'. A carceral approach contrasts with Indigenous Australian models of justice that emphasise censure and healing, rather than punishment. Where victims/survivors experience the state as repressive due to neocolonialism, state intervention in cases of domestic violence and abuse is not viewed as benign protection (Blagg & Anthony, 2019). Histories of colonialism are significant to contemporary policing, which needs to be understood in the context of policing domestic violence and abuse (Belknap & Grant, 2021).

Policies and legislation that expand definitions of domestic violence and abuse can further entrench criminalisation. Influenced by the concept of coercive control, the Domestic Abuse (Scotland) Act 2018 incorporates emotional and psychological abuse, and the cumulative effects of a course of behaviour, into its definition in order to help improve investigation and prosecution (Burman & Brooks-Hay, 2018). Burman and Brooks-Hay (2018) caution the incorporation of psychological abuse may criminalise women's attempts to protect themselves or their children from a male partner—a process described by Tolmie (2018) as 'mutualisation'. The wide scope of the definition risks over-criminalisation more generally. The imperative to expand legal definitions of violence and abuse to increase rates of arrest and prosecution is characteristic of a carceral approach, where protection and redress are pursued via the state. This approach means that ultimately action is taken on behalf of the state and not the victim/survivor.

Controlling and coercive behaviour within an intimate relationship was criminalised in England and Wales by the Serious Crime Act 2015 in order to recognise how abuse entails patterns of harm, as opposed to one-off events, and is broader than physical violence (Tolmie, 2018). The argued benefit of the legislation is that it more fully recognises the extent of the harm perpetrated by domestic violence and abuse and enables patterns of behaviours and incidents to be placed in the context of an ongoing abusive relationship (Bettinson, 2016). However, the criminal justice system, and adversarial legal systems particularly, are not well suited to appreciating the nuances of the diverse meanings of coercive and controlling behaviours in different relationships (Tolmie, 2018). Coupled with this problem is the need to distinguish between a 'normal' situation and an abusive one, especially in heterosexual relationships where male partners making major decisions and controlling the finances can be viewed as consistent with the gender norms of a 'traditional' relationship (Burman & Brooks-Hay, 2018; Tolmie, 2018). These issues mean that meeting legal evidentiary standards can be difficult (Tolmie, 2018).

Prosecution and conviction rates for coercive and controlling behaviour in England and Wales have so far been low, accounting for a minority of prosecutions for domestic violence related crime and only a small percentage of prosecutions have resulted in conviction (Barlow et al., 2019). Barlow et al.'s (2019) qualitative analysis of police files revealed police officers recorded evidence of isolated events rather than patterns of behaviour and were more willing to pursue prosecution for incidents that caused physical injury. Coercive and controlling behaviour was seen as hard to prove and coming down to one person's word against another. The barriers to prosecuting and convicting coercive control are not necessarily insurmountable but highlight how criminal justice responses can be inadequate or ineffective. Overcriminalisation is one risk of carceral approaches. Another is lack of meaningful action or change.

Tapia (2020) examined criminal courts in Ecuador that specialise in cases of violence against women. The criminalisation of domestic violence and abuse and the development of special courts followed Ecuador's new Constitution in 2008, which deems gender-based violence to be a human rights violation. This framing was influenced by the growth of international human rights discourse and expansion of NGOs working on gender-based violence. Ecuadorian feminist groups did not push for the strategy of criminalisation. Cases of violence against women have a high attrition rate as victims/survivors want protection but frequently do not want the perpetrator to be punished. Tapia (2020) argues criminalisation in Ecuador has not led to penal expansion but has restricted victim/survivors' access to support from social services. Attrition and indifference in the criminal justice system mean that women are neglected and their needs are not met.

The involvement of the state is not essential, or even desirable, in order to provide support for the victims/survivors of domestic violence and abuse. Critics of carceral feminism highlight the success of grassroots organisations in the United States such as INCITE!, Survived and Punished and Creative Interventions, which remain autonomous and do not seek public funding (Creek & Dunn, 2011; Kim, 2018; Richie et al.,

2021). Founded in 2000, INCITE! works to address violence against women of colour whether perpetrated within their communities, such as rape and domestic violence, or against their communities, such as police brutality and colonial violence. Embracing principles of abolitionist feminism and transformative justice, INCITE! organises with and within communities to encourage safety and support and to transform the abusive behaviour of individuals and the political conditions that sustain violence against women of colour. INCITE! works with abolitionist group Critical Resistance to oppose prisons as sites of gender and race based violence (INCITE!, 2021). Grassroots organisations have formed task forces to inform the provision of services at state and national level, particularly with regard to meeting the needs of women of colour (Richie et al., 2021).

Black Lives Matter, initiated by three queer Black women and drawing on legacies of Black feminism, campaigns to end police brutality against Black people (Belknap & Grant, 2021; Collins, 2017). BLM was established in the United States in 2013 and has since grown into a decentralised network active in Canada and Britain (BlackLivesMatter, 2021). Calls to defund or abolish the police are seen as necessary to reduce the violence experienced by communities and adopt a similar analysis of the interrelatedness of different forms of violence to Collins (1998, 2017). Whereas the police might symbolise protection for white cis women, for Black women, women of colour and trans women they represent threat.

Principles of transformative justice emphasise the need to bring about change at individual and structural levels. Rather than imposing professional expertise or prescribing solutions, transformative approaches are community-based and require collective engagement. Work takes place separately from the state and the formal voluntary sector and includes the people who are affected by violence to bring change about (Kim, 2018). Creative Interventions in San Francisco was founded in 2004 by Mimi Kim, a critic of carceral feminism, to develop community-based approaches to reducing intimate violence.

Polavarapu (2019) notes that, via international human rights networks, carceral feminism as a way of tackling intimate violence has developed global reach. International documents favour state, over community, solutions. However, there are examples of non-state and criminal justice responses in the Global South that could inform alternative approaches in the Global North. The Ugandan constitution encourages reconciliation as an important aspect of custom. Redress for intimate violence can be sought through the courts or through reconciliation and mediation. Reconciliation happens in various different ways but is characterised by the involvement of third parties such as family and community members. Polavarapu (2019) argues reconciliation can fill gaps left by court-based approaches. There are drawbacks; customary systems tend to have developed to benefit men primarily and do not resolve structural inequalities. Nevertheless, the Ugandan example represents an alternative to solely state or criminal justice based models.

Terwiel (2020) disputes the definition of carceral feminism as it has been applied to interventions in gender-based violence. She argues the women's movement in the United States did not bring about the carceral state and questions whether all feminist-led attempts at law reform in relation to gender-based violence should be labelled as carceral feminism, as if any such effort inescapably extends control and punishment. According to Terwiel (2020) critics of carceral feminism present a binary choice between informal community-based solutions and criminal justice approaches, which portrays the state as inevitably punitive. There could be models of state intervention in intimate violence that prioritised welfare over criminal justice. This point is important, but welfare is also a site of punitive control and violence as attested by historical examples such as child removal from Indigenous communities or contemporary examples of sanctioning in relation to finding employment. However, the state is an essential actor in effecting widespread structural change such as social and economic redistribution of wealth. Threadcraft and Miller (2017) contend activist groups can challenge state violence but cannot do its job as they cannot match the state for resources. Debates over state involvement in the prevention of domestic violence and abuse demonstrate the complexity of the issue. Intersectional critiques of carceral solutions reveal both the dangers of overcriminalisation and relative inaction by the state.

Homicide

Homicide between men in violent confrontations can be interpreted as an extreme way of achieving masculinity. Homicidal violence is a masculine resource deployed to establish dominance over other men in confrontational situations where a man perceives challenge to his honour or status (Messerschmidt, 2012; Polk, 1994). Such situations tend to take place in public and frequently involve heavy consumption of alcohol (Alder & Polk, 1996). Brookman and Maguire (2005) argue alcohol fuelled 'masculinity honour contests' account for a substantial proportion of homicides in England and Wales. Breaking the link between drunkenness and masculine bravado would be effective for reducing lethal violence. Alder and Polk (1996) state that men's lethal violence is not always a means to accomplish masculinity. Their research into men who kill their children found these homicides often derived from desperation and despair.

The notion of accomplishing or shoring up hegemonic masculinity is significant in understanding hate crime homicides. The motivation for fatal violence in these cases ranges from establishing dominance over putatively weaker men, expressing outrage at the perceived transgressive gender identity or sexuality of the victim or as a response to humiliation over feeling a deficit of masculinity. Anti-LGBTQ hate crime murders are characterised by a 'tone of outrage' at the perceived failure of others to embody ideals of masculinity, and/or their subversion of masculine gender identity (Kelley & Gruenewald, 2015; Tomsen, 2009). Lee and Peter (2014) examine the 'trans panic defence' to murder, whereby the defendant claims they thought the victim was cis not trans and this 'deception' provoked into them into outrage. Such defences bear the influence of cultural constructions of queerness as 'unmanly' and transphobic stereotypes about the inauthenticity of trans people's gender identities. Hate crime murders of homeless men can shore up the perpetrator's sense of hegemonic masculinity via exerting domination over a 'weaker' man and can also express disgust for the victim's perceived failure to achieve masculinity (Allison & Klein, 2021).

Episode 'Double Lives' of documentary series *Love and Hate Crime* (2018–2019) explores the murder in Mississippi of Mercedes

Williamson, a young trans woman, by her cis gender boyfriend Josh Vallum. He initially claimed 'trans panic' as his motive, but it emerged that he knew Mercedes was trans and did not want his friends to find out. *Boys Don't Cry* (1999) dramatises the story of Brandon Teena, a trans man murdered by two cis men in a small town in Nebraska in 1993. A few days before the murder, Teena's killers had forcibly disrobed and raped him. *Boys Don't Cry* portrays the rape and murder of Brandon Teena as hate crimes, whereby his attackers are both attracted and repelled by his trans identity (Barron, 2005). The film also shows how Teena was humiliated by the police in relation to his gender identity when he reported the rape. It has been criticised for casting a cisgendered female actor as Teena and for potentially feeding transphobic voyeurism by depicting a brutal rape of a trans man (Bendix, 2019).

Kalish and Kimmel (2010) assess the significance of hegemonic masculinity to mass shootings in educational institutions. The cultural standard of hegemonic masculinity induces aggrievement—and humil-iation—in some boys and young men who feel they do not match up. Their response is excessive violence to achieve the status to which they feel entitled. Scaptura and Boyle (2020) examine how some mass shooters, such as Elliot Rodger, were members of online 'incel' commu-nities. Incels are young men who identify as 'involuntarily celibate' and embrace misogynistic constructions of gender identity, which position men as naturally superior to women. The social progress of women is viewed as a threat to men and masculinity. Mass shooters who identify as incels react to gender role stress with homicidal violence as an extreme display of masculinity.

Case study:

Elliot Rodger was a 22 year old man who killed six people, two women and four men, and injured several others in Isla Vista in 2014 before shooting himself. He used a YouTube video and manifesto to explain his motives as hatred of women and of men who were successful in having relationships with women, particularly men of colour. Vito et al. (2018) interpret Rodger as feeling a sense of 'aggrieved entitlement' stemming from his adherence to ideals of hegemonic masculinity, which he felt he could not meet. Documentary *Inside the Secret World of Incels* (2019) examines the subculture of incels online and the connection between this subculture and mass shootings and hate crimes.

The sense of entitlement that characterises investment in hegemonic masculinity is a constituent part of constructions of white masculinity. Seal and O'Neill (2017) discuss two young adult novels, which address intersections of race, class and masculinity in school shootings. These novels challenge the racialisation of violent crime in the United States and highlight how aggrieved entitlement, underpinned by misogyny, racism and homophobia, is a toxic expression of white masculinity.

Woman Killing and Femicide

Women's death through homicide is more likely to take place in private and domestic settings than men's deaths. Gartner and McCarthy (1991) found this held over time in their research into the killing of women in Vancouver and Toronto between 1920 and 1988. In the United States, women are a quarter of murder victims, a third of whom are killed by a male partner. Only three per cent of male murder victims are killed by female partners. Worldwide, 40% of women homicide victims are killed by a male partner, with only six per cent of male victims killed by women partners (Stockl et al., 2013). Indigenous women aged 25–44 in Canada are five times more likely to die as a result of violence than other women. Distinctly from non-Indigenous women, they are as likely to be killed by a stranger as an intimate partner (Hargreaves, 2017). Walklate et al. (2020) emphasise that intimate partner homicide is a significant risk for women worldwide and is a marker of gender inequality. Political and media attention focuses more on the threat of global (non-state) terrorism, which pales in comparison in terms of extent of victimisation.

The murders of women in intimate relationships often follow years of domestic violence and abuse. Leaving an abusive relationship is a particularly high-risk time (Taylor & Jasinski, 2011). In Turkey, half of women's murders are by an intimate partner, with sexual jealousy and controlling violence in relation to infidelity being the most common motive (Toprak & Ersoy, 2017). Cullen et al. (2019) identified similar patterns in Australia, where more than half of women's murders were by a male partner. The biggest risk factors were previous experience of intimate violence and ending or being estranged from a relationship. Intimate murders do not always proceed from a situation of escalating physical violence in a relationship; jealousy and controlling behaviour are also significant precursors (Johnson et al., 2019). Messerschmidt (2017) argues intimate partner killing is a way of restoring dominant masculinity where men perceive it to have been undermined.

The term 'femicide' was popularised in the mid-1970s by feminist Diana Russell to refer to the misogynistic murders of women, or the killing of women by men *because* they are women (Radford & Russell, 1992). In Latin America, the term was translated as 'feminicidio' and its meaning expanded to include the structural violence of gender inequality (Corradi et al., 2016). In the mid-2000s, Mexican city Ciudad Juarez became internationally notorious for the high murder rates of women and girls there since the early 1990s. In the 1990s, feminist activists in Mexico deployed feminicidio to encompass how the murders of women and girls were not simply 'private' tragedies but consequences of structural violence in a failed state that did not adequately intervene to ensure women's safety (Corradi et al., 2016; Wright, 2011). Activists highlighted the imbalance of power between women and men and interpreted this imbalance as entailing an inferior form of citizenship for women. Feminists framed the murders of women and girls as a political issue and argued the conditions that made the murders possible needed to be tackled. These conditions included the neoliberalised economy, which rendered workers disposable, and an attitude that the experience of violence was 'normal' for women (Wright, 2011).

Bordertown (2006) is based on failed investigations into the Ciudad Juarez murders. Eva is a fifteen year old Indigenous girl who works at a factory, or maquiladora. Travelling home one day, the driver of her bus takes her to a remote spot and along with another man rapes, violently attacks and leaves her for dead. Lauren, a Mexican–American journalist, travels to Ciudad Juarez to investigate the femicides. She meets Eva and goes undercover as a factory worker in an attempt to bring the attackers to justice. Monnet (2017) argues the film portrays the relevance of neoliberalism to femicide in Ciudad Juarez through Eva's back story of being forced off her family land and sent to work in a maquiladora in a free trade zone because her family could not afford to pay land taxes. As Indigenous women living precarious lives in a border city, Eva and her mother were vulnerable to violence. The refusal of Lauren's newspaper to publish her story underlines that political and economic considerations take precedence over Mexican women's lives. Jeffries (2013) analyses how, to counter the failure of the state to prevent femicide, social organisations and documentary filmmakers investigated instead, bringing the murders to international attention. She highlights *Senorita Extraviada* (2001) as a political intervention, which countered the state's narrative about the missing women and challenged the impunity surrounding the femicides.

Carey and Torres (2010) argue in Guatemala violence against women constitutes, rather than tears, the social fabric. Political economy is crucial to the context in which this violence takes place. The conditions of globalisation, neoliberalism and economic crises increased levels of violence and helped to normalise it. The Brazilian penal code has included 'feminicide' as a specific type of homicide since 2015. Femicide in Brazil is connected to structural violence; the regions with the worst socioeconomic indicators have higher rates of interpersonal violence and femicide (Martins-Filho et al., 2018).

Shalhoub-Kevorkian (2003) interprets femicide in Palestine as sociopolitical, resulting from economic legacies and interwoven with colonialism. Women in the West Bank are subordinated within the patriarchal family, the maintenance of which is an attempt to preserve power in the face of Israeli settler colonialism. 'Honour' crimes against Palestinian women, which express denunciation for shaming the family or community, are interlinked with the nationalist struggle and exacerbated by occupation. Palestinian women are also endangered by the Israeli occupation and are vulnerable to military violence. Shalhoub-Kervorkian (2003) argues dominant narratives in the Global North designate the intimate murders of women by Western men 'crimes of passion', whereas the murders of women by Eastern men are 'crimes of honour', demarcating less 'civilised' cultures. This construction results from Orientalism, the Western assumption of superiority. Attributing 'honour crimes' to 'cultural norms' rather than social, political and economic factors is another form of colonial abuse.

The NiUnaMenos (translates as 'not one less') movement in Latin America originated in Argentina in 2015 following street protests in 2014 against femicide and violence against women. The slogan was coined during public readings at protest marches and the hashtag #NiUnaMenos was widely used on Twitter (Belotti et al., 2021). The movement radiated out from Argentina to other Latin American countries and NiUnaMenos became a network. Activists criticised the lack of official information on disappeared women, state inaction on violence against women and state complicity with violence (Chenou & Cepeda-Másmela, 2019). The movement incorporates feminist issues beyond femicide and physical violence against women. #NiUnaMenos has become a 'mother tag' for a range of demands, including expanded reproductive rights, affordable living, an end to racist migration laws and to the criminalisation of Indigenous people (Belotti et al., 2021; Langlois, 2020).

Women Who Kill

Women who kill elicit a high degree of cultural fascination. They violate norms of femininity such as gentleness, nurturance and care, which transgresses the gender order (Kilty & Frigon, 2016; Seal, 2010). Portrayals and representations of this transgression rely on entrenched stereotypes and archetypes of deviant womanhood, proving how difficult it is culturally to do without these stereotypes (Maury & Roche, 2020). The sexually assertive femme fatale is a persistent archetype and a staple of film noir and neo noir, from *Double Indemnity* (1944), to *Fatal Attraction* (1987) and *Basic Instinct* (1992), to *Gone Girl* (2014). The femme fatale is an evil woman adept at hiding her true nature, partly because of her physical beauty, and able to seduce men and engineer their destruction (Couch, 2021). Cultural archetypes such as the femme fatale exude misogynistic fears but do not represent the reality of women's homicide.

Female perpetrated homicide is comparatively rare, comprising around 15–20% of convictions worldwide. Women's killing usually takes place in domestic space and they very rarely kill strangers, patterns which hold historically (Callahan, 2013; Pretorius & Morgan, 2013). Women's most likely victims are their own children, followed by a male partner. Neonaticide, the killing of a newborn within the initial 24 hours of its life, is almost exclusively committed by women. There are around seven cases per year in the UK, although neonaticide is difficult to prove and likely to be more prevalent than this figure indicates. Neonaticides frequently follow a concealed pregnancy, although not always. Sometimes such cases are the result of failure to seek medical attention, rather than intentional killing (Brennan & Milne, 2018). Weare (2017) analyses legal narratives of women who kill their children, arguing they reinforce stereotypes of femininity. The ideology of motherhood dictates that to be a good woman, a woman must be a good mother. If women who kill their children can be portrayed as 'mad' or 'sad'—acting under the influence of psychosis, severe depression or limiting life circumstances—their femininity can be preserved as their behaviour has a culturally recognisable explanation. However, the 'bad' woman narrative is absolute and leaves no room for complexity. The social conditions of motherhood and the cultural and emotional ambivalence that comes along with it are denied.

In *I've Loved You So Long* (2008) Juliette, a former doctor, leaves prison after serving a fifteen year sentence for murdering her son. The film depicts Juliette rebuilding and re-establishing relationships with family members, including her nieces, transcending suspicion that she poses a threat. *I've Loved You So Long* presents Juliette as a fully realised human being, eschewing stereotypes. Comedy-drama series *Back to Life* (2019–present) concerns Miri, a woman who returns to her parents' home after spending eighteen years in prison for killing her best friend when she was a teenager. Miri is portrayed as sensitive and resilient despite the opprobrium she receives from people in her town. As a comedy, *Back to Life* is tonally different from *I've Loved You So Long* but is similar in drawing a woman who has killed as a fully realised character.

When women kill their male partners, it is frequently in the context of an abusive relationship. Legal reforms in several countries to make it easier for women to use evidence of the effects of ongoing abuse to support a defence to murder entail deploying medical evidence and psychological explanations. Battered Woman Syndrome is a mental health condition argued to develop in response to long term abuse in a relationship. It induces feelings of helplessness and fatalism, whereby women who kill their partners perceive homicide to be the only way out. Documentary *The Perfect Victim* (2015) focuses on the stories of four women in Missouri who were convicted of murdering their abusive husbands and received long sentences before the courts had started to hear evidence related to BWS.

Battered Woman Syndrome has been used to support defences of diminished responsibility in Scotland, which reduce murder to manslaughter if successful. McPherson (2020) argues the problem with Battered Woman Syndrome (BWS) is that it pathologises women, potentially making them less sympathetic to juries. The connection between helplessness and taking the extreme action of killing someone is difficult to reconcile. In Scotland, there is a move to present evidence of Post Traumatic Stress Disorder instead (McPherson, 2020). Ho and Chantagul (2017) conducted a public opinion survey about women who kill abusive partners in Thailand. Evidence of Battered Woman Syndrome did not have a positive influence on how people interpreted women's actions. They suggest that BWS pathologises women who kill abusive partners, but also that women who kill could not be viewed as 'good' women.

Women killing other women can be the outcome of an abusive relationship, but in these cases the woman who kills is also the abuser. Women who kill female partners have often deployed abusive and controlling behaviours in the relationship (Glass et al., 2004). Goel (2015) examines Indian 'dowry murders', where mothers-in-law perpetrate or are accomplices to the murders of their daughters-in-law motivated by dissatisfaction with their dowry (the transfer of money, gifts or property from the bride's family to her husband's). Goel (2015) interprets such murders as the misuse of the limited power women can exert as mothers-in-law—limited because ultimately the family is a patriarchal institution.

Historically recurrent discourses and narratives of femininity play a role in how women who kill are represented and treated. Women who were found guilty of murder by poisoning in nineteenth-century England faced stricter sentences than men. The 'bad' woman was judged harshly and did not have a single guise—women were bad for reasons such as being greedy, manipulative or working as prostitutes (Nagy, 2015). Women in late eighteenth and early nineteenth-century London were often convicted of manslaughter rather than murder, a form of benevolence that meant they escaped capital sentencing. However, women who worked as servants or prostitutes, and unmarried women, faced harsh punishment, demonstrating benevolence was not available for women seen as low status and/or disreputable (Callahan, 2013).

Black (2020) examines discourses of pathology in cases of women convicted of murder in mid twentieth-century Ireland, arguing that such women were seen as 'difficult' rather than dangerous. The interpretations of women's pathology that circulated in the criminal justice system drew on contemporary understandings of 'degeneracy', 'feeble-mindedness' and hereditary insanity. Black (2018) explains women convicted of murder were often released to Magdalene laundries—church run women only institutions—after prison, or sometimes sent to a laundry as an alternative to prison. At first glance, this would appear to constitute lenient treatment, but its effect was to confine women for longer than they would have been solely through a prison sentence. Black's work highlights how discourses of feminine pathology do not necessarily confer leniency.

Discourses and narratives of femininity continue to influence whether women who kill are portrayed sympathetically or with condemnation. Easteal et al. (2015) analysed representations of women who kill in studies of news media across six countries. They identified recurrent tropes of bad motherhood, flawed motherhood, helpless victims and monstrous women, depending on the type of case reported. Seal (2010) argues discourses of femininity in relation to women who kill both recur and shift in meaning over time. Women's sexuality, respectability, domesticity and motherhood are culturally judged and regulated—not in the same way, everywhere, but they retain symbolic potency. Seal (2010) explores five recurrent discourses of women who kill: the masculine woman, the muse or mastermind dichotomy, the damaged personality, the respectable woman and the witch. These representations of womanhood are intersectional; race, class, age and sexuality are all highly significant to their narration.

Different types of interpersonal violence sustain social hierarchies and bind forms of domination together. The gendered aspects of interpersonal violence need to be understood in relation to other interlocking elements of social identity. Interpersonal violence is not separate from other forms of violence, something which an intersectional analysis makes clear.

References

Alder, C. M., & Polk, K. (1996). Masculinity and child homicide. *British Journal of Criminology, 36*, 396–411.

Allison, K., & Klein, B. R. (2021). Pursuing hegemonic masculinity through violence: An examination of anti-homeless bias homicides, *Journal of Interpersonal Violence, 36*, 6859–6882.

Anitha, S. (2019). Understanding economic abuse through an intersectional lens: Financial abuse, control, and exploitation of women's productive and reproductive labor. *Violence against Women, 25*, 1854–1877.

Bailey, F. Y. (2009). Screening stereotypes. In D. Humphries (Ed.), *Women, violence, and the media: Readings in feminist criminology.* Northeastern University Press.

Bair-MErritt, M. H., Shea Crowne, S., Thompson, D. A., Sibinga, E., Trent, M., & Campbell, J. (2010). Why do women use intimate partner violence? A systematic review of women's motivations. *Trauma, Violence, & Abuse, 11*, 178–189.

Barlow, C., Johnson, K., Walklate, S., & Humphreys, L. (2019). Putting coercive control into practice: Problems and possibilities. *The British Journal of Criminology, 60*, 160–179.

Barron, A. (2005). Productive discomfort in the classroom. *New Review of Film and Television Studies, 3*, 75–84.

Belknap, J., & Grant, D. (2021). Domestic violence policy: A world of change. *Feminist Criminology, 16*, 382–395.

Belotti, F., Comunello, F., & Corradi, C. (2021). Feminicidio and #NiUna Menos: An analysis of Twitter conversations during the first 3 years of the Argentinean movement. *Violence against Women, 27*, 1035–1063.

Bendix, T. (2019, October 9). Boys Don't Cry 20 years later: For trans men, a divisive legacy. *New York Times.*

Bettinson, V. (2016). Criminalising coercive control in domestic violence cases: Should Scotland follow the path of England and wales? *Criminal Law Review, 3*, 165–180.

Black, L. (2018). "On the other hand the accused is a woman…": Women and the death penalty in post-independence Ireland. *Law and History Review, 36*, 139–172.

Black, L. (2020). The pathologisation of women who kill: Three cases from Ireland. *Social History of Medicine, 33*, 417–437.

BlackLivesMatter. (2021). About - Black Lives Matter, https://blacklivesmatter.com/about/

Blagg, H., & Anthony, T. (2019). *Decolonising criminology*. Springer.

Brennan, K., & Milne, E. (2018). Criminalising neonaticide: Reflections on law and practice in England and Wales. In K. Brennan, E. Milne, N. South & J. Turton (Eds.), *Women in the criminal justice system*. Palgrave.

Brookman, F., & Maguire, M. (2005). Reducing homicide: A review of the possibilities. *Crime, Law and Social Change, 42*, 325–403.

Brubaker, S. (2020). Identifying influences in intimate partner violence in LGBTQ relationships through an ecological framework. In B. Russell (Ed.), *Intimate partner violence and LGBTQ+ community: Understanding power dynamics*. Springer.

Burman, M., & Brooks-Hay, O. (2018). Aligning policy and law? The creation of a domestic abuse offence incorporating coercive control. *Criminology & Criminal Justice, 18*, 67–83.

Callahan, K. (2013). Women who kill: An analysis of cases in late eighteenth- and early nineteenth-century London. *Journal of Social History, 46*, 1013–1038.

Carey, D., & Torres, M. G. (2010). Precursors to femicide: Guatemalan women in a vortex of violence. *Latin American Research Review, 45*, 142–164.

Chencu, J.-M., & Cepeda-Másmela, C. (2019). #NiUnaMenos: Data activism from the Global South. *Television & New Media, 20*, 396–411.

Chiu, T. Y. (2017). Marriage migration as a multifaceted system: The intersectionality of intimate partner violence in cross-border marriages. *Violence against Women, 23*, 1293–1313.

Clark, A. (2000). Domesticity and the problem of wife beating in nineteenth century Britain. In S. D'Cruze & I. Crewe (Eds.), *Everyday violence in Britain, 1850–195–*. Routledge.

Collins. P. H. (1998). The tie that binds: Race, gender and US violence. *Ethnic and Racial Studies, 21*, 917–938.

Collins, P. H. (2017). On violence, intersectionality and transversal politics. *Ethnic and Racial Studies, 40*, 1460–1473.

Corradi, C., Marcuello-Servós, C., Boira, S., & Weil, S. (2016). Theories of femicide and their significance for social research. *Current Sociology, 64*, 975–995.

Couch, R. (2021). The "Gone Girl effect": "Girling" the femme fatale in Gillian Flynn's Gone Girl. In C. Beyer (Ed.), *Contemporary crime fiction: Crossing boundaries, merging genres*. Cambridge Scholars Publishing.

Cramer, E. P., & Plummer, S.-B. (2009). People of color with disabilities: Intersectionality as a framework for analyzing intimate partner violence in social, historical, and political contexts. *Journal of Aggression, Maltreatment & Trauma, 18*, 162–181.

Creek, S. J., & Dunn, J. L. (2011). Rethinking gender and violence: Agency, heterogeneity, and intersectionality. *Sociology Compass, 5*, 311–322.

Crenshaw, K. (1991). Mapping the margins: Intersectionality, identity politics, and violence against women of color. *Stanford Law Review, 43*(6), 1241–1299.

Crockett, C., Cooper, B., & Brandl, B. (2018). Intersectional stigma and late-life intimate-partner and sexual violence: How social workers can bolster safety and healing for older survivors. *The British Journal of Social Work, 48*, 1000–1013.

Cullen, P., Vaughan, G., & LI, Z., Price, J., Yu, D. & Sullivan, E. (2019). Counting dead women in Australia: An in-depth case review of femicide. *Journal of Family Violence, 34*, 1–8.

Day, A. S., & Gill, A. K. (2020). Applying intersectionality to partnerships between women's organizations and the criminal justice system in relation to domestic violence. *The British Journal of Criminology, 60*, 830–850.

Dobash, R. E., & Dobash, R. (1979).*Violence against wives: A case against patriarchy*. Free Press.

Donovan, C., & Barnes, R. (2020). Help-seeking among lesbian, gay, bisexual and/or transgender victims/survivors of domestic violence and abuse: The impacts of cisgendered heteronormativity and invisibility. *Journal of Sociology, 56*, 554–570.

Donovan, C., & Hester, M. (2015). *Domestic violence and sexuality: What's love got to do with it?* Policy Press.

Durfee, A. (2021). The use of structural intersectionality as a method to analyze how the domestic violence civil protective order process replicates inequality. *Violence against Women, 27*, 639–665.

Easteal, P., Bartels, L., Nelson, N., & Holland, K. (2015). How are women who kill portrayed in newspaper media? Connections with social values and the legal system. *Women's Studies International Forum, 51*, 31–41.

Frankland, A., & Brown, J. (2014). Coercive control in same-sex intimate partner violence. *Journal of Family Violence, 29*, 15–22.

Gartner, R., & MCCarthy, B. (1991). The social distribution of femicide in urban Canada, 1921–1988. *Law & Society Review, 25*, 287–311.

George, J., & Stith, S. M. (2014). An updated feminist view of intimate partner violence. *Family Process, 53*, 179–193.

Glass, N., Koziol-Mclain, J., Campbell, J., & Block, C. R. (2004). Female-perpetrated femicide and attempted femicide: A case study. *Violence against Women, 10*, 606–625.

Goel, R. (2015). Women who kill women. *The William & Mary Journal of Women and the Law, 22*, 549.

Hamilton, P. (1939). *Gas light*. Constable.

Hamilton, S. (2001). Making history with Frances Power Cobbe: Victorian feminism, domestic violence, and the language of imperialism. *Victorian Studies, 43*, 437–460.

Hargreaves, A. (2017). *Violence against indigenous women: Literature, activism, resistance*. Wilfrid Laurier University Press.

Hester, M. (2012). Portrayal of women as intimate partner domestic violence perpetrators. *Violence against Women, 18*, 1067–1082.

Hester, M. (2013). Who does what to whom? Gender and domestic violence perpetrators in English police records. *European Journal of Criminology, 10*, 623–637.

Ho, R. T. K., & Chantagul, N. (2017). An exploration of Thai public perceptions of defenses in cases of women who kill their domestically violent spouses. *Australian & New Zealand Journal of Criminology, 50*, 602–622.

Hsu, V. J. (2019). (Trans)forming #MeToo: Toward a networked response to gender violence. *Women's Studies in Communication, 42*, 269–286.

INCITE!. (2021). About INCITE!, https://incite-national.org/history/

Jeffries, F. (2013). Documentary noir in the city of fear: Feminicide, impunity and grassroots communication in Ciudad Juarez. *Crime, Media, Culture, 9*, 301–317.

Johnson, H., Eriksson, L., Mazerolle, P., & Wortley, R. (2019). Intimate femicide: The role of coercive control. *Feminist Criminology, 14*, 3–23.

Josephson, J. (2002). The intersectionality of domestic violence and welfare in the lives of poor women. *Journal of Poverty, 6*, 1–20.

Kalish, R., & Kimmel, M. (2010). Suicide by mass murder: Masculinity, aggrieved entitlement, and rampage school shootings. *Health Sociology Review, 19*, 451–464.

Kelley, K., & Gruenewald, J. (2015). Accomplishing masculinity through anti-lesbian, gay, bisexual, and transgender homicide: A comparative case study approach. *Men and Masculinities, 18*, 3–29.

Kilty, J. M., & Frigon, S. (2016). *The enigma of a violent woman: A critical examination of the case of Karla Homolka*. Routledge.

Kim, M. E. (2018). From carceral feminism to transformative justice: Women-of-color feminism and alternatives to incarceration. *Journal of Ethnic & Cultural Diversity in Social Work, 27*, 219–233.

Kim, M. E. (2020). The carceral creep: Gender-based violence, race, and the expansion of the punitive state, 1973–1983. *Social Problems, 67*, 251–269.

Langlois, A. (2020). #NiUnaMenos: Countering hegemonies in Argentina. *Engenderings* [Online]. Available from https://blogs.lse.ac.uk/gender/2020/02/10/niunamenos-countering-hegemonies-in-argentina/. Accessed 8 July 2021.

Larance, L. Y., Goodmark, L., Miller, S. L., & Dasgupta, S. D. (2019). Understanding and addressing women's use of force in intimate relationships: A retrospective. *Violence against Women, 25*, 56–80.

Lee, C., & Kwan, P. (2014). The trans panic defense: Masculinity, heteronormativity, and the murder of transgender women. *Hastings Law Journal, 66*, 77.

Martins-Filho, P. R. S., Mendes, M. L. T., Reinheimer, D. M., Do Nascimento-Júnior, E. M., Vaez, A. C., Santos, V. S., & Santos, H. P. (2018). Femicide trends in Brazil: Relationship between public interest and mortality rates. *Archives of Women's Mental Health, 21*, 579–582.

Maury, C., & RochE, D. (2020). Introduction. In D. Roche, D., & C. Maury (Eds.), *Women who kill: Gender and sexuality in film and series of the postfeminist era*. Bloomsbury.

McCarrick, J., Davis-MCCabe, C., & Hirst-Winthrop, S. (2016). Men's experiences of the criminal justice system following female perpetrated intimate partner violence. *Journal of Family Violence, 31*, 203–213.

McLaughlin, C. (2019). Shirleen has lost 3 close family members to violence. If it happened anywhere else, it would be a national emergency. *MamaMia*.

McPherson, R. (2020). Battered woman syndrome, Diminished responsibility and women who kill: Insights from Scottish case law. *The Journal of Criminal Law, 83*, 381–393.

Mehrotra, G. R., Kimball, E., & Wahab, S. (2016). The braid that binds us: The impact of neoliberalism, criminalization, and professionalization on domestic violence work. *Affilia, 31*, 153–163.

Messerschmidt, J. (2012). *Gender, heterosexuality, and youth violence: The struggle for recognition.* Rowman and Littlefield.

Messerschmidt, J. W. (2017). Masculinities and femicide. *Qualitative Sociology Review, 13.*

Messinger, A. A. (2017). *LGBTQ intimate partner violence: Lessons for policy, practice, and research.* University of California Press.

Messinger, A. A., & Roark, J. (2019). LGBTQ partner violence. In W. S. Dekeseredy, C. M. Rennison, & A. K. Hall-Sanchez (Eds.), *Routledge handbook of violence studies.* Routledge.

Monnet, A. S. (2017). Border gothic: Gregory Nava's Bordertown and the dark side of NAFTA. In L. Blake, & A. S. Monnet (Eds.), *Neoliberal gothic: International gothic in the neoliberal age.* Manchester University Press.

Nagy, V. (2015). *Nineteenth-century female poisners: Three English women who used arsenic to kill.* Palgrave.

Nichols, A. J. (2013). Meaning-making and domestic violence victim advocacy: An examination of feminist identities, ideologies, and practices. *Feminist Criminology, 8*, 177–201.

Nixon, J., & Humphreys, C. (2010). Marshalling the evidence: Using intersectionality in the domestic violence frame. *Social Politics: International Studies in Gender, State & Society, 17*, 137–158.

Parson, N. (2010). "I Am Not [Just] a Rabbit Who Has a Bunch of Children!": Agency in the midst of suffering at the intersections of global inequalities, gendered violence, and migration. *Violence against Women, 16*, 881–901.

Polavarapu, A. (2019). Global carceral feminism and domestic violence: What the West can learn from reconciliation in Uganda. *Harvard Journal of Law and Gender, 42*, 123.

Polk, K. (1994). Masculinity, honour, confrontational homicide. In T. Newburn, & E. Stanko (Eds.), *Just boys doing business? men, masculinities and crime*, 166–188. Routledge.

Pretorius, G., & Morgan, B. (2013). Women who kill in post-apartheid South Africa A content analysis of media reports. *Journal of Psychology in Africa, 23*, 393–400.

Radford, J., & Russell, D. (1992). *Femicide: The politics of woman killing.* Twayne.

Ramsey, C. B. (2011). Domestic violence and state intervention in the American West and Australia, 1860–1930. *Indiana Law Journal, 86*, 185.

Renzetti, C. (1992). *Violent betrayal: Partner abuse in lesbian relationships.* Sage.

Richie, B. E., & Eife, E. (2021). Black bodies at the dangerous intersection of gender violence and mass criminalization. *Journal of Aggression, Maltreatment & Trauma, 30,* 1–12.

Richie, B. E., Kanuha, V. K., & Martensen, K. M. (2021). Colluding with and resisting the state: Organizing against gender violence in the U.S. *Feminist Criminology, 16,* 247–265.

Ristock, J. (2002). *No more secrets: Violence in lesbian relationships.* Routledge.

Ristock, J., Zoccole, A., Passante, L., & Potskin, J. (2019). Impacts of colonization on Indigenous two-spirit/LGBTQ Canadians' experiences of migration, mobility and relationship violence. *Sexualities, 22,* 767–784.

Rogers, M. (2019). Challenging cisgenderism through trans people's narratives of domestic violence and abuse. *Sexualities, 22,* 803–820.

Rogers, M. M. (2019). Exploring the domestic abuse narratives of trans and nonbinary people and the role of cisgenderism in identity abuse, misgendering, and pathologizing. *Violence against Women.* https://doi.org/10.107 7801220971368.

Scaptura, M. N., & Boyle, K. M. (2020). Masculinity threat, "Incel" traits, and violent fantasies among heterosexual men in the United States. *Feminist Criminology, 15,* 278–298.

Scheer, J. R., & Poteat, V. P. (2021). Trauma-informed care and health among LGBTQ intimate partner violence survivors. *Journal of Interpersonal Violence, 36,* 6670–6692.

Seal, L. (2010). *Women, murder and femininity: Gender representations of women who kill.* Palgrave.

Seal, L., & O'Neill, M. (2017). Transgressive imaginations. In E. Carrabine & M. Brown (Eds.), *Oxford research encyclopedia of criminology and criminal justice.* Oxford University Press.

Shalhoub-Kevorkian, N. (2003). Reexamining femicide: Breaking the silence and crossing "scientific" borders. *Signs: Journal of Women in Culture and Society, 28,* 581–608.

Shoos, D. L. (2017). *Domestic violence in Hollywood film.* Springer.

Smollin, L. M. (2016). "You want fireworks? I'll show you fireworks!": Or not—Woman-to-woman violence on Sex and the City, The L Word, and The O.C. *Sexuality & Culture, 20,* 214–235.

Smye, V., Varcoe, C., Browne, A. J., Dion Stout, M., Josewski, V., Ford-Gilboe, M., & Keith, B. (2021). Violence at the intersections of women's lives in an urban context: Indigenous women's experiences of leaving and/or staying with an abusive partner. *Violence against Women, 27,* 1586–1607.

Sokoloff, N. J. (2008). Expanding the intersectional paradigm to better understand domestic violence in immigrant communities. *Critical Criminology, 16*, 229.

Stark, E. (2013). Coercive control. In N. Lombard & L. McMillan (Eds.), *Violence against women: Current theory and practice in domestic abuse, sexual violence and exploitation.* Jessica Kingsley.

Stark, E., & Hester, M. (2019). Coercive control: Update and review. *Violence against Women, 25*, 81–104.

Stockl, H., Devries, K., Rotstein, A., Abrahams, N., Campbell, J., Watts, C., & Garcia Moreno, C. (2013). The global prevalence of intimate partner violence: A systematic review. *The Lancet, 382*, 859–865.

Subirana-Malaret, M., Gahagan, J., & Parker, R. (2019). Intersectionality and sex and gender-based analyses as promising approaches in addressing intimate partner violence treatment programs among LGBT couples: A scoping review. *Cogent Social Sciences, 5*, 1644982.

Syrett, N. L. (2021). Responding to domestic violence in the nineteenth-century United States. *Journal of Women's History, 33*(1), 158–162.

Tapia, S. T. (2020). Beyond carceral expansion: Survivors' experiences of using specialised courts for violence against women in Ecuador. *Social & Legal Studies.* 0964663920973747.

Taylor, R., & Jasinski, J. L. (2011). Femicide and the feminist perspective. *Homicide Studies, 15*, 341–362.

Terwiel, A. (2020). What Is carceral feminism? *Political Theory, 48*, 421–442.

Threadcraft, S., & Miller, L. L. (2017). Black women, victimization, and the limitations of the liberal state. *Theoretical Criminology, 21*, 478–493.

Tolmie, J. R. (2018). Coercive control: To criminalize or not to criminalize? *Criminology & Criminal Justice, 18*, 50–66.

Tomsen, S. (2009). *Violence, prejudice and sexuality.* Routledge.

Toprak, S., & Ersoy, G. (2017). Femicide in Turkey between 2000 and 2010. *PLOS One, 12*.

United Nations. (2021). *Ending violence against women and girls*, https://www.un.org/sustainabledevelopment/ending-violence-against-women-and-girls/

Vito, C., Admire, A., & Hughes, E. (2018). Masculinity, aggrieved entitlement and violence: considering the Isla Vista mass shooting. *International Journal for Masculinity Studies, 13*, 86–102.

Walklate, S., Fitz-Gibbon, K., McCulloch, J. & Maher, J. (2020). *Towards a Global Femicide Index: Counting the Costs.* Routledge.

Waller, B. Y., Harris, J. & Quinn, C. R. Caught in the crossroad: An intersectional examination of African American women intimate partner violence survivors' help seeking. *Trauma, Violence, & Abuse.* 1524838021991303.

Watego, C., Macoun, A., Singh, D., & Strakosch, E. (2021, May25). Carceral feminism and coercive control: When Indigenous women aren't seen as ideal victims, witnesses or women. *The Conversation.*

Weare, S. (2013). "The Mad", "The Bad", "The Victim": Gendered constructions of women who kill within the criminal justice system. *Laws, 2,* 337–361.

Weare, S. (2017). Bad, mad or sad? Legal language, narratives, and identity constructions of women who kill their children in England and Wales. *International Journal for the Semiotics of Law - Revue Internationale De Sémiotique Juridique, 30,* 201–222.

World Health Organization. (2021). *Violence against women,* https://www.who.int/news-room/fact-sheets/detail/violence-against-women

Wright, M. W. (2011). Necropolitics, narcopolitics, and femicide: Gendered violence on the Mexico-U.S. border. *Signs: Journal of Women in Culture and Society, 36,* 707–731.

3

Sexual Violence

Sexual violence secures and reproduces inequalities of gender and race, as well as other hierarchies of power related to class, sexuality, dis/ability and citizenship (Armstrong et al., 2018; Collins, 1998; Heberle, 2014). The previous chapter discussed Collins's (1998, 2017) argument that violence binds together different forms of domination, making it an important entry point for understanding intersectionality. Sexual violence is enabled and perpetrated by individuals, organisations and states, with interconnections between these different levels. What binds them together is their support of wider systems of gendered and racialised domination. This chapter discusses universities as an example of how organisations can have negative cultures that perpetuate existing power differentials and facilitate sexual violence. States sanction sexual violence during wartime, as explored in Chapter 6, but also in state-run institutions such as prisons and other secure institutions, through invasive body searches, sexual abuse by prison staff and inadequate protection from sexual abuse by other inmates (Jenness & Fenstermaker, 2016; VanNatta, 2010).

Sexual violence refers to rape, sexual assault and sexual harassment. It incorporates a range of actions and experiences which, as with other

© The Author(s), under exclusive license to Springer Nature Switzerland AG 2022
L. Seal, *Gender, Crime and Justice*,
https://doi.org/10.1007/978-3-030-87488-9_3

forms of violence, are linked by their relationship to reinforcing and recreating existing patterns of domination and inequality. The prevalence of sexual violence worldwide is high: 35% of women experience physical or sexual violence from an intimate partner or someone else in their lifetime and 7% of women are sexually assaulted by someone other than an intimate partner during their lifetime (WHO, 2021; World Bank, 2019). Rates of sexual violence are highest among young women 16–24, trans people and people with disabilities (World Bank, 2019). Less than 40% of women who experience sexual violence seek help, and less than 10% report their assault to the police (World Population Review, 2021). It is likely that statistics, even from victim report surveys, do not fully capture the extent of the problem.

Since the 1970s, dominant feminist understandings of sexual violence, particularly rape, emphasise it as a primary means through which men subjugate women (Brownmiller, 1975). Not all men commit rape and not all women are raped, but the threat of sexual violence subjugates all women through persistent fear. Men benefit as the threat of sexual violence holds in place their power over women. This understanding identifies the link between sexual violence and domination, but does not acknowledge intersectional differences between different groups of women and men (Heberle, 2014). Rates of sexual violence are higher among people of colour, poor, queer, and LGBTQ people, which is missed by homogenising experiences (Armstrong et al., 2018; Wooter, 2015). The dominant feminist understanding also perceives sexual violence as something done to women by men. While sexual violence is disproportionately experienced by women and perpetrated by men ignoring the victimisation of men and perpetration by women not only denies the experiences of male victims and women attacked by other women, it also essentialises gender differences, and makes the binary of masculine power and feminine victimisation seem inevitable (Mack & McCann, 2018). Perpetration and victimisation beyond the gender binary ends up being ignored.

What Is Sexual Violence?

The term sexual violence encompasses a wide range of experiences. What connects them is lack of consent from the victim/survivor to sexualised acts, behaviour or comments. Boyle (2019) stresses the importance of 'continuum thinking' in relation to sexual violence, an adaptation of Kelly's (1988) concept of a continuum of sexual violence, ranging from groping and 'catcalling' to rape. What connects these experiences is that they result from male domination. Kelly (1988) argued it was important feminists did not establish a hierarchy of experiences of sexual violence. Victim/survivors are not always affected in the same way by the same actions; they may not always perceive themselves as having been victimised. The context in which sexual violence takes place is crucial to how it is experienced and perceived. Boyle (2019) states there are a range of connections and continuums between different experiences. There is a continuum of sexual violence, and also a continuum of what counts as sex. Constructions of consent, desire and identity are all significant to what counts as sex and as sexual violence (Heberle, 2014). There is no dichotomy between sex and violence, rather a web of connections between them (Boyle, 2019).

This nuanced understanding of sexual violence is not the one which is culturally dominant. The law, the criminal justice system, the media and public understandings of sexual violence are influenced by, and reproduce, harmful myths and stereotypes. A dominant popular understanding of what constitutes 'real rape' has been particularly tenacious. 'Real rape' is committed by a male stranger against a woman or girl and involves vaginal penetration. There is an expectation that the victim/survivor would report the crime to the authorities as soon as possible afterwards (Estrich, 1987). The ideal victim of real rape is white and heterosexual (Serisier, 2018). The 'real rape' myth is inaccurate—victim/survivors usually know their attacker, the vast majority do not report their attack to the police (or any authority), white heterosexual women are not proportionately at the highest risk (Armstrong et al., 2018; Serisier, 2018). However, this myth influences views on what counts as sexual violence, both culturally and in the criminal justice system. Victim/survivors who do not fit the stereotype may be disbelieved and devalued; perpetrators who depart from it may not be recognised as such.

Other prevalent rape myths include the belief that victim/survivors provoke sexual violence through their dress and behaviour, that false claims are frequent and more likely to be made in relation to sexual violence than other crimes, that sex workers cannot be raped, or are unaffected by rape, and that Black women are promiscuous and 'unrapeable' (Khan et al., 2020; Sprankle et al., 2018). In the popular imagination, rape and sexual violence are crimes committed by an identifiable individual, or group of individuals. This perception means the role of organisations and states in enabling and perpetrating sexual violence is not acknowledged (Harris, 2013).

An exception to the focus on individuals as the perpetrators of sexual violence is the attention to the role of the Catholic Church, in different countries, in hiding the sexual abuse of children by priests. *Spotlight* (2016) dramatises the *Boston Globe*'s investigative reporting in 2002 into the sexual abuse of boys by priests in Boston. When complaints about certain priests were made, they were moved to new parishes and were able to continue abusing children. This theme of cover up and institutional complicity in sexual violence is effectively portrayed in the film.

Understandings of sexual violence relate to divisions between public and private space. 'Real rape' is perceived as taking place somewhere public but deserted, usually after dark. Datta (2016) examines divisions between public and private debates in relation to sexual violence interventions in India. She discusses the 'Badaun rapes' of 2014 when two Dalit (low caste) girls were raped, murdered and hanged from a tree after going into a dark field at night. This crime was interpreted as resulting from the girls' lack of safety in having no access to a toilet and needing to use the field at night. However, the assumption that women and girls are safe at home obfuscates how most sexual violence takes place in private space. Datta (2016) highlights that Indian law does not recognise spousal rape. She also emphasises that Dalit women and girls are especially likely to have their claims of sexual violence ignored by the police, or to have the police collude with their attackers.

Perceptions that women and girls are unsafe when alone in public space, particularly at night, and should regulate their movements accordingly is an aspect of 'rape culture'. Rape culture refers to a cultural context that normalises, encourages, or even permits, sexual violence (Fanghanel, 2019). Victim blaming implies that sexual violence was excusable in a given context, such as a woman not taking due care to avoid being alone at night, not to be drunk and not to be provocatively dressed. Other elements of rape culture are the objectification and sexualisation of certain groups in ways that devalue them and make sexual violence permissible (Fanghanel & Lim, 2017).

Rape culture is underpinned by normative constructions of femininity and masculinity that encode feminine submissiveness and masculine dominance, and by racialised understandings of gender that construct white women as more virtuous and vulnerable than women of colour, and white men as entitled to the sexual use of women's bodies. It is also heteronormative, constituting sexualities beyond heterosexuality, and genders beyond the gender binary, as of low worth and/or as shameful. Rape culture and rape myths are not monolithic and are not the same in all times and places. However, many of the key elements such as divisions between public and private space and the significance of norms of gender, race and class are recurrent and enduring.

The term 'rape culture' has entered popular culture, which has become an important site for debates about issues of consent, victim blaming and rape myths (Phillips, 2016). This can mean these concepts are employed more broadly in popular cultural forms than they are in academic literature. However, the concept of rape culture has entered the mainstream. Phillips (2016) highlights *Game of Thrones* (2011–2019) as an example of a television show that became controversial because of its frequent and gratuitous depictions of sexual violence. Multiple news outlets criticised it for perpetuating rape culture by glamorising sexual violence. In particular, an episode from season four, 'Breaker of Chains' (2014), depicted the rape of Cersei by her brother Jaime. The episode's director, Alex Graves, commented 'It becomes consensual by the end' (Lyons, 2014). This statement demonstrated a lack of understanding of consent and bore the influence of the myth that women are masochistic, secretly wanting to be raped (Phillips, 2016).

Rape culture is perpetuated online by framing how words and images are understood and through propagating misogynistic tropes and narratives of victim blaming (Dodge, 2016; Lumsden & Morgan, 2017). Online spaces and new technologies can facilitate new expressions of sexual violence and extend experiences of offline violence. Technology facilitated sexual violence includes the creation of sexualised images without consent, disseminating sexualised images without consent, forms of digital harassment such as receiving unwanted text and/or images, and receiving abusive gendered and/or sexualised responses on social media—trolling frequently combines sexual harassment with racist, homophobic and transphobic abuse (Lumsden & Morgan, 2017; McGlynn et al., 2017; Powell & Henry, 2019). Online/offline is not a binary; an abusive partner may perpetrate image-based abuse or digital harassment as well as physical violence and offline harassment (Powell & Henry, 2019). Powell and Henry's (2019) survey of Australian adults' experiences of technology facilitated sexual violence found that 62% of 18–54 year olds had experienced it at least once, with digital harassment and stalking by intimate partners being the most frequently experienced examples.

Race and Sexual Violence

Intersections between race and gender are crucial in terms of securing racial, as well as gender, domination through sexual violence. Under the forms of chattel slavery practised in the Caribbean and United States, enslaved Black women had no protection from sexual violence from white slave owners and overseers. High levels of sexual violence were part of the institution of slavery. Toni Morrison's novel *Beloved* (1987) (adapted into a film in 1998) portrays the haunting of Sethe, a Black woman who escaped slavery, by Beloved her dead child. Sethe killed her daughter aged two to save her from the sexual violence of white men. Her haunting by this infanticide, and by the experience of sexual violation when she was enslaved, highlights the collective trauma of institutionalised rape under slavery (Barnett, 1997).

This legacy from slavery needs to be understood in terms of contemporary Black American women's experiences of sexual violence and the criminal justice system, and the cultural portrayal of Black victim/survivors of sexual violence (Wooten, 2015). Negative 'controlling images' in the media of Black women as especially promiscuous and therefore provocative, or as 'naturally' strong and able to withstand sexual violence, echo nineteenth-century stereotypes that continue to disadvantage Black women (McGuffey, 2013). White women as the 'ideal victims' of sexual violence means that Black women's narratives are less likely to be heard or taken seriously (Serisier, 2018). Overall, sexual violence against Black women is under-reported in the American media and other cultural portrayals rarely centre Black women's experiences (Moorti, 2002).

Docuseries *Surviving R Kelly* (2019–2020) features interviews with women recounting their experiences of being domestically and sexually abused by the R&B singer, as well as interviews with victims' family members, journalists and experts on violence and abuse. It is notable in focusing on the voices and experiences of Black women. Acquitted of charges of child pornography in 2008, multiple women, over several years, have described being abused and controlled by R Kelly as teenagers. The series makes the point that as Black girls, his accusers were not 'ideal victims' and were ignored. It also highlights the Mute R Kelly campaign, founded by Orinike Odeleye, to boycott his music. After the first series of Surviving R Kelly was broadcast, the singer faced numerous new charges of sexual assault and sexual abuse and was convicted of sex trafficking and racketeering in New York in 2021.

British drama *I May Destroy You* (2020) forefronts Black people's experiences of sexual violence through the stories of two women and a man. Benson-Allott (2020) argues its intersectional representations give greater depth and nuance than most televised portrayals of rape, and illuminate by comparison the privileging of whiteness in media portrayals of rape and sexual violence. The characters' experiences of rape are mediated by gender, sexuality and race and inflected by racism. Formally innovative, *I May Destroy You*'s use of flashback and intercutting of scenes highlights patterns in the characters' experiences related to their social positioning. The series portrays four different incidents of sexual violence, which Benson-Allott (2020) contends represent the systemic nature of rape and sexual violence.

In the period following the abolition of slavery in the United States, accusations that Black men had raped white women were central to denying full citizenship rights to Black men and to upholding white supremacy (Freedman, 2013). Lynching—the extrajudicial murder of Black men—secured racial domination through extreme violence. Men were targeted for political activity as well as rape accusations, but stereotypes of Black men as sexually predatory underpinned the justification of lynching. Carter (2012) argues that lynching was itself a type of sexual violence, demonstrated by the perpetrators' obsession with Black men's sexuality and practices of genital mutilation of victims. The circulation of images of Black suffering in white culture to elicit pleasure from white viewers has a sexualised aspect to it (Ferreday, 2017). The sexual demorisation of Black men highlights the problem with over-reliance on criminal justice and punishment-based approaches to redressing sexual violence. Protection of white women is prioritised above that of other victims. This includes victimised Black men. As Mack and McCann (2018) argue, sexual violence is rampant in prisons; prisons do not reduce sexual violence.

The Central Park Five were five Black and Lantino teenage boys wrongly convicted of raping and violently attacking Trisha Meili a white woman in Central Park, New York in 1989. The case became a notorious example of how decades after lynching accusations of sexual violence against white women could lead to miscarriages of justice against Black men and other men of colour. At the time, violent crime was high and cultural anxieties manifested in racialised stereotypes of dangerous Black 'predators'. This particular crime was interpreted as an example of social breakdown. Donald Trump, at the time a real estate developer in New York, published newspaper adverts headlined 'Bring Back the Death Penalty'. The boys gave coerced confessions, which they retracted. In 2002, convicted murderer and rapist Matias Reyes confessed to the crime and the Central Park Five were released (Chancer, 2005). Documentary *The Central Park Five* (2012) and the semi-fictionalised series *When They See Us* (2019) tell the story, highlighting the dynamics of gendered racial injustice.

The legacy of European colonialism is significant to intersections of race and gender in relation to sexual violence. In nineteenth-century

South Africa, rape accusations by Black women against white men were discounted, despite the pervasive nature of rape. Black women were not regarded as respectable complainants (Scully, 1995). This history affects Black women in present-day South Africa as a stereotype of Black women as unworthy victims persists, as does their constitution as sexual subjects in relation to white men, white women and Black men (Gouws, 2018). The myth of the hypersexual rapist of colour was not confined to the United States, but was widespread across different British colonies, including India and Jamaica (Scully, 1995).

Histories of settler colonialism influence Indigenous women's experiences of sexual violence and of reporting it to the authorities. High levels of sexual violence against Indigenous women have historically been ignored in the United States, Canada, Australia and Scandinavian countries (Kuokkanen, 2015). Colonisers' portrayals of Indigenous societies as pathological contributed to women's fear of reporting sexual violence or accessing services, which risked implicating the whole community (Bubar, 2014). Smith and Ross (2004) argue that colonialism itself is a type of sexual violence as it entails violation, and is practised through violence against Indigenous people.

Colonial histories of sexual violence shape contemporary understandings and international media portrayals. Patil and Purkayastha (2015) compare the reporting in the *Times of India* and the *New York Times* of the rape and murder of Jyoti Singh in Delhi and the rape of a high school girl in Steubenville, Ohio in 2012. Both cases involved multiple attackers. They argue the *New York Times* contextualized the Delhi case in relation to patriarchy and rape culture in India, and the toxicity of local football culture to the Steubenville case—but without scaling this up to reflect national American culture. Unlike the *Times of India*, the *New York Times* attributed the Delhi case to clashes between modernity and tradition in India. Patil and Purkayastha (2015) attribute these differences in reporting to racialised, colonial understandings of India as less civilised and less advanced than the United States.

Case study:

Jyoti Singh, a 23 year old student, and her male friend took a privately run bus after going to see a film. Singh was gang-raped and violently attacked by five men and one boy on the bus and her friend was beaten. She died from her injuries in hospital. The crime was reported internationally and sparked protests as it raised issues about women's lack of safety in public and semi-public spaces, even when accompanied by a man. Laws on sexual assault in India were subsequently reformed to make penalties harsher. One of the perpetrators died in prison; the minor was sentenced to three years in prison and the other four adults were executed in 2020. Documentary *India's Daughter* (2015) portrays the protests that took place in Indian cities after Singh's murder and includes an interview with the bus driver. Miniseries *Delhi Crime* (2019) explores the crime, the police investigation and the case's aftermath, contextualising it in relation to pervasive sexual violence and socioeconomic inequality.

Gender, Sexuality and Heteronormativity

Experiences of sexual violence and responses to it are shaped by constructions of gender and sexuality. Rape myths stem from heteronormative and heterosexist understandings of sex and sexuality, according to which sex is something a man does to a woman—he is the active partner and she is the recipient. This perception is consonant with gender norms of masculinity as active/dominant and femininity as passive/submissive. Men who are victim/survivors of sexual violence and women who perpetrate it transgress this conceptualisation.

'Male rape myths' include incorrect beliefs such as men cannot be raped, or women cannot rape, only gay men get raped by other men, and rape does not affect men as badly as it does women (Turchik & Edwards, 2012). Men who are raped or sexually assaulted by women may be seen as not 'really' victimised, or even as having enjoyed the attack (Turchik & Edwards, 2012). Men are not the 'ideal victims' of sexual violence and women do not fit the stereotype of perpetrator (Weare, 2018). These myths are influenced by gender stereotypes of masculinity as incompatible with victimisation. Gay men who are raped by other men may be 'doubly victimised' through facing homophobic attitudes that they are not 'real' men and are somehow blameworthy (Javaid, 2018).

In many places, the law surrounding sexual violence is itself gendered. In England and Wales, the law did not recognise anal penetration without consent as a crime until 1994. Before that, rape was a crime for which only women could be legally recognised as victims (Graham, 2006). The Sexual Offences Act 2003 defines rape as penile penetration of the vagina, anus or mouth without consent. This definition means that men who are forced to penetrate someone else are not legally recognised as having been raped. Instead, such acts can be prosecuted as sexual assault or sexual activity without consent, which both attract lighter penalties than rape (Weare, 2018).

People often find it hard to believe or accept that women can commit sexual violence (Girschick, 2002). Phillips (2016) discusses the difficulty of naming women's sexual violence towards men in relation to the television show *Transparent* (2014–2019). One storyline portrays the relationship between character Josh and an older woman, Rita. Rita was the family's babysitter and began a sexual relationship with Josh when he was fifteen. This particular storyline received little public discussion and Phillips (2016) argues that this reflected limitations in being able to conceptualise such a relationship as abusive.

Coupled with heterosexist legal definitions of rape, people who have been raped or sexually attacked by women may find it difficult to access support services, or be taken seriously by the police (Girschick, 2002; Weare, 2018). Woman to woman sexual violence is particularly invisible. It challenges both gender stereotypes about women's caregiving nature and certain feminist assumptions about lesbian relationships as non-violent. These perceptions mean there are significant barriers to victims' disclosure—even to themselves—and specific psychological impacts (Gilroy & Carroll, 2009; Girschick, 2002; Wang, 2011).

Trans women experience particularly high levels of sexual violence. Research in the United States found 69% of trans women had been victims of sexual violence, with victimisation especially high for women of colour, sex workers and homeless trans women. Transmisogyny is a factor in sexual violence, with trans women experiencing sexual violence motivated by attackers fetishising or objectifying their gender identity, or expressing hatred of their identity. Trans women also experience sexual violence and harassment similarly to cis women, such as catcalling in public and sexual violence as an expression of masculine domination (Matsuzaka & Koch, 2019).

Sexual violence against individuals from certain social groups remains disproportionately hidden. Disabled women experience sexual violence at higher rates than non-disabled women, including in institutions and care settings, and disablist hate crime. However, prevailing stereotypes about disabled people as asexual, not sexually desirable or unable to provide reliable testimony contribute to silencing them (Balderston, 2013; Mitra et al., 2011). As victim/survivors who do not fit the 'real rape' stereotype, older people are also rendered invisible as victim/survivors of sexual violence. Assumptions that older women (who are more likely to experience sexual violence than men) are asexual and sexually undesirable influence this invisibility, as does a perception of 'elder abuse' as physical but not sexual (Bows, 2019). Academic research and public and policy discussions of sexual violence tend to focus on young women as victims, as do media representations (Bows, 2018).

Street Harassment

Street harassment encompasses unwanted sexualised verbal and non-verbal behaviours in public and semi-public places. It has historically gained less attention than other forms of gender-based violence, including workplace harassment, but this has begun to change with the emergence of international initiatives and social activism devoted to tacking the problem (Logan, 2015; Vera-Gray, 2016). Gender-based street harassment can be experienced by men, particularly gay men, but it is disproportionately experienced by women and girls. Some studies have found 100% of women have experienced street harassment at some point and most street harassment is perpetrated by men (Logan, 2015). Vera-Gray (2016) defines street harassment as 'men's stranger intrusions' on women in public spaces.

The street is a gendered space and a point of convergence for different social groups (Ilahi, 2009). Harassment is commonplace and 'everyday' but can limit women and girls' access to, and freedom within, public space (Vera-Gray, 2016). It is linked to fear of sexual violence and other crimes, and in itself is an unwelcome experience (Adur & Jha, 2018). In relation to street harassment in Cairo, Ilahi (2009) argues that to improve their safety women seek male accompaniment if going out at night, but this reinforces traditional gender norms and male power—the very factors underpinning street harassment.

Certain social groups experience higher levels of harassment than others. Adur and Jha's (2018) appraisal of the implementation in Delhi of the UN's 'Safer Cities' programme to tackle violence against women and girls highlights that the programme was heterosexist because it did not include reducing harassment of LGBTQ people. Dalit (low caste) women and women perceived as 'Westernised' were also especially subject to street harassment, demonstrating the need for an intersectional understanding. Muslim women in the UK who wear the niqab (face veil) experienced frequent sexual and Islamophobic harassment in public spaces, which resulted from intersections of race, religion and gender. The niqab made them very visible and was interpreted by white men both as a symbol of oppression and as an indication of terrorism (Mason-Bish & Zempi, 2019).

Sexual Violence and the Criminal Justice System

Gendered understandings of sexual violence and 'rape myths' are significant in the criminal justice system, particularly in terms of explaining the low reporting of sexual violence and the high attrition rate of rape cases. Sexual violence is reported at lower rates than other violent crimes (Spohn & Tellis, 2012). A minority of rapes are reported to the police—around 10% in the United Kingdom and New Zealand, for example, and 'real rapes' i.e. those committed by a stranger or with a weapon are more likely to be reported (Jordan, 2011). Reporting of rape in intimate relationships is very low, although this type of victimisation is very prevalent. Stranger rape is also more likely to proceed to prosecution than cases where the victim knew the attacker (Jordan, 2011; Hohl &

Stanko, 2015). From the small minority of rapes that are reported to the police, only around 7% in England and Wales end in conviction. Greater reporting has not led to more convictions (Hohl & Stanko, 2015).

Police are the initial gatekeepers in relation to whether a crime is recorded and whether reports of rape proceed through the criminal justice system (Spohn & Tellis, 2012). A study from Denmark found that the police closed 62% of rape cases without proceeding to prosecution and studies from the UK and New Zealand have found the police close around a third to half (Hansen et al., 2015; Jordan, 2011). Victim/survivors withdrawing their complaint is one of the biggest reasons for cases not to proceed, and police officers making victim/survivors feel validated and not disbelieved is significant to whether they proceed with a complaint (Hohl & Stanko, 2015; Spohn et al., 2014). A study from South Korea established that police frequently believed rape myths, such as that victim/survivors were partly responsible for their attack if they were drunk, did not fight back 'enough' or wore 'provocative' clothing (Lee et al., 2011).

Cultures of scepticism among police about reports of rape and sexual violence, informed by rape myths, inhibit cases' progress in the criminal justice system (Jordan, 2011). Shaw et al. (2017) analysed rape myths about victims in police sexual assault case records, finding that perceptions individuals were not acting like victims, or negative stereotypes based on notions of sexual promiscuity and 'bad reputation', affected whether police continued with cases. A further negative perception of victim/survivors as unwilling to assist with investigations was mobilised to blame victims for unsuccessful investigations in certain cases. Javaid (2018) notes that police cultures are significant to the negative reporting experience of male rape victims, who might not be taken seriously when they report. Black women and women of colour face barriers to reporting due historical and personal experiences of racism (Belknap, 2010). Specialised units to deal with sex offences, which have been introduced in several countries, have improved victims' experiences of disclosing sexual violence but largely have not increased the number of charging decisions or convictions (Hansen et al., 2015; Hohl & Stanko, 2015; Spohn & Tellis, 2012).

After the police, the prosecutor or prosecution service further sifts cases, creating another major point for attrition. In Hansen et al.'s (2015) Danish study, 54% of the rape cases referred by the police were closed by the prosecution. Hohl and Stanko (2015) found the London-based Metropolitan Police Service deployed notions of 'credible criminals' and 'credible victims' in relation to choosing which cases to refer to the Crown Prosecution Service. Victim/survivors were seen as less credible if they had mental health problems or learning disabilities, or had been drinking at the time of the attack. Identification of a 'credible criminal' was the most important factor in terms of the Crown Prosecution Service of England and Wales deciding to prosecute. 'Credible criminals' included men with previous convictions for sex offences and men of colour.

The final stage of the road to gaining a conviction is the trial, where there is around a 50–60% chance of success (Jordan, 2011). Trials for rape and sexual assault have been notorious for the degrading cross-examination of victim/survivors and for circulation of sexist and derogatory stereotypes about victims' dress and behaviour. Lees's (1997) courtroom observation of rape trials in England twenty-five years ago revealed the prevalence of rape myths, such as warnings from the judge to the jury about the possibility of false claims. Adversarial systems, which have a prosecution and defence offering opposing arguments about what took place, over simplify complex events and work to undermine reform measures for improvement (Jordan, 2011; Smith & Skinner, 2017).

Changes to the law on rape and sexual assault, and to the practice of adversarial trials, have not eliminated the presence of rape myths. In Australia there is an affirmative standard of consent, meaning the defendant must show the steps they had taken to ensure consent, rather than the victim/survivor needing to show they did not give consent. However, this is phrased as the defendant ensuring a 'reasonable belief' in consent. This notion of 'reasonable belief' enables derogatory stereotypes about the victim/survivors' behaviour as flirtatious or promiscuous to be deployed (Burgin & Flynn, 2021). Burgin and Flynn (2021) found women's actions such as dancing with the defendant, walking home with the defendant, or even sitting next to him on a park bench had been suggested as evidence in trials as justifying reasonable belief in consent.

Legal and cultural understandings of 'reasonableness' lead to assessments of victims/survivors' behaviour as divisible into 'normal' or 'abnormal'. Where they are perceived to have acted irrationally or abnormally—for example through giving inconsistent accounts, or where there is evidence of contact with the defendant after the attack—there is less chance of conviction (Smith & Skinner, 2017).

Assumptions about credible criminals and credible victims also influence juries. Smith and Skinner's (2017) courtroom observation of rape trials in England revealed that judges and prosecution lawyers did sometimes refute rape myths. However, the same lawyers when acting for the defence sometimes mobilised rape myths on behalf of the defendant Ellison and Munro (2009) researched how far expert testimony to dispel rape myths and negative stereotypes about victim/survivors affects juries. Their mock jury study found that stereotypes about victim/survivors as seeming too calm and not distressed enough, and beliefs that delayed reporting indicated the rape claim was false, were diminished by expert evidence but assumptions that rape would cause physical injury remained.

Most feminist and criminological work on sexual violence has focused on criminal trials and the criminal justice system, but Baillot et al. (2009) argue similar issues about the barriers to hearing victims' narratives pertain to Asylum and Immigration Tribunals in the UK. Many women claiming refugee status have experienced sexual violence in their home country but the closed question and answer format of the tribunal impedes effective communication of their story. Rape myths about victim credibility such as lack of appropriate demeanour, disclosing 'too late' and suspicion about inconsistent narratives were present in asylum cases.

A minority of victim/survivors report their experience(s) of sexual violence to the police—the criminal justice system is usually not involved. Specialist support services are crucial for addressing victims' needs and helping their recovery (Hester & Lilley, 2017). However, such services are frequently underfunded and face cutbacks in eras of restricted public spending (Jordan, 2011). Trans and gender non-conforming people may find they are excluded from and discriminated against by women-only services, or that they have difficulty accessing services appropriate for their needs—for instance, lack of understanding of the context of experiences of sexual violence together with transphobia (Jordan et al., 2019). There are few support services specifically for male victims of sexual violence, and many are women-only. Some men report encountering homophobia and ageism when attempting to access support (Javaid, 2018; Lowe, 2018).

One of the most internationally successful police procedural television dramas, *Law & Order: SVU* focuses on police detective work into sex-based crimes as part of a Special Victims Unit in New York and the prosecution of those crimes. The show has been praised for challenging rape myths about consent and for portraying sexual violence as a violation of power. Audience reception studies have identified *Law & Order: SVU* as a show that lowers viewers' rape myth acceptance and increases their understanding of consent (Hust et al., 2015). Although the detectives do not prevail in every episode, usually the perpetrator is discovered and convicted as a result of their investigation. As such, the show presents the criminal justice system, and carceral punishment, as the solution to sexual violence (Moorti & Cuklanz, 2017). The nature of the show, which pursues investigation and prosecution of sexual violence, means that it does not portray the reality, in New York and elsewhere, of under-reporting and case attrition.

Sexual Violence on Campus

The issue of sexual violence within large organisations and how they do (or do not) respond to it can be explored through the example of universities. The United States is distinct in having federal (national level) legislation against sex discrimination in the educational system, which incorporates sexual violence. Institutions must compile and publish statistics about crime on campus and their policies to tackle it and are required to have policies to tackle sexual assault (Dauber & Warner, 2019; Klein, 2018). Many universities have adopted mandatory reporting policies, which means when students disclose experience of sexual violence to someone employed by the institution, that person must report it to the university officially.

As with all victim/survivors of sexual violence, the vast majority of students who experience sexual violence do not report it and may not want to (McMahon & Seabrook, 2019). This means that mandatory reporting policies can inhibit disclosure (Gronert, 2019), a problem Durbach and Grey (2018) note also applies in Australia. In particular, LGBTQ students and students of colour are reluctant to disclose experiences of sexual violence to their institution, fearing they will either not be believed, or not be recognised as credible victims (McMahon & Seabrook, 2019). Harris (2017) argues American universities employ a heterosexist understanding of sexual violence, which is inadequate to recognise the experiences of many students.

Potential exclusions created by legislation and policies are exacerbated by their narrow focus on student-to-student violence and formal reporting (Klein, 2018). The targets are individual perpetrators rather than the wider cultures in which sexual violence in universities takes place. The prizing of masculine athletic culture in American universities, for example, is frequently based on heteronormative, racist and misogynistic values and the sexualised objectification of women (Harris, 2013). In the UK, university-based 'lad cultures' emphasise sporting prowess, drinking to excess and sexist and homophobic 'banter', the latter of which often manifests as harassment. Lad cultures also privilege whiteness, and middle-class laddism is not seen as threatening or deviant in the same way as the perceived hypermasculinity of Black men (Phipps, 2018).

Penalising individuals does not transform underlying cultures. Klein (2018) argues that sexualised peer cultures among students need to be challenged, as do university governance structures dominated by middle-aged white men. Drawing on critiques of carceral feminism, Phipps (2018) maintains racialised and working-class men are more vulnerable to punitive treatment via university disciplinary measures than their more privileged counterparts. The legislative and policy framework governing sexual violence in the United States fosters technical and procedural compliance but does not encourage cultural change. Recognising sexual violence as a form of organisational violence is rare (Harris, 2013).

Case study:

The Stanford Rape Case exhibited a number of the issues salient to sexual violence on university campuses. In January 2015, Chanel Miller was sexually assaulted on the Stanford University campus by Brock Turner, a student at the university who was also a member of the swimming team. In 2016, Turner was sentenced to six months in prison for the assault and was released after three. His sentence was widely perceived as insufficiently lenient and attributed to his status as a white male athlete at an elite university. In protest, Miller's victim impact statement was published under the name 'Emily Doe' by Buzzfeed in 2016 and was viewed millions of times within a few days. Public outrage led to a successful campaign to recall and unseat the judge in the case and the introduction of mandatory minimum sentences for sexual assault in California (Mack & McCann, 2019; Serisier, 2018). Turner seemed to exemplify white masculine privilege, but Mack and McCann (2019) argue that calls for harsher punishment ultimately reinforce a criminal justice system weighted against people of colour. The prosecution of privileged young men is the exception in a system that largely impacts on the marginalised. In 2019, Miller waived her anonymity and published a memoir, *Know My Name* (2019).

Documentary *The Hunting Ground* (2015) examines the ubiquity of rape and sexual assault on American university campuses and the inadequacy of institutional responses. It implicates the masculinist culture of college football in encouraging the perpetration of rape and sexual assault and highlights the impunity experienced by footballing 'stars' accused of sexual harm. *The Hunting Ground* has been screened widely at American, Australian and British universities and helped to spark discussion of the issue of sexual violence on campus (Anitha & Lewis, 2018).

Feminist Activism in the Era of #MeToo

The trope of Black men as a sexual threat to white women underpinned European colonialism. Colonial fears of Black men's sexual violence to white women created so called 'Black Peril scares' in British African colonies such as Kenya, Rhodesia and South Africa in the early twentieth century (Anderson, 2010). Historically, protest against sexual violence has constituted disparate movements, not all of them connected to feminism or notions of improving women's rights. In the nineteenth-century United States, the social purity and temperance movements campaigned against sexual violence, as did women's rights organisations. Opposition to sexual violence was expressed by anti-lynching campaigners, but also white supremacists who portrayed Black men as a threat to white women (Freedman, 2013). This historical context means the protection of white women in particular has frequently been centred in movements against sexual violence in North America and Europe (Phipps, 2020).

During the American civil rights movement, Black women attested to their experiences of sexual violence from white men. Civil rights campaigners pursued the issue of rape accusations against Black men being used as justification for racism, racist violence and harsh punishment (Freedman, 2013; Serisier, 2018). In the 1970s, rape was redefined as a feminist issue and as a form of violence against women. Women articulated and shared personal experiences of sexual violence as part of feminist consciousness raising. Rape crisis centres and telephone hotlines were established and Take Back the Night/Reclaim the Night protest marches drew attention to sexual and gendered violence as a mechanism for controlling women (Freedman, 2013; Mendes, 2015). However, the dominant feminist narrative privileged the experiences of white women and was inattentive to the significance of racism to sexual violence and erased Black women's organising and political activism (Linder, 2017; Serisier, 2018; Wooten, 2015).

By the 1980s, a feminist interpretation of sexual violence as a harmful social problem could be found in mainstream cultural portrayals such as daytime television programmes and magazines aimed at women. In 1988, *The Accused* portrayed issues of victim blaming in relation to gender and class-based stigma (Serisier, 2018). Based on a real case of gang rape, *The Accused* was a cultural landmark in being a mainstream Hollywood film that addressed rape, gender and class. Widely interpreted as feminist, it portrays the violence of rape, the cultural objectification of women and the difficulty a 'disreputable' woman faces in being heard and believed in the legal system (Fuchs, 1989). Feminist critiques have highlighted that the film's prolonged rape scene is interspersed with the courtroom testimony of a male witness, meaning that ultimately the story of the rape rests on male authority, not the words of the female victim (Horeck, 2004; Young, 2009).

Popularised in the 1990s, the term 'date rape' referred to nonconsensual sex where the victim knew her attacker and physical injuries were not necessarily sustained. Feminists argued that such rapes were frequently misunderstood as 'seduction' rather than sexual violence (Pineau, 1989). Conservative 'backlash' discourses argued that feminism had gone 'too far', framing simple flirtation as sexual harassment and awkward interactions as sexual violence. Postfeminist assessments of date rape and 'rape crisis narratives' in the 1990s such as Roiphe (1993) criticised activism against sexual violence like Take Back the Night for disempowering women by positioning them as vulnerable victims. Gill and Donaghue (2013) define postfeminism as a sensibility which accepts certain feminist principles and arguments, while repudiating others. For example, an emphasis on empowerment and sexual autonomy exists alongside the belief young women make false rape claims because they have accepted a view of themselves as victims.

High-profile, media savvy twenty-first century protests against sexual violence such as SlutWalk marches and Femen's naked protests received widespread media coverage and spread from their countries of origin (Canada and Ukraine, respectively) via social media (Mendes, 2015). Both movements centred the gendered body as a site of protest, using nakedness or sexualised clothing to argue for women's autonomy and control over their sexuality. This focus prioritised young, slim white women's bodies and did not tackle intersectional specificities related to race, age, size and dis/ability, arguably underwriting rather than subverting heteronormative ideals of feminine appearance (O'Keefe, 2014).

Contemporary social movements against sexual violence are notable for their mixing of digital and direct action. The #EndRapeCulture campaign originated at Rhodes University in South Africa in 2016 when a group of Black women students posted online the names of eleven male students who were alleged rapists to protest the university's inaction on sexual violence (Gouws, 2018). In addition to this strategy of naming, they organised topless marches which spread to other campuses. These marches were inspired by anti-colonialism and a tradition of naked protest by African women. The campaign highlighted the sexualisation of Black women's Blackness and stereotypes of Black women as hypersexual, which relate to the exoticisation and eroticisation of skin colour rather than dress (Gouws, 2018).

Young women in particular have mobilised against sexual violence through digital feminism and using social media to create networks and connections (Boyle, 2019; Keller et al., 2018). At the same time, online spaces have facilitated the expression of misogyny and new mediations of sexual violence (Keller et al., 2018; Phipps et al., 2018). Hashtags such as #BeenRapedNeverReported and #YesAllWomen, which encouraged the online reporting of experiences of sexual violence and harassment, created possibilities for community and connection between women, and highlighted the pervasiveness of sexual violence. Keller et al. (2018) argue that such participation in online activism can help women to develop feminist consciousness. The use of hashtags has raised issues of erasure and exclusion if they become associated with only documenting the experiences of relatively privileged white middle class cis women. A Muslim woman initiated #YesAllWomen but distanced herself from the hashtag after she faced abuse online and when it appeared the experiences of women of colour and trans women were not being recognised through its circulation (Rodino-Colocino, 2014).

Feminist digital activism has also mobilised against street harassment, with the hashtag #YouOkSis, and websites such as Hollaback, Stop Street Harassment and the Everyday Sexism Project providing online venues for sharing experiences and also examples of effective responses to harassment, as well as encouraging intervention. These responses range from ignoring harassment and walking away, to resisting physically, to employing satire to mock harassers (Fleetwood, 2019). Such websites seek to challenge the misogynistic underpinnings of street harassment (Logan, 2015). Fleetwood (2019) describes the London version of Hollaback! as 'storytelling activism' that offers women possibilities of resistance and agency. Sharing stories enables women to rework their gendered habitus away from vulnerability. Shared narratives open 'counter cultural public spheres' where victims of street harassment can gain recognition and bear witness to harms (Fileborn, 2017; Salter, 2013). Online spaces offer possibilities for informal justice but reproduce exclusions. Fileborn (2017) found gender diverse and disabled women who shared experiences of harassment via websites and social media did not always feel heard; disabled women encountered safety advice that presumed being able-bodied. She argues such activism can achieve a form of partial justice, but does not recognise everybody equally, or hold perpetrators to account.

The most successful and culturally impactful example of digital activism against sexual violence is #MeToo—which has entered everyday language. Activist Tarana Burke coined 'MeToo' on social networking site MySpace in 2006 after a young woman of colour disclosed to her that she had been sexually assaulted. The phrase was an expression of shared experience and solidarity, and intended to facilitate conversation about sexual violence against Black women and women of colour. The following year, Burke developed workshops for survivors of sexual violence in Alabama also under the concept 'Me Too'. In 2017, actor Alyssa Milano posted a tweet suggesting that women share their experiences of sexual abuse and harassment using #MeToo. Milano was inspired by the multiple allegations of sexual violence and harassment made against film producer Harvey Weinstein, including by famous actors. Her invocation prompted millions of tweets across the world, with the emergence of Chinese, French, Italian and Spanish variations on the hashtag (Fileborn & Loney-Howes, 2019).

Case study:

Between October 2017 and February 2018 numerous women publicly accused film producer Harvey Weinstein of sexually harassing, sexually assaulting and raping them, with allegations stretching back over 30 years. Weinstein was charged with rape and other counts of sexual abuse in New York in May 2018, with further charges added in subsequent months. He was found guilty of a criminal sexual act and third degree rape in February 2020 and sentenced to 23 years in prison in March 2020. His name has become a byword for sexual harassment and predatory sexual violence. Documentary *Untouchable: The Rise and Fall of Harvey Weinstein* (2019) depicts the complicity of the Hollywood film industry and the wider media in Weinstein's abusive behaviour. The allegations against him were widely known but did not hinder his career and for years remained unreported until investigative journalism by Jodi Kantor and Megan Twohey for the *New York Times* and Ronan Farrow for the *New Yorker*.

#MeToo's association with celebrity made it newsworthy and assisted its proliferation. It opened up discussion of sexual violence on social media, in traditional media and beyond. However, in North America, Australia and Europe, it also demonstrated the same shortcomings of previous digital feminism around hashtags in prioritising the experiences of white, privileged women. When #MeToo exploded, Tarana Burke was not initially credited with coining the term and her intersectional arguments about the need to place women of colour at the centre of campaigns against sexual violence were not heeded (Boyle, 2019; Ryan, 2019). In 2017 Time magazine chose 'The Silence Breakers' as its Person of the Year. The silence breakers had become a term for people who spoke out against sexual harassment and/or sexual assault. The accompanying cover featured actor Ashley Judd, singer Taylor Swift, Uber engineer Susan Fowler, and strawberry picker Isabel Pascuel, all of whom in some way exposed sexual violence in their professions, as well as the arm of an anonymous woman to symbolise those unable to speak. Inside, the magazine featured interviews with more people, including Tarana Burke. Nathaniel (2019) questions why Burke, as the founder of MeToo, was not on the front cover and argues the omission was symptomatic of her displacement in favour of rich white women.

Ryan (2019) highlights how Aboriginal and Torres Strait Islander women in Australia spoke out both about Black women's experiences of sexual violence and the erasure of Black women's voices in the #MeToo movement. #MeToo and its offshoot #TimesUp concentrate predominantly on sexual violence in the workplace, but the conceptualisation of work focuses on the official labour market, ignoring the lived reality of millions of women worldwide in the informal economy. As Kagal et al. (2019) note, globally women are disproportionately represented in the informal economy and in insecure and precarious work. Migrant women are especially likely to work in informal sectors. Campaigns for labour rights and organisation of workers into trade unions are vital in order to reduce sexual violence against workers, and to address wider structural inequalities (Kagal et al., 2019).

Sexual violence binds different forms of domination together. This includes inequalities of gender, race and class among others, which is crucial to appreciate in terms of gaining a nuanced understanding of sexual violence and of the best ways to campaign against it. Criminal justice responses are inadequate and frequently harmful, raising the question of whether it is possible for the criminal justice system to be effective at preventing and reducing sexual violence, or whether alternatives are needed.

References

Adur, S. M., & Jha, S. (2018). (Re)centering street harassment—An appraisal of safe cities global initiative in Delhi, India. *Journal of Gender Studies, 27*(1), 114–124.

Anderson, D. M. (2010). Sexual threat and settler society: 'Black Perils' in Kenya c. 1907–30. *Journal of Imperial and Commonwealth History, 38,* 47–74.

Anitha, S., & Lewis, R. (2018). Introduction: Some reflections in these promising and challenging times. In S. Anitha & R. Lewis (Eds.), *Gender based violence in university communities* (pp. 1–19). Policy Press.

Armstrong, E. A., Gleckman-Krut, M., & Johnson, L. (2018). Silence, power, and inequality: An intersectional approach to sexual violence. *Annual Review of Sociology, 44*(1), 99–122.

Baillot, H., Cowan, S., & Munro, V. E. (2009). Seen but not heard? Parallels and dissonances in the treatment of rape narratives across the asylum and criminal justice contexts. *Journal of Law and Society, 36*(2), 195–219.

Balderston, S. (2013). Victimized again? Intersectionality and injustice in disabled women's lives after hate crime and rape. In *Gendered perspectives on conflict and violence: Part A* (Vol. 18A, pp. 17–51). Emerald Group Publishing Limited.

Barnett, P. E. (1997). Figurations of rape and the supernatural in Beloved. *Pmla/publications of the Modern Language Association of America, 112*(3), 418–427.

Belknap, J. (2010). Rape: Too hard to report and too easy to discredit victims. *Violence Against Women, 16*(12), 1335–1344.

Benson-Allott, C. (2020). How i may destroy you reinvents rape television. *Film Quarterly, 74*(2), 100–105.

Bows, H. (2018). Sexual violence against older people: A review of the empirical literature. *Trauma, Violence, & Abuse, 19*(5), 567–583.

Bows, H. (2019). *Sexual violence against older people*. Routledge.

Boyle, K. (2019). What's in a name? Theorising the inter-relationships of gender and violence. *Feminist Theory, 20*, 19–36.

Brownmiller, S. (1975). *Against our will: Men, women and rape*. Simon & Schuster.

Bubar, R. (2014). Indigenous women and sexual assault: Implications for inter-sectionality. In H. N. Weaver (Ed.), *Social issues in contemporary Native America: Reflections from Turtle Island* (pp. 169–186). Ashgate.

Burgin, R., & Flynn, A. (2021). Women's behavior as implied consent: Male "reasonableness" in Australian rape law. *Criminology & Criminal Justice, 21*(3), 1748895819880953.

Carter, N. M. (2012). Intimacy without consent: Lynching as sexual violence. *Politics & Gender, 8*(3), 414–421.

Chancer, L. S. (2005). *High-profile crimes*. University of Chicago Press.

Collins, P. H. (1998). The tie that binds: Race, gender and US violence. *Ethnic and Racial Studies, 21*(5), 917–938.

Collins, P. H. (2017). On violence, intersectionality and transversal politics. *Ethnic and Racial Studies, 40*, 1460–1473.

Datta, A. (2016). The intimate city: Violence, gender and ordinary life in Delhi slums. *Urban Geography, 37*, 323–342.

Dauber, M. L., & Warner, M. O. (2019). Legal and political responses to campus sexual assault. *Annual Review of Law and Social Science, 15*(1), 311–333.

Dodge, A. (2016). Digitizing rape culture: Online sexual violence and the power of the digital photograph. *Crime, Media, Culture, 12*(1), 65–82.

Durbach, A., & Grey, R. (2018). Grounds for concern: An Australian perspective on responses to sexual assault and harassment in university settings. In S. Anitha & R. Lewis (Eds.),*Gender based violence in university communities: Policy, prevention and educational initiatives* (pp. 83–104). Policy Press.

Ellison, L., & Munro, V. E. (2009). Turning mirrors into windows? Assessing the impact of (mock) juror education in rape trials. *British Journal of Criminology, 49*, 363–383.

Estrich, S. (1987). *Real rape.* Harvard University Press.

Fanghanel, A. (2019). *Disrupting rape culture: Public space, sexuality and revolt.* Bristol University Press.

Fanghanel, A. and Lim, J. (2017). Of 'Sluts' and 'Arseholes': Antagonistic desire and the production of sexual vigilance. *Feminist Criminology, 12*, 341–360.

Ferreday, D. (2017). 'Only the Bad Gyal could do this': Rihanna, rape-revenge narratives and the cultural politics of white feminism. *Feminist Theory, 18*(3), 263–280.

Fileborn, B. (2017). Justice 2.0: Street harassment victims' use of social media and online activism as sites of informal justice. *British Journal of Criminology, 57*, 1482–1501.

Fileborn, B., & Loney-Howes, R. (2019). Introduction: Mapping the emergence of #MeToo. In B. Fileborn & R. Loney-Howes (Eds.), *#MeToo and the politics of social change* (pp. 1–18). Palgrave.

Fleetwood, J. (2019). Everyday self-defence: Hollaback narratives, habitus and resisting street harassment. *British Journal of Sociology, 70*, 1709–1729.

Freedman, E. B. (2013). *Redefining rape.* Harvard University Press.

Fuchs, C. (1989). The Accused. *Cinéaste, 17*(1), 26–28.

Gill, R., & Donaghue, N. (2013). As if postfeminism had come true: The turn to agency in cultural studies of 'sexualisation'. In S. Madhok, A. Phillips, & K. Wilson (Eds.), *Gender, agency, and coercion* (pp. 240–258). Springer.

Gilroy, P. J., & Carroll, L. (2009). Woman to woman sexual violence. *Women & Therapy, 32*, 423–435.

Girschick, L. B. (2002). *Woman-to-woman sexual violence: Does she call it rape?* Northeastern University Press.

Graham, R. (2006). Male rape and the careful construction of the male victim. *Social & Legal Studies, 15*, 187–208.

Gouws, A. (2018). #EndRapeCulture campaign in South Africa: Resisting sexual violence through protest and the politics of experience. *Politikon, 45*(1), 3–15.

Gronert, N. M. (2019). Law, campus policy, social movements, and sexual violence: Where do we stand in the #MeToo movement? *Sociology Compass, 13*(6), e12694.

Hansen, N. B., Nielsen, L. H., Bramsen, R. H., Ingemann-Hansen, O., & Elklit, A. (2015). Attrition in Danish rape reported crimes. *Journal of Police and Criminal Psychology, 30*(4), 221–228.

Harris, K. L. (2013). Show them a good time: Organizing the intersections of sexual violence. *Management Communication Quarterly, 27*(4), 568–595.

Harris, K. L. (2017). Re-situating organizational knowledge: Violence, intersectionality and the privilege of partial perspective. *Human Relations, 70*(3), 263–285.

Heberle, R. (2014). Sexual violence. In R. Gartner & B. McCarthy (Eds.), *The Oxford handbook of gender, sex, and crime* (pp. 59–76). Oxford University Press.

Hester, M., & Lilley, S.-J. (2017). More than support to court: Rape victims and specialist sexual violence services. *International Review of Victimology, 24*(3), 313–328.

Hohl, K., & Stanko, E. A. (2015). Complaints of rape and the criminal justice system: Fresh evidence on the attrition problem in England and Wales. *European Journal of Criminology, 12*(3), 324–341.

Horeck, T. (2004). *Public rape: Representing violation in film*. Routledge.

Hust, S. J. T., Marett, E. G., Lei, M., Ren, C., & Ran, W. (2015). Law & Order, CSI, and NCIS: The association between exposure to crime drama franchises, rape myth acceptance, and sexual consent negotiation among college students. *Journal of Health Communication, 20*(12), 1369–1381.

Ilahi, N. (2009). Gendered contestations: An analysis of street harassment in Cairo and its implications for women's access to public spaces. *Surfacing: An Interdisciplinary Journal of Gender in the Global South, 2*, 56–59.

Javaid, A. (2018). The criminal justice system and male rape: Processing male rape cases. In *Male rape, masculinities, and sexualities* (pp. 195–230). Springer.

Jenness, V., & Fenstermaker, S. (2016). Forty years after Brownmiller: Prisons for men, transgender inmates, and the rape of the feminine. *Gender & Society, 30*(1), 14–29.

Jordan, J. (2011). Here we go round the review-go-round: Rape investigation and prosecution—Are things getting worse not better? *Journal of Sexual Aggression, 17*(3), 234–249.

Jordan, S. P., Mehrotra, G. R., & Fujikawa, K. A. (2019). Mandating inclusion: Critical trans perspectives on domestic and sexual violence advocacy. *Violence Against Women*, 1077801219836728.

Kagal, N., Cowan, L., & Jawad, H. (2019). Beyond the bright lights: Are minoritized women outside the spotlight able to say #MeToo? In B. Fileborn & R. Loney-Howes (Eds.), *# MeToo and the politics of social change* (pp. 133–149). Springer.

Keller, J., Mendes, K., & Ringrose, J. (2018). Speaking 'unspeakable things': Documenting digital feminist responses to rape culture. *Journal of Gender Studies, 27*, 22–36.

Kelly, L. (1988). *Surviving sexual violence.* Polity Press.

Khan, S., Greene, J., Mellins C. A., & Hirsch, J. S. (2020). The social organization of sexual assault. *Annual Review of Criminology, 3*, 139–163.

Klein, R. (2018). Sexual violence on US college campuses: History and challenges. In S. Anitha & R. Lewis (Eds.), *Gender based violence in university communities: Policy, prevention and educational initiatives* (pp. 63–82). Policy Press.

Kuokkanen, R. (2015). Gendered violence and politics in Indigenous communities. *International Feminist Journal of Politics, 17*(2), 271–288.

Lee, J., Lee, C., & Lee, W. (2011). Attitudes toward women, rape myths, and rape perceptions among male police officers in South Korea. *Psychology of Women Quarterly, 36*(3), 365–376.

Lees, S. (1997). *Ruling passions: Sexual violence, reputation and the law.* Open University Press.

Linder, C. (2017). Re-examining our roots: A history of racism and antirape activism. In J. C. Harris & C. Linder (Eds), *Intersections of identity and sexual violence on campus.* Stylus Publishing.

Logan, L. S. (2015). Street harassment: Current and promising avenues for researchers and activists. *Sociology Compass, 9*(3), 196–211.

Lowe, M. (2018). Male sexual assault survivors: Lessons for UK services. *Journal of Aggression, Conflict and Peace Research, 10*(3), 181–188.

Lumsden, K., & Morgan, H. (2017). Media framing of trolling and online abuse: Silencing strategies, symbolic violence, and victim blaming. *Feminist Media Studies, 17*(6), 926–940.

Lyons, M. (2014). Yes, of course that was rape on last night's Game of Thrones, Vulture. https://www.vulture.com/2014/04/rape-game-of-thrones-cersei-jaime.html. 21 April.

Mack, A. N., & McCann, B. J. (2018). Critiquing state and gendered violence in the age of #MeToo. *Quarterly Journal of Speech, 104*(3), 329–344.

Mack, A. N. and McCann, B. J. (2019). Recalling Persky: White rage and publicity after Brock Turner. *Journal of Communication Inquiry, 43*, 379–393.

Mason-Bish, H., & Zempi, I. (2019). Misogyny, racism, and Islamophobia: Street harassment at the intersections. *Feminist Criminology, 14*(5), 540–559.

Matsuzaka, S., & Koch, D. E. (2019). Trans feminine sexual violence experiences: The intersection of transphobia and misogyny. *Affilia, 34*, 28–47.

McGlynn, C., Rackley, E., & Houghton, R. (2017). Beyond 'revenge porn': The continuum of image-based sexual abuse. *Feminist Legal Studies, 25*(1), 25–46.

McGuffey, C. S. (2013). RAPE AND RACIAL APPRAISALS: Culture, intersectionality, and Black women's accounts of sexual assault. *Du Bois Review: Social Science Research on Race, 10*(1), 109–130.

McMahon, S., & Seabrook, R. C. (2019). Reasons for nondisclosure of campus sexual violence by sexual and racial/ethnic minority women. *Journal of Student Affairs Research and Practice*, 1–15.

Mendes, K. (2015). *SlutWalk: Feminism, activism and media*. Palgrave.

Mitra, M., Mouradian, V. E., & Diamond, M. (2011). Sexual violence victimization against men with disabilities. *American Journal of Preventive Medicine, 41*(5), 494–497.

Moorti, S. (2002). *Color of rape: Gender and race in television's public spheres*. SUNY Press.

Moorti, S., & Cuklanz, L. (2017). *All-American TV crime drama: Feminism and identity politics in Law and Order: Special Victims Unit*. Bloomsbury Publishing.

Nathaniel, A. (2019). #Metoo mishaps: Black bodies, bloody grounds. *South Central Review, 36*, 52–67.

O'Keefe, T. (2014). My body is a manifesto! SlutWalk, Femen and femmenist protest. *Feminist Review, 107*, 1–19.

Patil, V., & Purkayastha, B. (2015). Sexual violence, race and media (in)visibility: Intersectional complexities in a transnational frame. *Societies, 5*(3) 598–617.

Phillips. N. D. (2016). *Beyond blurred lines: Rape culture in popular media*. Rowman and Littlefield.

Phipps, A. (2018). 'Lad culture' and sexual violence against students. In *Gender based violence in university communities: Policy, prevention and educational initiatives* (p. 41).

Phipps, A. (2020). *Me, not you: The trouble with mainstream feminism*. Manchester University Press.

Pineau, L. (1989). Date rape: A feminist analysis. *Law and Philosophy, 8*, 217–243.

Powell, A., & Henry, N. (2019). Technology-facilitated sexual violence victimization: Results from an online survey of Australian adults. *Journal of Interpersonal Violence, 34*(17), 3637–3665.

Phipps, A., Ringrose, J., Renold, E., & Jackson, C. (2018). Rape culture, lad culture and everyday sexism: Researching, conceptualizing and politicizing new mediations of gender and sexual violence. *Journal of Gender Studies, 27*, 1–8.

Rodino-Colocino, M. (2014). #YesAllWomen: Intersectional mobilisation against sexual assault is radical (again). *Feminist Media Studies, 14*, 1113–1115.

Roiphe, K. (1993). *The morning after: Sex, fear and feminism.* Little, Brown and Company.

Ryan, T. (2019). This black body is not yours for the taking. In B. Fileborn & R. Loney-Howes (Eds.), *# MeToo and the politics of social change* (pp. 117–132). Springer.

Salter, M. (2013). Justice and revenge in online counter-publics: Emerging responses to sexual violence in the age of social media. *Crime, Media, Culture, 9*, 225–242.

Scully, P. (1995). Rape, race, and colonial culture: The sexual politics of identity in the nineteenth-century Cape Colony, South Africa. *The American Historical Review, 100*(2), 335–359.

Serisier, T. (2018). *Speaking out: Feminism, rape and narrative politics.* Springer.

Shaw, J., Campbell, R., Cain, D., & Feeney, H. (2017). Beyond surveys and scales: How rape myths manifest in sexual assault police records. *Psychology of Violence, 7*, 602–614.

Smith, A., & Ross, L. (2004). Introduction: Native women and state violence. *Social Justice, 31*(4 (98)), 1–7.

Smith, O., & Skinner, T. (2017). How rape myths are used and challenged in rape and sexual assault trials. *Social & Legal Studies, 26*(4), 441–466.

Spohn, C., & Tellis, K. (2012). The criminal justice system's response to sexual violence. *Violence Against Women, 18*(2), 169–192.

Spohn, C., White, C., and Tellis, K. (2014). Unfounding sexual assault: Examining the decision to unfound and identifying false reports. *Law & Society Review, 48*, 161–192.

Sprankle, E., Bloomquist, K., Butcher, C., Gleason, N., & Schaefer, Z. (2018). The role of sex work stigma in victim blaming and empathy of sexual assault survivors. *Sexuality Research and Social Policy, 15*, 242–248.

Turchik, J. A., & Edwards, K. M. (2012). Myths about male rape: A literature review. *Psychology of Men and Masculinities, 13*(2), 211–226.

VanNatta, M. (2010). Conceptualizing and stopping state sexual violence against incarcerated women. *Social Justice, 37*, 27–52.

Vera-Gray, F. (2016). Men's stranger intrusions: Rethinking street harassment. *Women's Studies International Forum, 58*, 9–17.

Wang, Y. (2011). Voices from the margin: A case study of a rural lesbian's experience with woman-to-woman sexual violence. *Journal of Lesbian Studies, 15*, 166–175.

Weare, S. (2018). 'Oh you're a guy, how could you be raped by a woman, that makes no sense': Towards a case for legally recognising and labelling 'forced-to-penetrate' cases as rape. *International Journal of Law in Context, 14*(1), 110–131.

Wooten, S. C. (2015). *Heterosexist discourses: How feminist theory shaped campus sexual violence policy* (pp. 33–51). Routledge.

World Bank. (2019). *Gender-based violence (violence against women and girls).* https //www.worldbank.org/en/topic/socialsustainability/brief/violence-against-women-and-girls. Last accessed 17 Sept 2021.

World Health Organization. (2021). *Violence against women.* https://www.who.int/news-room/fact-sheets/detail/violence-against-women. Last accessed 17 Sept 2021.

World Population Review. (2021). *Rape statistics by country 2021.* https://worldpopulationreview.com/country-rankings/rape-statistics-by-country. Last accessed 17 Sept 2021.

Young, A. (2009). *The scene of violence: Cinema, crime, affect.* Routledge-Cavendish.

4

Sex Work and the Night-Time Economy

The city is a space of the commodification of sex, entertainment and hedonism. This chapter discusses two different but interlinked topics related to the experience and regulation of selling and buying sexual and night-time entertainment services: sex work and the night-time economy. There are spaces where sex work and the night-time economy overlap, such as lap-dancing and strip clubs, but they also entail distinct issues. Both, however, relate to conceptualisations of moral geography and questions of who belongs in which spaces and how they should behave within them. Moral geography refers to the moral judgements about spaces and people that shape regulation and processes of inclusion and exclusion (Domosh, 2001; Seal & O'Neill, 2019).

Moral geographies create and recreate norms of gender, as well as norms of race and class, particularly around designations of respectability and legitimacy. Sex work is governed by attitudes towards appropriate sexual behaviour but also related norms of appropriate womanhood and understandings of legitimate relationships. The night-time economy is based on the sale of entertainment and pleasure, mediated by the purchase and consumption of alcohol, possibly alongside illicit drugs.

© The Author(s), under exclusive license to Springer Nature
Switzerland AG 2022
L. Seal, *Gender, Crime and Justice,*
https://doi.org/10.1007/978-3-030-87488-9_4

As such both phenomena are subject to moral regulation and moral anxiety. They are also both affected by neoliberal economics and modes of governance that entwine with gendered morality.

Sex Work

Weitzer (2009) describes sex work as 'polymorphous' because it encompasses a range of occupations, working arrangements, worker experiences and power relations. This diversity includes selling sex from one's home or a brothel, working on the street, as an escort, stripping, phone sex, internet-based camera work and the porn industry. The definition of sex work is not clear-cut and has fuzzy boundaries (Kempadoo, 2001). Some argue sex work also incorporates sexual relationships that are based on one party providing accommodation, gifts and other financial support for the other, such as 'mistresses', 'kept boys' and 'sugar babies' (Kempadoo, 2001; Scull, 2020; Weitzer, 2009). Street-based sex work has been the most extensively researched form of sex work, and there is more research about cis women who sell sex than men or trans sex workers (Weitzer, 2009). The diversity of sex work and of sex workers is represented in *Whispers and Moans* (2007), which comprises vignettes about characters who work in different aspects of the sex trade in Hong Kong—as mistresses, nightclub hostesses, in brothels and on the streets. One of those portrayed who work on the streets is Jo, a trans woman, and her boyfriend Tony (Veg, 2007).

The term 'sex worker' was coined by activist Carol Leigh to exemplify that sex work is a form of labour and to replace the stigmatising label of 'prostitute'. 'Sex worker' is a potentially unifying term as it can encompass a range of different jobs (Kempadoo & Doezema, 1998). Kempadoo and Doezema (1998) stress involvement in sex work is not someone's whole identity; it is one aspect of their life. People might do sex work for a short time, sporadically or alongside other employment. People's reasons for engaging in sex work vary, but are primarily material (O'Neill, 2010; Smith & Mac, 2018). Sex work can compare favourably with other work in terms of pay, flexibility and degree of autonomy (Benoit et al., 2018).

Sex work entails a wide range of experiences. Foley (2019) conducted ethnographic research with women who engaged in sex work in Senegal. The rural economy in Senegal collapsed, reducing employment available in the formal sector. Men were more able than women to migrate in search of work to different areas or countries. Particularly where women experienced a triggering event, such as divorce or the death of their husband, sex work was the best available option because it paid better than other available jobs, like domestic work. Similarly, women and men in the Caribbean worked in the tourism-based sex trade as it was better paid and often safer than alternatives such as domestic work, street vending and fishing (Kempadoo, 2001).

For educated middle-class women employed in different aspects of the sex industry in San Franscisco, sex work was more highly paid than other service sector work such as waitressing or retail, and could also be combined with other activities like postgraduate study or creative practice (Bernstein, 2007). Bernstein (2007) argues that due to structural gender inequality, well-qualified women were more likely to be pushed into low skill, low wage work than well-qualified men. The women she interviewed did not engage in sex work for bare survival, but as an option that had advantages over the others available. *The Girlfriend Experience* (2009) depicts the professional life of Chelsea, a 'high end' sex worker whose customers are men drawn from New York's financial elite. They pay to spend time with her hence her business is the 'girlfriend experience'. Her professional environment is Manhattan's expensive apartments, hotels and restaurants. Stewart and Pine (2014) interpret Chelsea as a member of the economic precariat—she can make decent money but has no security. The film was adapted as an anthology series for television (2016–ongoing), which have storylines based on women doing escort work alongside burgeoning careers in law and the tech industry.

The focus of this chapter is on paid sex as a form of labour, which applies in many places in the Global South and North. However, it is accepted that this interpretation does not have universal applicability. Wardlow (2004) contends that payment for sex cannot be universally understood as a form of labour and that 'sex work' is not a term that applies globally. Huli 'passenger' women in Papua New Guinea had sex in exchange for money or goods, but in Huli culture non-reproductive sex was not understood as work as women's sexuality was associated with reproductive potential. Passenger women were not motivated by financial necessity, but often as a form of protest against their families for not protecting them from violence. Wardlow's (2004) argument highlights the diversity of practices and meanings of selling sex across different cultures.

Like other forms of paid work, there are inequalities in sex work. Trans women and Black women are overrepresented in street-based sex work, which is the riskiest form of sex work as well as the most stigmatised and most dangerous (Kempadoo & Doezema, 1998; Weitzer, 2009). Kattari and Begun (2017) found that trans women and gender nonconforming people in the United States were more likely to engage in survival sex—sex in exchange for resources—than cis women. This was connected to trans people's higher rates of homelessness, resulting from transphobia and family rejection. Trans sex workers also faced barriers in terms of accessing shelters, which were often segregated by gender, and drug treatment services.

Tangerine (2015) gained attention due to its portrayal of Sin-Dee and Alexandra, two Black trans women engaged in sex work in Los Angeles, over the course of one day, which happens to be Christmas Eve. Yep et al. (2019) argue the film offers multidimensional portrayals of working class Black trans women, who are frequently invisible in cinema and mainstream society. While trans people's stories are now told more frequently in the media than in the past, the stories of poor trans women and trans women of colour have less visibility (Yep et al., 2019). *Tangerine* depicts the women's experiences of hardship and transphobic harassment, but also the depth of their friendship and their arts of survival.

The exoticisation of racialised women as objects of sexual desire in the white Western imagination reflects legacies of colonialism (Kempadoo & Doezema, 1998). Whiteness is the hegemonic standard of beauty and white women are better represented in the safe and more well-paid parts of the sex industry. Garcia (2010) found that in Cuba, Black women and women of colour were often assumed to participate in the tourism-based sex industry and were subject to surveillance and regulation by the authorities. This assumption rested on stereotypes about women of colour as exotic and erotic others.

The majority of sex workers are women, but men also do sex work. Whowell (2010) notes that in England and Wales, men are absent from policies on sex work, which focus on women. Male sex work has gained greater visibility following the emergence of new online and offline sites via which it can be advertised. Social media such as Grindr and Instagram have made a significant contribution to this increased visibility (Ryan, 2016). Ryan (2016) contextualises the raised profile of male sex work against social and cultural changes such as the commodification of the masculine body and the greater social acceptability of gay identities. In the Global North, male sex work has historically been stigmatised as effeminate. Kempadoo (2001) argues that Black Caribbean men who sell sex to female tourists are not denied masculinity and can maintain an identity consistent with notions of 'real' manhood. O'Shaughnessy (2017) discusses films exploring the sex tourism of women from the Global North in countries of the Global South. *Heading South* (2005), set in Haiti, and *Paradise: Love* (2012), set in Kenya, show the privileged white women tourists as 'empowered' consumers unaware of and uninterested in the emotional labour performed by those in the tourist industry who facilitate their experiences, and oblivious to the colonial histories shaping their encounters.

Stigma

Sex work is heavily stigmatised, and the figure of the woman who sells sex on the streets has been a particular target for this stigma. Women who sell sex have been negatively portrayed across different places and times as symbols of immorality, disease and disorder and their presence in public space has been contested (O'Neill, 2010; O'Neill et al., 2008). Pheterson (1993) conceptualises this as 'whore stigma', the assumption that women who sell sex are dishonourable and bearers of shame. This stigma has grave consequences as it is expressed in the various ways sex work is regulated to reduce sex workers' freedom and in the social designation of sex workers as unworthy.

Although men who sell sex are also stigmatised, whore stigma has historically been attached to women and was a component part of constructing respectable femininity. The 'whore' or prostitute was the opposite of a respectable woman and a danger to morality. Levine (1993) examines how in Victorian and Edwardian England, commentaries referred to prostitution as a 'social evil' and pathologised women who sold sex as different and distinct from women who laboured as textile workers or matchmakers. The motives of women were believed to need special explanation beyond financial necessity, or they were assumed to have been coerced. Street-based women became targets of regulation as they were public symbols of deviant womanhood. The association between sex workers, disease and contagion was instantiated in law by the Contagious Diseases Acts of the 1860s. These stipulated that in certain districts, women suspected of prostitution must undergo genital examinations and receive compulsory treatment if found to have venereal disease. Refusing examination was punishable with imprisonment (Levine, 1993; Walkowitz, 1980). The Acts were part of the state's regulation of gender, sexuality and space.

In a more recent context, the stigmatisation of sex workers as vectors for disease has centred on the transmission of HIV, particularly in relation to women from the Global South (O'Neill et al., 2008; Scambler & Paoli, 2008). As the sex industry globalised, the stereotype of foreign sex workers as bringers of disease and a threat to public health developed (O'Neill et al., 2008; Scambler, 2007). Derogatory attitudes towards sex work are entwined with views on race, migration and upholding national borders, but these anxieties are often hidden beneath the expression of other concerns, for instance in relation to sex trafficking. The foreign sex worker as bringer of disease stereotype is likely to be mobilised in arguments for stricter immigration controls (Smith & Mac, 2018). Like Pheterson (1993), Smith and Mac (2018) highlight that 'whore stigma' is deployed metaphorically in ways that are antithetical to sex workers' rights. They argue for a focus on practical and material issues that affect sex workers, such as poverty, criminalisation and immigration laws.

Stigma negatively affects sex workers' lives and both contributes to and is reproduced by policies that regulate the sale of sex (Benoit et al., 2019). All forms of sex work are stigmatised to an extent, although stigma is more intense in relation to street-based sex work, and to poor, racialised and trans sex workers (Benoit et al., 2018; Weitzer, 2018). Lyons et al.'s (2017) research with trans sex workers in Vancouver, Canada identified that transphobia and criminalisation contributed to the violence their participants experienced. Trans sex workers faced violence from transphobic clients, as well as from the police. This physical violence was underpinned by the structural violence of poverty and the symbolic violence of transphobic stigma.

Research into sex workers' experiences finds that stigma is one of sex work's main disadvantages in comparison with other types of work. Women in Canada and Senegal stated that sex work compared favourably with other kinds of available work in terms of pay and autonomy, but was stigmatised in ways that other types of service work were not (Benoit et al., 2019; Foley, 2019). In Senegal, sex workers could register with authorities to receive medical care, but many women avoided doing so due to fear of stigma (Foley, 2019). Scambler (2007) interviewed Eastern European women working as escorts in London. They were highly aware of the stigma associated with sex work, and to mitigate this association distanced themselves from a sex worker identity, stressing that it was a short-term option to make money.

Film and television have created cultural imaginaries of sex work and sex workers with progressive, regressive and transgressive effects. One recurrent portrayal is the location of sex workers of different genders in sleazy urban milieu, as in New York set *Midnight Cowboy* (1969) and *Taxi Driver* (1976), where sex work is one type of survival indexing the socially decaying city. *The Deuce* (2017–2019) revisits this setting to explore the sex industry and developing drug trade in 1970s and 80s Manhattan. In series one, street-based sex worker Eileen Merrell begins working with a director of porn films to make a film centring on female desire. From there, she develops a career directing feminist pornography. Her portrayal resists many of the on-screen stereotypes about sex workers as in need of rescue or as hypersexual and fetishised. The final scene of the final episode of *The Deuce* shows one of the characters in old age moving through present-day Times Square—a commercialised and sanitised space in comparison with the 1970s. Rather than presenting

Manhattan in the 1970s as a site of urban social decay, it depicts it as one of possibility, albeit where survival is hard.

O'Neill (1998) analyses three westerns that feature representations of sex workers. She argues fictional worlds offer the opportunity for audiences to immerse themselves in the lifeworlds and processes of frontiers people. In *Unforgiven* (1992), there is some departure from stereotypical portrayals of 'whores' as women who must either be killed or redeemed. The women who work in the brothel support each other and offer care to marginalised men on the frontier. They defend one another and resist mistreatment. They play a role in the development of frontier society and in maintaining the social order in that society.

Regulation

There are four models for regulating sex work: criminalisation, partial criminalisation, legalisation and decriminalisation. Criminalisation is where either the sale of sex and/or related activities, such as solicitation and running a brothel, are against the criminal law. This approach conceives of selling and buying sex as harmful and deserving of punishment. Partial criminalisation focuses on the purchase of sex. Legalisation recognises sex work as legitimate work and means that sex workers gain employment rights and contracts are legally enforceable. It also means that sex work is likely to be formally regulated by the state, for instance through registration and licensing. Decriminalisation removes laws and penalties related to selling and purchasing sex but does not entail special requirements such as registration and licensing. Jurisdictions usually adopt mixed models for regulating sex work (Aronowitz, 2014; Phoenix, 2009).

Major reforms to the regulation of sex work tend to occur episodically and during periods of socio-economic change (Scoular, 2010). Nineteenth century reforms such as the Contagious Diseases Acts, which applied in Britain and British colonies, took place when British cities were rapidly expanding and when the Empire was growing. Concerns over sexual and spatial regulation within Britain, and sexual and racial regulation in the colonies, undergirded the Acts (Howell, 2000). Scoular (2010) highlights globalisation and neoliberalism as significant shifts that are relevant to contemporary policymaking in relation to sex work. Crucially, she emphasises that in the twenty-first century, different European regimes of regulation are underpinned by the politics of security. The contemporary conflation of sex work with sex trafficking, the illicit drug trade and migration continues the longstanding tendency for sex work to be treated as a metaphor for other phenomena.

In the twenty-first century, models of criminalisation have frequently been justified via the supposed interlinking of sex work and trafficking. In the United States, the Victims of Trafficking and Violence Prevention Act 2000 interpreted 'prostitution' as responsible for causing sex trafficking (Jackson, 2016). The evidence for this connection is not strong, and research demonstrates that coerced sex work is comparatively rare (Benoit et al., 2019). However, this legislation had a significant policy impact, resulting in punitive approaches towards sex workers such as arrests, court appearances, compulsory rehabilitation programmes and deportations for migrant sex workers. It also instantiated the portrayal of sex workers as victims without agency, a portrayal reinforced by the 'rescue industry' of feminist and religious organisations (Agustin, 2007; Jackson, 2016; Weitzer, 2010). While such groups profess sympathy for sex workers, supporting policies of criminalisation has had severe consequences and reinscribed stigma. American government funding was funnelled into expanding arrests and carceral outcomes, and NGOs doing international work had to state their opposition to sex work in order to be eligible for American funding.

Films about sex trafficking are frequently based on a 'rescue narrative' in which a naïve young woman is abducted or tricked by an evil trafficker, only to be rescued by a white male saviour (Baker, 2014). Baker identifies *Taken* (2010), in which Bryan, a former CIA investigator, rescues his daughter from Albanian traffickers, as a prominent and commercially successful example. The rescue restores masculinity—and by association patriarchal authority—to Bryan. The rescue narrative constructs women and girls as in need of protection and paternal authority.

Wahab and Panichelli (2013) provide an example of the harmful effects of the 'rescue industry'. The Arizona-based project 'Reaching Out to the Sexually Exploited' was a collaboration between the Phoenix Police Department and the School of Social Work at Arizona State University. The police conducted raids targeting the sex industry, during which they arrested sex workers. Eligible sex workers could attend a social worker-led six-month diversion programme as an alternative to criminal charges. Eligibility required that sex workers had no prior arrests for sex work, no outstanding warrants for their arrest, were not in possession of drugs and were legal residents of the United States. Wahab and Panichelli (2013) state the majority of women arrested did not meet these eligibility rules and were criminalised and/or subjected to immigration control. The authors contend that even where women could avail themselves of the social work programme, compulsory rehabilitation under threat of criminalisation violates social work's ethical codes of needing informed consent from the participants of such programmes.

Neoabolitionist approaches seek to use the criminal law to remove sex work, but (in theory) target the male purchasers of sex rather than the female sellers (Ward & Wylie, 2017). This model neglects male sex workers (Chu & Glass, 2013). Sweden's Violence Against Women Act 1998 pioneered the neoabolitionist approach and was based on radical feminist conceptualisations of sex work as a violent expression of patriarchal power. It linked sex work and sex trafficking together and perpetuated an understanding of sex workers as vulnerable coerced victims (Hubbard et al., 2008; Ward & Wylie, 2017). In practice, the criminalisation of purchasers meant that sex workers needed to be less visible to attract customers, which made their reliance on pimps stronger and their working conditions less safe (Grenfell et al., 2016; Hubbard et al., 2008; Levy & Jakobsson, 2014). Convictions for sex trafficking have remained low (Heber, 2018).

The Swedish (or Nordic) model has nevertheless been influential and versions of it have been adopted in Finland, Norway, Iceland, Canada, Ireland, Northern Ireland and France. Ward and Wylie (2017) argue the perception of Sweden as a state with high levels of gender equity has given neoabolitionism legitimacy. Swedish politicians promoted this model to other European Union countries and feminist violence against women activists advocated for it through transnational activist networks. Concerns about sex trafficking dovetail with states' concerns about migration and this has also given strength to neoabolitionism (Ward & Wylie, 2017). The body of the sex worker becomes an emblem of the state's violated borders, with her putative vulnerability to exploitation symbolising that of the state. These anxieties reflect a racist imaginary of others as a threat to national purity and safety (Hubbard et al., 2008). Documentary *Buying Sex* (2013) outlines debates about the regulation of sex work as they pertained in Canada at the time, presenting the neoabolitionist Swedish model and decriminalisation in New Zealand as divergent possible policy directions. The Protection of Communities and Exploited Persons Act 2014 criminalised the purchase of sex and certain activities related to the sale of sex (Haak, 2018).

England and Wales has a complicated regulatory regime surrounding sex work, which exposes sex workers to criminalisation in several ways. Selling sex is not illegal, which means that sex workers can be autonomous, register as self-employed and pay taxes. Sex work is heavily stigmatised so sex workers often choose to hide their employment status (Pitcher & Wijers, 2014). Brothels, known as massage parlours, can offer safe working conditions as they have security measures such as CCTV and receptionists who can screen customers. However, collective working is illegal and any collective working situation, even just two women working from the same accommodation, can count as a brothel (Pitcher & Wijers, 2014; Sanders & Campbell, 2007). Sex workers are also governed via anti-social behaviour legislation, according to which they can be compelled to attend rehabilitation meetings focused on exiting sex work. Failure to comply results in punishment (Munro & Scoular, 2012). Criminologists have theorised compulsory rehabilitation as a form of responsibilisation, whereby individuals must work to overcome the structural disadvantages they face. The onus to reform and become 'respectable' is placed on the individual sex worker (Sanders, 2009; Scoular and O'Neill, 2007).

The Netherlands legalised sex work in 2000, removing penalties for running brothels and pimping. Brothels are regulated through licencing. The number of available licences is limited, which means that there are few opportunities for sex workers to be independently employed;

rather they work for brothels and escort agencies (Pitcher & Wijers, 2014). Local municipalities can impose their own standards and the police can demand to check sex workers' documents (Hubbard et al., 2008). Sex workers who cannot meet regulatory standards, or who are undocumented migrants, are pushed into the illegal sector. Legalisation has improved working conditions for some, but lowered them for others (Scoular, 2010). Scoular (2010) describes the Netherlands' model of regulation as one that favours profitability and is consistent with capitalism.

The Nordic model, England and Wales and the Netherlands represent different regulatory regimes with similar underlying logics (Hubbard et al., 2008). Priorities of neoliberal governance are reflected in their regulation of space. All three regimes control where sex workers can(not) be present and visible. Spatial governance supports the gentrification of city centres, and clears them for the profitmaking legitimate sex industry—legalised brothels in the Netherlands or lap-dancing clubs in England and Wales (Hubbard et al., 2008). Sex workers are conceptualised as vulnerable and in need of state protection, whether this is through attempting to abolish sex work, 'reform' sex workers or to oversee their working situation, and the state presents itself as benevolent (Munro & Scoular, 2012; Scoular, 2010). However, these regulatory approaches variously expose sex workers to criminalisation, unsafe working conditions, lower autonomy and greater control through pimps, and deportation.

The mobilisation of immigration law is particularly significant as, although the conflation of sex work and sex trafficking is presented as concern for vulnerable migrant women, the regulation of sex work exposes them to detention and removal from their country of residence. In addition to a portrayal of benevolence, the state positions itself as vulnerable, with sex work and/or sex workers representing a threat to security and the integrity of national borders (Munro & Scoular, 2012). Ultimately, these models of regulation uphold the exclusion and banishment of those deemed undesirable (Scoular, 2010). Pickering and Ham (2013) conducted observation and carried out interviews with immigration officers at an Australian airport in order to assess the micropolitics of interactions at the border. Sex work was legal in the jurisdiction in which the airport was based. Immigration officers sought to identify trafficking victims and those suspected of working illegally, and in relation to both concentrated especially on women they identified as sex workers. Pickering and Ham (2013) argue officers made judgements based on assumptions about the nationality and race of Asian women. These judgements were not a reliable means of identifying trafficked women, but were a process of racialised social sorting.

Decriminalisation is the model of regulation favoured by sex worker activists, advocates and global organisations such as Amnesty International and the World Health Organization (Weitzer, 2018). New Zealand's Prostitution Reform Act 2003 fully decriminalised sex work, despite the wider global trend of neoabolitionism (Armstrong, 2016). Armstrong (2016) explored how decriminalisation changed interactions between the police and street-based sex workers, the most heavily criminalised group of sex workers. Decriminalisation had greatly improved the picture, with sex workers feeling that they could report violence to the police and that they had safer working conditions. It did not mean police abuse of powers disappeared completely. Smith and Mac (2018) highlight the strongest benefit of decriminalisation as improving working conditions. Indoor workers can work collectively without being prosecuted for brothel keeping and, where they work in a managed brothel, their employers are subject to labour laws. Sex workers can communicate boundaries to their clients without resorting to euphemism and are more able to refuse clients. Smith and Mac (2018) emphasise that the New Zealand approach to decriminalisation is a starting point rather than a perfect model. Drugs and immigration laws mean there are still ways in which many sex workers can be criminalised and subjected to repressive measures.

There is no clear link between the type of state (for example, democratic or authoritarian) and its regime for regulating sex work (Ward & Wylie, 2017). Scholars like Bumiller (2008) and Bernstein (2010) highlight the intersection between carceral feminist politics and neoliberalism, which underpins the conflation of sex work with sex trafficking and the consequent greater criminalisation of sex work. However, Sweden, which pioneered neoabolitionism, did so in the context of state welfarism and New Zealand decriminalised sex work against the backdrop of neoliberalism (Ward & Wylie, 2017). The social control of sexuality, and by association of gender, class and race, operated before the predominance of neoliberal capitalism and is not dependent on it. White (1990) argues sex work was not caused by capitalism, but under capitalism sex work took the form of commoditised labour. This argument can be extended to neoliberal capitalism: it shapes and affects the form of different approaches to the regulation of sex work in diverse and contradictory ways (Rivers-Moore, 2014). The neoliberal emphasis on self-governance means the regulation of sex work can take place through licencing, rather than repression, as in the Netherlands (Scoular, 2010). Rivers-Moore (2014) argues that in Costa Rica, the neoliberal governance of sex workers operates through inadequate provision of health services and immigration raids that affect migrant women, rather than through the threat of imprisonment. What these different approaches share is deployment for the social control of gender and sexuality.

Sex Worker Activism

Sex worker activism has a long history but the current international sex worker rights movement has grown in strength since the 1980s. This movement argues for labour rights and safer working conditions for sex workers and criticises the harms caused by criminalising sex work (Smith & Mac, 2018). As Smith and Mac (2018) argue, sex workers are experts on their working conditions and on the nature of the sex industry. They do not make their arguments from an abstracted or symbolic position, but from one of being able to focus on practical issues. Sex worker activists have provided a counter story to the portrayal of sex workers as helpless victims (Jackson, 2016). They have shown that sex workers are people with agency and deserving of a voice. Activists have challenged the presumptions of the 'rescue industry' by highlighting that carceral approaches based on arrest and deportation are deeply harmful to the very people they are supposed to 'protect' (Jackson, 2016). Rather than rescue or punishment, activists stress the need for labour rights. Smith and Mac (2018) argue that labour centred analyses and activism do not need to come from the position that work is inherently good, or necessarily fulfilling. Instead, they need to challenge labour exploitation and argue for workers' rights.

Hardy and Rivers-Moore (2018) examine unionisation and self-organisation among sex workers in Latin America. Such groups have drawn attention to sex workers' health-based needs and advocated for decriminalisation. Fundamentally, they use the language of class to make claims about sex workers' labour rights and build bridges with other parts of the labour movement. In Argentina, sex worker rights unions have forged links with other workers, such as teachers and those employed in the informal sector. In Nicaragua, where 65% of workers are employed in the informal sector, the formally recognised sex worker union Girasoles has allied with workers such as street vendors and market traders (Hardy & Rivers-Moore, 2018). Such alliances highlight the similarities between sex work and other types of work. This both challenges the stigmatisation of sex work as something exceptional or morally suspect and shows how demanding rights for sex workers can be made in solidarity with demands for labour rights more broadly. Labour-based activism offers a wider critique of working conditions in the context of capitalist exploitation. *Sunflowers of Nicaragua* (2017) follows eighteen members of the Girasoles collective who were given legal powers in 2015 to act as mediators for small conflicts without resorting to the police.

Sex worker unions in Latin America also protest against police and paramilitary violence against sex workers (Hardy & Rivers-Moore, 2018). Activists highlight how criminalisation makes sex workers vulnerable to violence, which is exacerbated by lack of action by the state on their behalf. Transgender Equality Uganda opposes gender-based violence against trans sex workers, as well as forced health tests and compulsory rehabilitation (Lusimbo & Bryan, 2018). In Canada, the annual Women's Memorial March in the Downtown Eastside (DTES) of Vancouver/Unceded Coast Salish Territories, led by Indigenous women, brings attention to the murdered and missing women from this area, who are disproportionately Indigenous, poor and involved in sex work (Seal & O'Neill, 2019). The march is also part of the campaign to decriminalise sex work in Canada, particularly since the purchase of sex was criminalised in 2014 (Seal & O'Neill, 2019). Documentary *Survival, Strength and Sisterhood: Power of Women in the Downtown Eastside* (2011) examines the origins and history of the women's march and the lives of the women activists. *Finding Dawn* (2006) tells the stories of three missing Indigenous women from British Columbia and Saskatchewan. Hargreaves (2015) argues *Finding Dawn* is an example of Indigenous feminist research practice, which performs holistic analysis through storytelling to enact remembrance of gendered colonial violence.

The next part of this chapter explores the significance of gender to nightlife and the night-time economy, which involves the applicability of concepts such as moral geography and the regulation of space.

Gender and the Night-Time Economy

Since the 1990s, commercial night-time leisure spaces, such as pubs, bars and clubs, have become significant elements of urban economies around the world. The expansion of the night-time economy in Europe, Australia and New Zealand was characterised by longer opening hours for venues and comparatively cheaply priced drinks (Measham & Østergaard, 2009). Central and waterfront districts underwent redevelopment, with disused buildings such as warehouses being transformed into entertainment venues. Such districts formed new economic centres, publicised by city authorities as evidence of a region's vibrancy (Tomkins, 2005). Depending on local legal and regulatory frameworks, the mix of businesses can also include sexual entertainment venues such as lap-dancing clubs (Hubbard & Colosi, 2015a). Chew (2009) argues that in China commercial sex is integral to the night-time economy as regular clubs and bars are interlinked with the sex industry.

Night-time leisure spaces offer escape from everyday routines and the chance to have fun. Many of the rules of comportment and social interaction that govern daily life are suspended or relaxed, allowing excessive behaviour that would be unacceptable in a different context (Ayres & Treadwell, 2012; Briggs & Ellis, 2017). In this sense, night-time leisure spaces are liminal and on the margins of the usual social order (Hobbs et al., 2003; Turner, 1987). They are sites of carnival—of pleasure-taking and time out of normal life (Presdee, 2003). Hobbs et al. (2003) describe nightlife as 'patterned liminality' as it takes place in designated, commodified spaces that are carefully demarcated as the zones in which excessive behaviour can take place. These zones are profit-making and serve the priorities of consumer capitalism. The rowdy behaviour that ensues from drinking too much in a convivial setting can be interpreted as social conformity, rather than rebellion, as it is shaped by commercially driven notions of what constitutes a good time (Briggs & Ellis, 2017).

The liminal and carnivalesque nature of night-time leisure spaces, coupled with commercial imperatives, provides the context for the reproduction of gender identity. The night-time economy combines regulation and deregulation—people may feel their behaviour can be freer than usual, but gendered norms and power differences are still in place (Sheard, 2011). Reality television shows about British-based tourists on holiday in Spain and Greece evoke the 'anything goes' carnivalesque atmosphere of nightlife in tourist destinations (Williams-Burnett et al., 2018; Casey, 2020). Such shows portray nights out on holiday as a means of doing working class heterosexual masculinity as well as solidifying young men's friendship networks (Casey, 2020). Nights out that include drinking to excess followed by deviant behaviour offer a sense of masculine affirmation, although this deviance is in keeping with accepted rituals and codes of masculinity as incorporating some 'bad' behaviour and 'laddishness' (Briggs & Ellis, 2017). Briggs and Ellis (2017) cite stag parties as a particularly apt example. Harder and Demant (2015) interviewed young men who frequented Danish nightclubs and used illegal drugs. Their participants reported that drugs such as cocaine, ecstasy and amphetamines enabled them to overcome shyness and anxiety, and gain the confidence to pick up women. This enhanced confidence fulfilled their idealised notions of being 'real' men.

The *Hangover* trilogy (2009–2013) portrays male bonding enacted via stag parties, with the first and second films set in the tourist destinations of Las Vegas and Bangkok. The concept of the movies is based on the liminal space the trips create for the characters and the release it offers from their normal bourgeois lives (Harbidge, 2012). The films locate the characters' carnivalesque experiences in the commercialised leisure industries associated with drinking, gambling and sex. Boyle (2014) argues the men's sense of entitlement over women is uncontested in the films and is constructed as a marker of their masculinity. In Part 2 (2011) especially, women working in Thailand's sex industry are portrayed as disposable along lines of class, race and gender identity, with comedic representations based on racist and transphobic stereotypes.

Nayak (2006) explored the significance of nights out for young working-class men in Newcastle, UK. Such young men experienced an insecure transition from childhood to adulthood in a post-industrial context in which employment was precarious. Newcastle city centre is renowned for its nightlife and the city has a reputation as a party centre. Participating in Newcastle's night-time economy, and concomitant drinking culture, was an important means for some young men to bond with one another. They recuperated a sense of masculinity from the shared rituals of a night out, and the funny stories it supplied. For young men in paid work, the enjoyment of nights out was consistent with a respectable working-class identity. Not all participants could afford to frequent city centre clubs and bars, or to purchase the clothing this required. Nayak (2006) observes that some working-class young men instead accrued embodied capital through physical stature, toughness and exhibiting 'hard masculinity'. Hard masculinity was associated with being 'rough', or not respectable. Such differences in masculine performance were shaped by and intersected with class-based identities.

Raymen and Smith (2017) highlight a transformed masculine life-course under consumer capitalism, which potentially extends 'youth' into men's thirties. Their ethnographic research with male 'lifestyle gamblers' revealed the importance of hedonism and consumption to these men, despite most being in long-term relationships and some being fathers. The gamblers' conception of the good life, and of their masculine identity, was shaped by consumerism. The role of hedonism in creating personal and collective masculine identities is explored by Ayres and Treadwell (2012) in their ethnography of English football fans. The men constructed a hypermasculine identity through excessively consuming alcohol and cocaine and engaging in violence. This took place during nights out in the liminal space of the night-time economy. Hypermasculinity required displays of physical strength and intimidation and was the basis for reinforcing feelings of togetherness among the football fans.

Night-time leisure spaces are also sites for performing femininity and for cementing female friendships. Nightclubs offer young women pleasurable experiences and feelings of freedom and empowerment. Publicly engaging in hedonistic behaviour potentially redefines 'traditional' femininity, which is identified with domesticity (Hutton et al., 2013; Nicholls, 2017). However, feminine performance in nightlife spaces often reproduces norms of gender through elements such as dress and drink choice. Nicholls (2017) found in her interviews with young women about 'girls' nights out' in Newcastle that wine and cocktails were understood as consistent with femininity, whereas pints of beer were not. Sharing a bottle of wine was an opportunity to collectively experience friendship and femininity. Griffin et al. (2013) highlight a contemporary 'hypersexual femininity' at work in young women's participation in night-time economies. On the one hand, this femininity is exuded through an attitude of independence and 'sassiness', looking 'sexy' and drinking to excess. On the other hand, such feminine performance is fraught with contradictions as it is important for young women not to appear overly sexual, or too assertive.

Hutton et al. (2016) conducted focus groups with friendship groups of young women in New Zealand about their drinking practices and nights out. Their participants engaged enthusiastically with the night-time economy and with the associated culture of intoxification. The young women identified with twenty-first century 'new femininities' that value empowerment, sexual assertiveness and individualism (Gill & Scharff, 2011), and enjoying a night out with friends was a way of enacting this femininity. However, they also articulated the need to exercise restraint and remain within boundaries of respectability. Participants disapproved of other women if they were too drunk, out of control or went 'too far'. Griffin et al. (2013) argue that out of control and excessively sexual behaviour is characterised as working class and disreputable, and as unfeminine.

Similar priorities were discussed by young women in Gunby et al.'s (2020) research conducted in Liverpool, UK. There was a line to be walked in the performance of femininity on nights out between fulfilling emphasised femininity by looking attractive and seeming fun, but not appearing promiscuous. Gunby et al. (2020) explored the range of young women's strategies for dealing with unwanted sexual attention in the night-time economy. These strategies included managing the emotions of troublesome men, invoking male protection, intervention from female friends or exhibiting a 'feisty femininity' of retaliation. Feisty femininity was influenced by feminism and demonstrated resistance to the sexist norms that enable harassment (Gunby et al., 2020).

Fileborn (2016) researched young people's safety strategies in the night-time economy in Melbourne, Australia. Typically, both women and men felt safe but had differently gendered strategies in order to achieve this. Women discussed not getting too drunk, going to familiar places and being with people they knew as ways of avoiding sexual violence on a night out. Fileborn (2016) argues that the responsibility for avoiding sexual violence is placed on women, who must manage their routines to avoid danger. Men, both heterosexual and gay, regarded safety as an issue that was more relevant to women and stated they were protected by their comparatively greater size and strength. Both genders identified groups of heterosexual men as posing the most danger. Fileborn (2016) observes that men's responses were shaped by normative masculinity and not wanting to seem fearful—it was possible safety was more of a concern than they admitted.

Night-time leisure spaces evoke a range of emotions, from happiness, desire and belonging, to anxiety and fear. Affective atmospheres influence how individuals feel when they participate in nightlife (Shaw, 2014). Race (2016) argues that for LGBTQ people, nightlife is an important part of emotional bonding and community formation. Shifts in the regulation of the night-time economy that lead to the closure of queer venues limit these community-building opportunities. Emotional experiences are shaped by gender, sexuality and race. Through ethnographic research, Held (2015) examined how feelings of comfort and fear during nights out in the Gay Village in Manchester, UK contributed to experiences of othering. Lesbian women could feel uncomfortable in and excluded from venues that were dominated by gay men and frequented by heterosexual women. However, lesbian women found gay spaces safer and more comfortable than straight venues. Black and Asian lesbian women experienced racism in gay spaces, which manifested in different ways, such as being ignored, or being fetishised as exotic. They also reported incidences of not being perceived as lesbians by white women and therefore viewed as not belonging in gay spaces. This othering was experienced through feelings of discomfort and exclusion. Held (2015) argues homonormative gay and lesbian identities were white, able-bodied and middle class, which had exclusionary effects.

Gender and Professional Identities

Night-time leisure spaces are sites of 'time out' from the daily routine for customers, but are also spaces of employment. Hobbs et al. (2003) researched the occupational habitus of male bouncers (door staff) in northern England. Bouncers embodied an aggressive working-class masculine identity demonstrated through exhibiting tough physicality and willingness to use violence. Understanding, pre-empting and intervening in violent interactions was central to the job and the bouncers drew on violence as a resource. Their occupational habitus was interwoven with a habitus of working-class masculinity. As working-class men, the bouncers were more likely than middle-class men to be socialised to regard violence as central to masculinity and a means for gaining respect (Hobbs et al., 2003). This valorisation of violence does not characterise all British working-class masculinities as historical research on the first half of the twentieth-century attests (Smith, 2015). Rather, the hard masculinity exhibited by bouncers should be understood as one masculine performance among many.

Tomkins (2005) carried out an ethnography of night-time establishments in Hobart, Tasmania, which included attention to the occupational masculinity of bouncers. Like the men in Hobbs et al.'s (2003) study, the bouncers drew on an aggressive working-class masculinity that prized physical strength. Bouncers who were adept at intervening in and controlling violence that occurred among customers attained a form of dominant masculinity, whereas men who were less skilled in violence were subordinate. However, Tomkins (2005) argues the dominant masculinity of 'successful' bouncers increased the risk of violence in night-time establishments as some male customers interpreted it as a challenge to their own masculine identity and reacted aggressively.

Bouncers have been the subjects of British reality television series, which portray their work as upholding social order and control in post-industrial cities, as well as offering a voyeuristic representation of young people behaving badly during nights out, such as *British Bouncers* (2013) and *Bouncers* (2019). *Bouncers* (2019) contextualises the work of security personnel as to an extent replacing what would previously have been done by the police. Documentary *Berlin Bouncers* (2019) focuses on three well-known bouncers from the Berlin club scene, their lives and the changing social and political context of the scene across their careers.

Not all bouncers are men. Hobbs et al. (2007) examined how female door supervisors in licensed establishments dealt with customers' aggression and how they mediated the potential contradictions between their professional role and their gender identity. Like male bouncers, women needed to understand violence and how it could be precipitated. They used a range of strategies to counter violent incidents, such as deploying local knowledge about how to defuse situations. Some women adopted a masculine habitus of toughness, which Hobbs et al. (2007) characterise as an alternative femininity distinct from—and transgressive of—normative middle-class femininity. Women door staff could gain status from their knowledge of violence and connections to violent men, as well as from their own willingness to engage in violence if needed.

Rickett and Roman's (2013) analysis of interviews with female bouncers highlights the discourse of the 'hard matriarch' as one frequently employed by their participants. The hard matriarch asserted a powerful identity through demonstrating capacity for violence but also exhibited maternal qualities of responsibility and duty. Women door staff rejected many of the markers of heterosexual femininity, but still faced restrictions in terms of gender. Hobbs et al. (2007) argue women bouncers were employed primarily to deal with other women and in this sense their occupational position was conventionally gendered. Rickett and Roman (2013) emphasise that to fit in with the masculine occupational culture of door work, female staff were the subject of sexist jokes and harassment.

In policing the door, bouncers play a significant role in choosing which groups of people are permitted to enter venues, and which groups are not. Castro (2013) recounts her experiences as a Black woman, accompanied by Black friends, of being turned away from nightclubs in the Zona Rosa area of Bogota, Colombia. She argues this exclusion highlighted the racialised spatial boundaries operating in this nightlife district. Although Bogota has a reputation as a 'cosmopolitan' city, racial hierarchies were significant to clubs' door policies. Søgaard's (2014) ethnography with bouncers in Aarhus, Denmark explores the 'ethnic governance' enacted by door staff, which involved the production and reproduction of ethnic boundaries and the creation of exclusive spaces. Bouncers turned away minority ethnic men on the grounds of 'security'. Like Castro (2013), Søgaard (2014) observes that portrayals of urban nightlife as cosmopolitan and culturally diverse mask the racism that takes place there. May (2014) describes nightlife spaces as characterised by 'integrated segregation'. Different social groups—in terms of race, class and culture—might share the same spaces, but they interact with people similar to themselves. In his ethnographic research in Georgia in the United States, he observed that social tensions, conflicts and exclusions along racial lines were at play night-time leisure spaces.

Portrayals of Gender and the Night-Time Economy

Perceptions of gendered behaviour and participation in the night-time economy delineate the boundaries of respectability and civilisation. Hubbard (2013) analysed British news articles that portrayed excessive drinking and bad behaviour during student nights in British cities. Such coverage of nightlife spaces revealed anxieties about breaches of the boundary between the civilised and uncivilised, which were integral to the liminality of nights out. Newspapers represented student nights as antisocial and troublesome. Young women were portrayed in contradictory ways: as vulnerable to victimisation when on a night out, as caretakers of drunken men and as drunk and out of control. These different portrayals demarcated lines between respectable and disreputable femininities. Concerns about women's behaviour in urban public space offer a parallel with anxieties about the moral geography of sex work.

Measham and Østergaard (2009) note that in the early 2000s, the British news media created a public spectacle of young women's drunkenness in night-time spaces. This spectacularised portrayal exhibited disapproval of the supposed new femininity of greater sexual assertiveness and increased 'masculine' type hedonistic behaviour from women. Rolando et al. (2016) analysed comments beneath Italian YouTube videos of female and male drunkenness and found double standards about drunkenness persisted in social media. Men's drunken behaviour was interpreted as having fun, whereas women's was stigmatised as sexual availability.

Hubbard and Colosi (2015a, 2015b) examine lap-dancing clubs as particularly contentious sites in the night-time economy of England and Wales. Local authorities can refuse to give sexual entertainment venues (SEVs) a licence and there have been organised feminist campaigns against such venues. Hubbard and Colosi (2015a) argue these campaigns problematically constructed women as vulnerable in the night-time city. They also researched the attitudes of local residents towards SEVs, finding that lap-dancing clubs were perceived as out of place in respectable areas, attracting loutish male clientele and victimising the women who worked within them (2015b). Disapproval of sexual entertainment venues was not based on first-hand knowledge of the experiences of performers. Such views created a moral geography, informed by perceptions of gender, class and sexuality, drawing boundaries around respectable communities and middle-class life as spaces in which sexualised entertainment was unwelcome.

Lap-dancing and strip clubs are ubiquitous in popular culture, as are portrayals of women working as strippers. Few such fictional portrayals include the women as developed characters. An exception is *Hustlers* (2019), a film about a group of women who work as strippers who, after business is damaged by the 2008 recession, drug and steal from the wealthy financiers who form their client base. The film is based on a real case and examines the close relationships between the women and their ability to outwit the men who are supposedly their social superiors. Short documentary *The Sisterhood of Strippers* (2016) features members of the East London Strippers' Collective, who discuss their adverse labour conditions, which were worsened by the introduction of licensing for sexual entertainment venues. They decided to organise to gain greater employment rights and to challenge stigma.

Consumption practices related to sex, tourism, leisure and entertainment are spatialised and regulated according to moral geographies. Such practices are also examples of the commodification of intimacy, relaxation and fun under neoliberal capitalism. This landscape of regulation and commodification shapes intersectional gender identities and what counts as gendered normativity and gendered transgression.

References

Agustin, L. (2007). *Sex at the margins: Migration, labour markets and the rescue industry.* Zed Books.

Armstrong, L. (2016). From law enforcement to protection? Interactions between sex workers and police in a decriminalized street-based sex industry. *The British Journal of Criminology, 57,* 570–588.

Aronowitz, A. (2014). To punish or not to punish: What works in the regulation of the prostitution market. In N. Persak & G. Vermeulen (Eds.), *Reframing prostitution: From discourse to description, from moralisation to normalisation.* Maklu.

Ayres, T. C., & Treadwell, J. (2012). Bars, drugs and football thugs: Alcohol, cocaine use and violence in the night time economy among English football firms. *Criminology & Criminal Justice, 12,* 83–100.

Baker, C. N. (2014). An intersectional analysis of sex trafficking films. *Meridians, 12,* 208–226.

Benoit, C., Jansson, S. M., Smith, M., & Flagg, J. (2018). Prostitution stigma and its effect on the working conditions, personal lives, and health of sex workers. *The Journal of Sex Research, 55,* 457–471.

Benoit, C., Smith, M., Jansson, M., Healey, P., & Magnuson, D. (2019). Unlinking prostitution and sex trafficking: Response to commentaries. *Archives of Sexual Behavior.*

Bernstein, E. (2007). Sex work for the middle classes. *Sexualities, 10,* 473–488.

Bernstein, E. (2010). Militarized humanitarianism meets carceral feminism: The politics of sex, rights, and freedom in contemporary antitrafficking campaigns. *Signs, 36,* 45–71.

Boyle, K. (2014). Buying and selling sex: Sexualization, commerce, and gender. In C. Carter, L. Steiner, & L. Mclaughlin (Eds.), *The Routledge companion to media & gender*. Routledge.

Briggs, D., & Ellis, A. (2017). The last night of freedom: Consumerism, deviance and the "stag party." *Deviant Behavior, 38*, 756–767.

Bumiller, K. (2008). *In an abusive state: How neoliberalism appropriated the feminist movement against sexual violence*. Duke University Press.

Casey, M. (2020). Shagaluf: Reality television and British working class hetero-sexuality on holiday in Mallorca. *Journal of Tourism and Cultural Change, 18*, 532–544.

Castro, F. W. (2013). Afro-Colombians and the cosmopolitcan city: New negotiations of race and space in Bogota, Colombia. *Latin American Perspectives, 40*, 105–117.

Chew, M. M. (2009). Research on Chinese nightlife cultures and night-time economies. *Chinese Sociology & Anthropology, 42*, 3–21.

Chu, S. K. H., & Glass, R. (2013). Sex work law reform in Canada: Considering problems with the Nordic model. *Alberta Law Review, 51*, 101–124.

Domosh, M. (2001). The 'women of New York': A fashionable moral geography. *Environment and Planning D: Society and Space, 19*, 573–592.

Fileborn, B. (2016). Doing gender, doing safety? Young adults' production of safety on a night out. *Gender, Place & Culture, 23*, 1107–1120.

Foley, E. E. (2019). "The prostitution problem": Insights from Senegal. *Archives of Sexual Behavior, 48*, 1937–1940.

Garcia, A. (2010). Continuous moral economies: The state regulation of bodies and sex work in Cuba. *Sexualities, 13*, 171–196.

Gill, R., & Scharff, C. (2011). Introduction. In R. Gill, & C. Scharff (Eds.), *New Femininities: Postfeminism, neoliberalism and subjectivity*. 1–20. Palgrave.

Grenfell, P., Eastham, J., Perry, G., & Platt, L. (2016). Decriminalising sex work in the UK. *BMJ, 354*, i4459.

Griffin, G., Szmigin, I., Bengry-Howell, A., Hackley, C., & Mistral, W. (2013). Inhabiting the contradictions: Hypersexual femininity and the culture of intoxification among young women in the UK, *Feminism and Psychology, 23*, 184–206.

Gunby, C., Carline, A., Taylor, S. & Gosling, H. (2020). Unwanted sexual attention in the night-time economy: Behaviors, safety strategies, and conceptualizing "feisty femininity". *Feminist Criminology, 15*, 24–46.

Haak, D. M. (2018, December 9). Canada's laws designed to deter prostitution, not keep sex workers safe. *The Conversation.*

Harbidge, L. (2012). Redefining screwball and reappropriating liminal spaces: The contemporary bromance and Todd Phillips' The Hangover DVD. *Comedy Studies, 3,* 5–16.

Harder, S. K., & Demant, J. (2015). Failing masculinity at the club: A post-structural alternative to intoxication feminism. *Substance Use & Misuse, 50,* 759–767.

Hardy, K., & Rivers-Moore, M. (2018). Compañeras de la calle: Sex worker organising in Latin America. *Moving the Social, 59,* 97–113.

Hargreaves, A. (2015). Finding Dawn and missing women in Canada: Story-based methods in antiviolence research and remembrance. *Studies in American Indian Literatures, 27,* 82–111.

Heber, A. (2018). The hunt for an elusive crime—An analysis of Swedish measures to combat sex trafficking. *Journal of Scandinavian Studies in Criminology and Crime Prevention, 19,* 3–21.

Held, N. (2015). Comfortable and safe spaces? Gender, sexuality and 'race' in night-time leisure spaces. *Emotion, Space and Society, 14,* 33–42.

Hobbs, D., Hadfield, P., Lister, S., & Winlow, S. (2003). *Bouncers: Violence and governance in the night-time economy.* Oxford University Press on Demand.

Hobbs, D., O'brien, K., & Westmarland, L. (2007). Connecting the gendered door: Women, violence and doorwork*. *The British Journal of Sociology, 58,* 21–38.

Howell, P. (2000). Prostitution and racialised sexuality: The regulation of prostitution in Britain and the British Empire before the contagious diseases acts. *Environment and Planning D: Society and Space, 18,* 321–339.

Hubbard, P. (2013). Carnage! Coming to a town near you? Nightlife, uncivilised behaviour and the carnivalesque body. *Leisure Studies, 32,* 265–282.

Hubbard, P., & Colosi, R. (2015a). Respectability, morality and disgust in the night-time economy: Exploring reactions to 'lap dance' clubs in England and Wales. *The Sociological Review, 63,* 782–800.

Hubbard, P., & Colosi, R. (2015b). Taking back the night? Gender and the contestation of sexual entertainment in England and Wales. *Urban Studies, 52,* 589–605.

Hubbard, P., Matthews, R., & Scoular, J. (2008). Regulating sex work in the EU: Prostitute women and the new spaces of exclusion. *Gender, Place & Culture, 15,* 137–152.

Hutton, F., Griffin, C., Lyons, A., Niland, P., & Mccreanor, T. (2016). "Tragic girls" and "crack whores": Alcohol, femininity and Facebook. *Feminism & Psychology, 26*, 73–93.

Hutton, F., Wright, S., & Saunders, E. (2013). Cultures of intoxication: Young women, alcohol, and harm reduction. *Contemporary Drug Problems, 40*, 451–480.

Jackson, C. A. (2016). Framing sex worker rights: How U.S. sex worker rights activists perceive and respond to mainstream anti-sex trafficking advocacy. *Sociological Perspectives, 59*, 27–45.

Kattari, S. K., & Begun, S. (2017). On the margins of marginalized: Transgender homelessness and survival sex. *Affilia, 32*, 92–103.

Kempadoo, K. (2001). Freelancers, temporary wives, and beach-boys: Researching sex work in the Caribbean. *Feminist Review, 67*, 39–62.

Kempadoo, K., & Doezema, J. (1998). *Global sex workers: Rights, resistance, and redefinition.* Routledge.

Levine, P. (1993). Women and prostitution: Metaphor, reality, history. *Canadian Journal of History, 28*, 479–494.

Levy, J. & Jakobsson, P. (2014). Sweden's abolitionist discourse and law: Effects on the dynamics of Swedish sex work and on the lives of Sweden's sex workers. *Criminology & Criminal Justice, 14*, 593–607.

Lusimbo, R., & Bryan, A. (2018). Kuchu resilience and resistance in Uganda a history. In R. Lusimbo, N. Nicol, A. Jjuuko, N. J. Mulé, S. Ursel, A. Wahab, & P. Waugh (Eds.), *Envisioning global LGBT human rights.* School of Advanced Study, University of London.

Lyons, T., Krüsi, A., Pierre, L., Kerr, T., Small, W., & Shannon, K. (2017). Negotiating violence in the context of transphobia and criminalization: The experiences of trans sex workers in Vancouver, Canada. *Qualitative Health Research, 27*, 182–190.

May, R. A. B. (2014). *Urban nightlife: Entertaining race, class, and culture in public space.* Rutgers University Press.

Measham, F., & Østergaard, J. (2009). The public face of binge drinking: British and Danish young women, recent trends in alcohol consumption and the European binge drinking debate. *Probation Journal, 56*, 415–434.

Munro, V. E., & Scoular, J. (2012). Abusing vulnerability? Contemporary law and policy responses to sex work in the UK. *Feminist Legal Studies, 20*, 189–206.

Nayak, A. (2006). Displaced masculinities: Chavs, youth and class in the post-industrial city. *Sociology, 40*, 813–831.

Nicholls, E. (2017). 'Dulling it down a bit': Managing visibility, sexualities and risk in the night time economy in Newcastle, UK. *Gender, Place & Culture, 24*, 260–273.

O'Neill, M. (1998). Saloon girls: Death and desire ill the American West. In J. Hassard & R. Holliday (Eds.), *Organization-representation: Work and organizations in popular culture.* Sage.

O'Neill, M. (2010). Cultural criminology and sex work: Resisting regulation through radical democracy and participatory action research (PAR). *Journal of Law and Society, 37*, 210–232.

O'Neill, M., Campbell, R., Hubbard, P., Pitcher, J., & Scoular, J. (2008). Living with the other: Street sex work, contingent communities and degrees of tolerance. *Crime, Media, Culture, 4*, 73–93.

O'Shaughnessy, M. (2017). Cinema, sex tourism and globalisation in American and European cinema. In E. Mazierska & L. Kristensen (Eds.), *Contemporary cinema and neoliberal ideology.* Routledge.

Pheterson, G. (1993). The whore stigma: Female dishonor and male unworthiness. *Social Text*, 39–64.

Phoenix, J. (2009). *Regulating sex for sale: Prostitution policy reform in the UK.* Policy Press.

Pickering, S., & Ham, J. (2013). Hot pants at the border: Sorting sex work from trafficking. *The British Journal of Criminology, 54*, 2–19.

Pitcher, J., & Wijers, M. (2014). The impact of different regulatory models on the labour conditions, safety and welfare of indoor-based sex workers. *Criminology & Criminal Justice, 14*, 549–564.

Presdee, M. (2003). *Cultural criminology and the carnival of crime.* Routledge.

Race, K. (2016). The sexuality of the night: Violence and transformation. *Current Issues in Criminal Justice, 28*, 105–110.

Raymen, T., & Smith, O. (2017). Lifestyle gambling, indebtedness and anxiety: A deviant leisure perspective. *Journal of Consumer Culture, 20*, 1469540517736559.

Rivers-Moore, M. (2014). Waiting for the state: Sex work and the neoliberal governance of sexuality. *Social Politics, 21*, 403–429.

Rickett, B., & Roman, A. (2013). 'Heroes and matriarchs': Working-class femininities, violence and door supervision work. *Gender, Work & Organization, 20*, 664–677.

Rolando, S., Taddeo, G., & Beccaria, F. (2016). New media and old stereotypes: Images and discourses about drunk women and men on YouTube. *Journal of Gender Studies, 25*, 492–506.

Ryan, P. (2016). #Follow: Exploring the role of social media in the online construction of male sex worker lives in Dublin, Ireland. *Gender, Place & Culture, 23*, 1713–1724.

Sanders, T. (2009). Controlling the 'anti sexual' city: Sexual citizenship and the disciplining of female street sex workers. *Criminology & Criminal Justice, 9*, 507–525.

Sanders, T., & Campbell, R. (2007). Designing out vulnerability, building in respect: Violence, safety and sex work policy. *The British Journal of Sociology, 58*, 1–19.

Scambler, G. (2007). Sex work stigma: Opportunist migrants in London. *Sociology, 41*, 1079–1096.

Scambler, G., & Paoli, F. (2008). Health work, female sex workers and HIV/AIDS: Global and local dimensions of stigma and deviance as barriers to effective interventions. *Social Science & Medicine, 66*, 1848–1862.

Scoular, J. (2010). What's law got to do with it? How and why law matters in the regulation of sex work. *Journal of Law and Society, 37*, 12–39.

Scoular, J., & O'Neill, M. (2007). Regulating prostitution: Social inclusion, responsibilisation and the politics of prostitution reform. *British Journal of Criminology, 47*, 764–778.

Scull, M. (2020). "It's Its Own Thing": A typology of interpersonal sugar relationship scripts. *Sociological Perspectives, 63*, 135–158.

Seal, L., & O'Neill, M. (2019). *Imaginative criminology: Of spaces past, present and future.* Bristol University Press.

Shaw, R. (2014). Beyond night-time economy: Affective atmospheres of the urban night. *Geoforum, 51*, 87–95.

Sheard, L. (2011). 'Anything could have happened': Women, the night-time economy, alcohol and drink spiking. *Sociology, 45*, 619–633.

Smith, H. (2015). Love, sex, work and friendship: Northern, working-class men and sexuality in the first half of the twentieth century. In A. A. J. Harris & T. Willem (Eds.), *Love and romance in Britain, 1918–1970.* Palgrave.

Smith, M., & Mac, J. (2018). *Revolting prostitutes: The fight for sex workers' rights.* Verso Trade.

Søgaard, T. F. (2014). Bouncers, policing and the (in) visibility of ethnicity in nightlife security governance. *Social Inclusion, 2*, 40–51.

Stewart, M., & Pine, J. (2014). Vocational embodiments of the precariat in the Girlfriend Experience and Magic Mike. *TOPIA: Canadian Journal of Cultural Studies, 30–31*, 183–206.

Tomkins, K. (2005). Bouncers and occupational masculinity. *Current Issues in Criminal Justice, 17*, 154–161.

Turner, V. (1987). Betwixt and between: The liminal period in rites of passage. In L. C. Mahdi, S. Foster, & M. Little (Eds.), *Betwixt and between: Patterns of masculine and feminine initiation*. Open Court.

Veg, S. (2007). Hong Kong by night: Prostitution and cinema in Herman Yau's Whispers and Moans. *China Perspectives*.

Wahab, S., & Panichelli, M. (2013). Ethical and human rights issues in coercive interventions with sex workers. *Affilia, 28*, 344–349.

Walkowitz, J. R. (1980). *Prostitution and victorian society: Women, class, and the state*. Cambridge University Press.

Ward, E., & Wylie, G. (2017). Introduction. In E. Ward & G. Wylie (Eds.), *Feminism, prostitution and the state: The politics of neo-abolitionism*. Taylor & Francis.

Wardlow, H. (2004). Anger, economy, and female agency: Problematizing "prostitution" and "sex work" among the Huli of Papua New Guinea. *Signs: Journal of Women in Culture and Society, 29*, 1017–1040.

Weitzer, R. (2009). Sociology of sex work. *Annual Review of Sociology, 35*, 213–234.

Weitzer, R. (2010). The movement to criminalize sex work in the United States. *Journal of Law and Society, 37*, 61–84.

Weitzer, R. (2018). Resistance to sex work stigma. *Sexualities, 21*, 717–729.

White, L. (1990). *The comforts of home: Prostitution in colonial Nairobi*. University of Chicago Press.

Whowell, M. (2010). Male sex work: Exploring regulation in England and Wales. *Journal of Law and Society, 37*, 125–144.

Williams-Burnett, N., Skinner, H., & Fallon, J. (2018). Reality television portrayals of Kavos, Greece: Tourists behaving badly. *Journal of Travel & Tourism Marketing, 35*, 336–347.

Yep, G. A., Alaoui, F. Z. C., & Lescure, R. M. (2019). Transing Sin-Dee Rella: Representations of trans women of color in sean baker's tangerine. In R. A. Lind (Ed.), *Race/gender/class/media: Considering diversity across audiences, content, and producers*. Routledge.

5

Street Crime, Gangs and Drugs

The street as public space is masculinised as a site of pleasure, danger and mundane daily activity. Negotiating the street is gendered; women and girls are arguably out of place in certain spaces and at certain times. The street refers to a physical place, a culture, a set of codes and behaviours and commodified style. There is a strong association between the street and crime, which is the focus of this chapter. The word 'crime' more readily evokes street crimes such as burglary, theft and drug dealing than it does other forms of crime. Street crime is heavily symbolic of crime and disorder in general, and of certain stereotyped associations such as masculine threat, particularly from young, racialised working-class men. The street should not, however, simply be conflated with crime and violence but understood as a space with multiple purposes and meanings (de la Tierra, 2016; Ilan, 2015; Ross, 2018). This chapter discusses gender in relation to street crime, including paying attention to gangs and drug markets, as well as issues of fear and victimisation.

© The Author(s), under exclusive license to Springer Nature
Switzerland AG 2022
L. Seal, *Gender, Crime and Justice*,
https://doi.org/10.1007/978-3-030-87488-9_5

Street Culture

Street culture is a product of social inclusion and exclusion (Ilan, 2015). It is associated with poor young men living in the inner city, particularly young men of colour, and is frequently understood as an adaptation to poverty and social exclusion. Anderson (1999) interprets the 'code of the street'—performative toughness and readiness to violence to secure respect—as an outcome of the abandonment of American inner cities by authorities and employers in the 1980s and 90s. The code of the street filled the breach left by weakened civil law and employment in the illicit drug economy replaced the manufacturing sector. Young Black men were aware that abiding by norms of respectability did not lead to social inclusion or financial stability and sought alternatives. Bourgois (2003) traces a similar role for street culture in the lives of young Puerto Rican men in New York City, with the values and beliefs of this culture offering an alternative route to personal dignity in the context of exclusion from mainstream society.

Although an outcome of marginalisation, street culture has strong symbolic power as a marker of authenticity, defiance and vitality—summarised by Ilan (2015) as cool. Street culture has a high level of symbolic inclusion, exhibited in music, television, film, computer games, fashion and language. Its new iterations get packaged and commodified. While defiance and rebelliousness are recurrent features, whether street culture represents a value system in opposition to mainstream values is debatable (Bourgois, 2003; Ilan, 2015). The premium placed on financial success and material acquisition, as well as individualism and responsibility for one's own success or failure, arguably reflect the dominant values of neoliberal consumer capitalism. Hallsworth (2005) describes street culture as a hybrid of conventional values, lawbreaking and violence. The prizing of hypermasculinity also reflects the wider gender order of subordinating both women and 'feminised' men (Connell, 2005). However, this picture is nuanced by studies that explore the significance of women and femininity to street culture, and that acknowledge the significance of a range of masculinities.

Rap music in particular is a cultural form associated with street culture, and is one which Kubrin (2005) argues extends the code of street and its prioritisation of violence and respect. This does not mean that rap causes violence, but has cultural influence. In the UK, drill rap music has been blamed for inciting knife crime and murder and criminalised in terms of prohibitions on the topics that lyrics can address in videos and performances (Fatsis, 2019). In 2019, two rappers received suspended prison sentences for performing one of their tracks live. Ilan (2020) analyses drill rap videos on YouTube, finding the lyrics address themes of drug dealing, violence and the desirability of luxury brands. Lyrics were a means to cultivate a criminal persona, but Ilan (2020) argues this should not be understood as a straightforward reflection of reality. Drill rap evinces masculine braggadocio but also offers the chance for emotional reflection. Criminalisation of drill as responsible for violence ignores its nuances and the significance of fiction and performance. This criminalisation of young Black men's cultural expression can be situated within a history of racist policing and social control (Fatsis, 2019). Documentary *Defending Digga D* (2020) follows the story of a British drill rapper who received a Criminal Behaviour Order controlling his creative output, meaning he could be arrested for his songs and videos if they breach the terms of the order.

Criminologists have stressed the context of neoliberal capitalism as crucial to the emergence of street culture as the predominant urban 'folk culture' of the late twentieth- and early twenty-first centuries (Ilan, 2015). Bakkali (2019) encapsulates neoliberalism as free market fundamentalism, minimal welfare provision and the marketisation of previously state operated sectors such as education, health and criminal justice. The effect has been increased insecurity and entrenched inequality. Inequalities of class, race, gender and sexuality precede the development of neoliberal capitalism in the latter part of the twentieth century, but take on distinct forms under it. The decline of manufacturing in Western states and the shift to service-based economies meant, particularly in urban settings, that stable employment in factories was replaced by insecure work in the service sector—or the absence of legitimate paid work. This affected the nature of street culture.

Street culture's commodification in fashion and media means that it is globalised, and aspects of its style and aesthetics are shared internationally (Ilan, 2015; Stapleton & Terrio, 2012). The codes and principles of street culture also find international expression, but with strong local variation (Heitmeyer et al., 2019; Holligan, 2015; Williams & Kamaludeen, 2017). Bakkali (2019) identifies 'road culture' as a UK specific form of street culture that has developed in multi-ethnic, working-class spaces of the city. As opposed to spectacular violence, it is based on everyday elements of urban life, such as leisure, friendship and material survival. Variation is important to consider as although neoliberal capitalism operates globally, its effect on the nature of the economy is different across different continents and regions. Van Hellemont and Densley (2019) describe the influence of landmark American portrayals of street culture and gang life such as *New Jack City* and *The Wire* as inspiring 'gang glocalization'—the convergence of mythmaking, style and sensibilities in urban gangs across international locations. However, these global cultural flows interact with local, nationally and regionally specific representations.

Space is a key aspect of the development of street culture, which often originates in urban areas of public or social housing that are demarcated by race and class (Brotherton, 2015; Ilan, 2015). As Ilan (2015) argues, the street exists even where services and facilities are absent. Such urban areas have a strong presence in the cultural imagination as sites of excitement, fascination and danger. The notion of 'dangerous' urban spaces is closely associated with fear of hypermasculine racialised working-class young men (Collins, 2005). In the United States, 'ghettos' and 'barrios', inner city neighbourhoods with a high proportion of Black and Latinx residents, have been understood as 'criminal spaces' (Fleury-Steiner et al., 2009). The French banlieues have a similar place in the cultural imagination as the home of supposedly criminal and terrorist young Muslim men, although are situated on the urban periphery, rather than the centre (Dikeç, 2011). In the Global South, self-built urban neighbourhoods, such as Brazilian favelas, symbolise difference and disorder (Penglase, 2014). Such neighbourhoods, whether originally public housing or self-built, are the outcome of government policies, socio-economic inequalities and practices of social control.

Films have represented racially demarcated urban spaces and situated them in the global cultural imagination. *Boyz N the Hood* (1991), set in a predominantly Black neighbourhood of South Central LA, was a landmark in terms of portraying relations of power in urban space (Massood, 1996). *La Haine* (1995) depicts life in a Parisian banlieue for three characters, all young Muslim men, over one day. Sharma and Sharma (2000) argue it presents a humanised representation of violence and marginalised masculinity, which seeks to induce empathy in the audience, but ultimately does not transcend a tendency towards Othering racialised urban space. *City of God* (2003) portrays the deepening entrenchment of the drug trade in a Brazilian favela. The *City of God* is depicted as segregated from the rest of Rio de Janeiro and run by violent young men. Internationally successful, the film further stimulated the tourism industry of organised tours of favelas (Freire-Medeiros, 2011).

British drama serial *Top Boy* (2011-ongoing) is set on the fictional Summerhouse council estate in Hackney, London. It depicts gang life, drug dealing and violence and related social issues of inadequate housing and poverty. Young Black men's involvement in drug dealing is motivated by the pursuit of wealth but—even if locally successful and rising to 'top boy'—they remain segregated on their housing estate and marginalised in terms of race and class (Özer, 2019). Özer (2019) argues the series also portrays Summerhouse as a place of community and solidarity, where residents support one another in the face of social neglect.

The space of the street is gendered. People of all genders are present in public urban spaces, but these spaces were designed primarily according to masculinist assumptions (Spain, 2014); for example, inner cities can be difficult to navigate with small children (Pain, 2001). Public and social housing was built for nuclear families comprising a woman, man and children in their own units. This does not necessarily reflect the familial arrangements of residents and inhibits communal living (Spain, 2014). Assumptions and conventions about who belongs in public space shape fear of crime and attitudes towards victimisation. They also affect the gendered commission of street crime. The binary of public masculine and domestic feminine space is too simplistic, however, as public and domestic activity are interrelated and interdependent, including in relation to crime. Shifts in illicit drug economies mean the criminological focus has widened from the inner city to include small towns and rural settings, which raises new issues about the relationship between gender, space and crime (Linnemann, 2010).

Gendered Social Networks

Street crime is male dominated. As numerous researchers have argued, this reflects the wider gender order of male domination in social, political and economic life. The motivation for engaging in street crime, including drug dealing, is usually similar for women and men but the extent of their involvement and the particular roles they enact are different. Mullins and Cherbonneau (2011) found that car thieves in St. Louis, USA were initiated via neighbourhood peers, who were typically male. This made it harder for women to become involved. Another limitation for women was that they were less likely to have the contacts needed in order to sell on stolen cars or their parts. Their methods of theft were not different but they did not profit as much as men did due to having lesser access to the social networks that made car theft profitable.

Women's involvement in street crime is usually low level and non-violent. Caputo and King (2011) identify shoplifting as a crime that women commit to earn money, and which is an alternative to male-dominated drug markets. Drug trafficking, robbery and burglary are all co-ordinated and enacted through male-dominated networks (Becker & McCorkel, 2011). Where women do participate in more serious crimes it is often as co-offenders with men, which broadens their criminal opportunities. Barlow and Weare's (2019) study of women in the English midlands who had participated in crimes such as shoplifting and drug-related offences found factors such as fear and coercion were intertwined with women's co-offending with men (but not with female friends) and needed to be considered alongside the notion of co-offending as a route to increased opportunities.

Maher's (1997) ethnography of illicit drug and sex markets in 1990s Brooklyn found them to be controlled by men, with women-centred networks operating as a resource in response to male domination, which aided street survival. Men were more likely to use their personal networks instrumentally than women. The women in Maher's study were peripheral to the drug market; their unequal position reflected women's unequal position in the formal labour market. She interprets drug and sex markets as sites of cultural reproduction mirroring wider structures of inequality.

Women's entry into drug dealing networks in West Scotland tended to be via family and intimate partner relationships, and they also played a role in recruiting other family members (Holligan et al., 2019).

Despite their marginalised and peripheral position in drug markets, women's involvement is crucial to these markets' operation. Anderson (2005) highlights providing housing, domestic and financial support to men, buying drugs and participating in drug dealing as activities carried out by women without which illicit drug markets would collapse. Such an argument is consistent with feminist theorisation of the gendered division of labour, whereby men's more prominent (and lucrative) roles in the labour market are supported and facilitated by women's performance of unpaid domestic labour. Anderson's (2005) argument also unsettles the dichotomy between public and domestic space in relation to street crime, in that the public activity of drug dealing relies on support provided in domestic space. Holligan et al. (2019) observed this straddling of public and domestic spheres in their research with Scottish women. There can be spatial differences in where women sell drugs compared with men. Women who sold crack in a small town in England conducted business in indoor or contained spaces such as supermarkets, benefit (welfare) offices and car parks (Fleetwood, 2014b).

The gendered division of labour in drug economies is affected by the structure and organisation of particular markets (Deitzer et al., 2019). Home-based production of methamphetamine in rural Missouri was more open to women being fully involved than inner city crack markets (Miller & Carbone-Lopez, 2015). Ingredients could be purchased from discount warehouse stores rather than needing to be trafficked. Deitzer et al.'s (2019) research into the production of 'shake and bake' methamphetamine in rural Alabama found its decentralised and closed nature meant that women could be autonomously involved as meth cooks, or participate in small teams that could be female headed. Shake cooking was easy to learn, could be carried out anywhere and was often for personal use rather than for profit. The risk of violence was lower than when dealing to strangers.

The portrayal of women drug dealers in television series tends to locate them within family networks but also places them in senior positions. In *ZeroZeroZero* (2021) Emma Lynwood becomes involved in drug trafficking and negotiating with cartels via employment in her father's shipping firm and in *Snowfall* (2017-ongoing) Lucia Villanueva develops her own drug business independently of her drug lord father. These depictions evince a popular version of the 'liberation theory' perspective, whereby women's greater representation in professional life is mirrored by greater representation in illegal markets (Simon, 1975). This is at odds with empirical findings about women's marginalised and peripheral positions in drug markets but has greater dramatic potential. Miller et al. (2019) argue Colombian narconovelas—soap operas about drug cartels and narco culture—underrepresent women as characters and portray them as weak and the targets of male violence. American Spanish-language narconovela *La Reina del Sur* (2011) follows a female empowerment narrative to chart the rise of Teresa Mendoza to cartel leader and female 'boss', who mobilises aspects of masculine gender performance (Dunn & Ibarra, 2015).

Respect and Survival

The link between garnering respect and accomplishing masculinity is a recurrent theme in studies of street crime. Anderson (1999: 9) describes the 'code of the street' as entailing a 'desperate search for respect' by young black men in inner city Philadelphia. He argues respect operated as a valuable form of social capital in a context where access to other forms of capital was low. Being respected meant having the capacity to be feared and demonstrating a willingness to engage in physical violence. Fighting, stealing and provoking retaliation were all ways to perform street masculinity. Anderson conceptualises respect garnered through violence and drug dealing as on the one hand a way for economically and racially marginalised young men to accomplish masculinity when other routes were blocked, and on the other necessary for survival in a context where civil law was weak.

Hollywood films from the early 1990s such as *Boyz N the Hood* (1991), *New Jack City* (1991) and *Menace II Society* (1993) portray young Black men's struggle for survival in New York and Los Angeles, including their deployment of street masculinity and violence. They also convey their experiences of state violence in the form of police brutality (Baker, 1999; Spohrer, 2018). Documentary *Crips and Bloods: Made in America* (2007) contextualises the emergence of gangs as a response to deindustrialisation in the 1970s and the ensuing urban poverty and unemployment. Gangs offered young Black men a sense of belonging and employment in the drug trade. *Bastards of the Party* (2005), made by a former member of the Bloods, traces the history of American anti-Black racism, from slavery to police brutality in the 1950s and 60s, as the backdrop to urban gangs. Against the decline of legitimate employment, drug dealing provided an income and possible route to wealth (Witherspoon, 2013).

The Puerto Rican crack dealers in Bourgois's (2003) ethnography needed to earn money to live, but they also wanted dignity and fulfilment, which entailed feeling respected. Contreras (2008) outlines 'street masculinity' as characterised by autonomy, self-sufficiency and taking action through crime. Zubillaga (2009) found that respect was fundamental to masculine identity for poor young men in Caracas, Venezuela. Violence and gang membership provided recognition and self-realisation, as well a sense of affiliation, in the face of threats to integrity and esteem wrought by poverty. Young men were under physical threat in the barrio—from other young men but also from police and military agents. Historical research on youth gangs in late nineteenth-century Manchester and Salford identifies gang violence as being associated with norms of 'hard' masculinity held in working-class communities. Hard men secured respect from peers and young women, particularly before they were old enough to assume the breadwinner roles occupied by their fathers (Davies (1998). This historical example demonstrates Brotherton's (2015) point that the codes and practices of gangs derive from the class, race and gender characteristics of the communities in which they are formed.

Peaky Blinders is a period drama about a criminal gang in Birmingham in the years following the First World War. 'Peaky blinder' was a term used to refer to members of youth gangs in Birmingham, deriving either from the practice of sewing razors into the peaks of their caps, or from pulling the peak of the cap low over the eyes (Davies, 2006). The show evokes working-class life in an industrial city, focusing on the criminal and 'disreputable' (Long, 2017). Larke-Walsh (2019) argues that *Peaky Blinders* portrays a narrow view of working-class masculine identity as synonymous with violent, self-destructive toxic masculinity. It depicts the young men as damaged by war but also glorifies their criminality. There are strong female characters but ultimately their role is to 'repair' damaged men, rather than challenge toxic behaviour.

Collins (2005) argues that, in addition to demonstrating manliness and gaining respect, poor Black men's use of violence is a means of asserting dominance. This is valued as an attribute of masculinity across race and class spectrums in the United States, but for men with few economic resources and lacking in other forms of social and cultural power, such dominance can only be attained through physical violence. Men who are privileged in race and class hierarchies secure dominance through symbolic violence, in terms of the exercise of bureaucracy or forms of cultural representation, and benefit from the racialised physical violence deployed by the state against poor Black men, for example by the police.

Male street thieves from an urban area in the southern United States expressed and performed situationally dependent masculinity—fighting was more likely in a bar than at home. Earning enough through theft to be autonomous and independent was important, and fulfilled ideals of masculinity (Copes & Hochstetler, 2003). Hallsworth (2013) describes the search for pleasure as a key aspect of street culture. Pleasure does not have to entail transgression, but rule breaking offers excitement and a break from the mundane. Conspicuous consumption and hedonistic partying are significant to pleasure seeking (Copes & Hochstetler, 2003), something Brookman et al. (2007) found from interviews with imprisoned street robbers in the UK. Copes and Hochstetler (2003) identified variations according to age—young men were more likely to emphasise risk and fun, those who were older and more experienced minimised risk.

de la Tierra (2016) cautions against a myopic focus on 'perilous masculinity', characterised by violence and risk-taking, in relation to street culture. This overlooks the range of masculinities expressed by men and underplays other important norms of masculinity, such as commitment to family or placing value on leading a principled existence. Such a focus is also in danger of conflating the street with criminality. Baird's

(2012) life history interviews with men in poor neighbourhoods in Medellin, Colombia reveal masculinity was integral to the reproduction of violence, but most young men were not gang members and rejected crime and violence.

Brotherton (2015) notes that gang members also exhibit a range of masculine identities, and hypermasculinity should not be assumed as the default. Some hypermasculine gangs allow openly gay and transgender members, and hypermasculine men are not always heterosexual (Brotherton, 2015; Panfil, 2017). Some gangs comprise solely LGBT members, and may use violence as a form of protection from homophobia (Panfil & Peterson, 2015). However, they also engage in criminally motivated violence against other gangs (Panfil, 2017). Panfil (2017) argues criminological research has been stuck in a 'heterosexual imaginary', with LGBT people considered only as passive victims. This means the construction of queer identities alongside criminal and gang member identities has been ignored. The Omar Little character in iconic crime series *The Wire* (2002–2008) is a gay stick-up man who robs drug dealers. He is at once macho and tough, but is also someone who demonstrates care to other characters. In this sense he subverts heteronormativity and embodies a queer subjectivity (Dhaenans and Van Bauwel, 2012).

Moonlight won the Oscar for Best Motion Picture in 2017, the first film with an all-Black cast to do so. It is a coming of age story depicting in three acts the childhood, adolescence and early adulthood of Chiron as he grows up in Miami. A shy child with a drug addicted mother, he faces homophobic bullying and is neglected and abused by his mother. As a teenager, he shares a sexual experience with his friend Kevin. After violently retaliating to a bully at school, Chiron is sent to a youth detention centre. In the final act, Chiron, now a drug dealer in Atlanta and hypermasculine in appearance, drives to Miami to meet with Kevin, who runs a diner. *Moonlight* represents the intersections of race, class and sexuality in Chiron's life (Copeland, 2018). In following his story from childhood, it avoids clichés about street life, crime and Black masculinity, and portrays multiple masculinities (Kannan et al., 2017).

Heinonen (2011) argues membership of gangs and use of violence was crucial to the survival of homeless street children in Addis Ababa, Ethiopia. Boys needed to resort to violence in order to appear manly and to avoid losing face, but did not do so for enjoyment. Heinonen outlines wider Ethiopian norms of masculinity as protecting and honouring family, but rather than emphasising independence and autonomy, suppression of feelings and meeting the needs of others were valued. Instead of respect, she identifies 'yilunta', which broadly, although not directly, translates as shame, or a sense of principle, as interacting powerfully with cultural constructions of Ethiopian masculinity. Such norms were held by children in street gangs who could not avoid crime and violence due to their poverty. Burnett (1999) similarly argues that gang violence was a survival strategy for poor young men of colour in Johannesburg, South Africa. In the context of living with the structural violence of poverty, domination through physical violence was the only way to achieve some measure of advantage.

A desire for respect, and the need to demonstrate toughness for survival, is also applicable to women and girls. Jones (2008) argues that for the inner city Black girls with whom she conducted research the appearance of vulnerability and willingness to retaliate to violence or disrespect were important. Feeling disrespected or humiliated was the most frequently mentioned reason for resorting to violence by imprisoned women in Minneapolis (Kruttschnitt & Carbone-Lopez, 2006). This was usually violence towards other women, a finding also supported by Mullins et al. (2004) in relation to street crime. Girls and young women in Cape Town found belonging, status and income through gang participation but also faced incarceration in prison and violent victimisation as a result of gang involvement (Dziewanski, 2020).

Laidler and Hunt (2001) examine the gendered meanings of respect for girls of colour in gangs in the San Francisco Bay Area in terms of how they interpreted femininity. Being able to retaliate and stand up for yourself was valued, but perceived acceptable conduct in terms of sexuality was an important component of being worthy of respect. De Coster and Heimer (2017) argue that girls in street gangs place value on certain conventional understandings of femininity and regulate the sexual behaviour of other girls. Gaining respect means exhibiting respectability.

Miller and Carbone-Lopez (2015) analyse women's routes into involvement in meth production and argue that understanding survival is key. Precocious transitions into adulthood and an acceleration of the lifecourse influenced women's meth use and involvement in production. This included leaving the family home at a young age due to experiencing abuse and having few options about where to go. Miller and Carbone-Lopez (2015) argue this should not be interpreted through individualised understandings of trauma, but in relation to the influence of poverty and social inequalities on the gendered lifecourse. This argument is illustrated by O'Grady and Gaetz's (2009) analysis of the survival techniques of street youth in Toronto, which incorporated a combination of street crime, sex work and activities such as begging. Girls were more at risk of sexual victimisation than boys, and more likely to have been in care, have previous experience of abuse and mental health problems. The street was a gendered space in which boys and men had power, even if this was within the context of extreme marginalisation.

Capital and Habitus

Criminologists have fruitfully employed Bourdieu's concepts of capital and habitus in their analyses of gender identity and street crime. Habitus refers to the dispositions and habits that people adopt over time and that are developed from their experiences and social position. Habitus shapes how they interpret the social world and how they act and react. This entails individual agency and strategic adoption of certain actions and reactions at certain times, although does not imply full consciousness or intent, or acting coherently (Ilan & Sandberg, 2019). Capital is a source of power that can enable success in areas of social life, or as Bourdieu terms them, fields. Street capital is accrued through adopting the right demeanour, willingness to engage in violence and the ability to strike the best deals and come out on top (Sandberg, 2008). A hypermasculine or 'hard man' habitus is linked to gaining street capital. The importance of respect is consistent with this Bourdieusian approach—respect is a form of street capital.

Violent masculinity is a resource for street crime as it can be deployed to frighten and intimidate rivals and potential victims (Brookman et al., 2007). Street capital is more easily accrued by men, but women adopt a range of strategies and gendered performances as a means of gaining capital and surviving the street (Brookman et al., 2007; Dziewanski, 2020; Grundetjern & Sandberg, 2012). One of these is to downplay feminine gender performance in favour of a masculine habitus in order to be 'one of the guys'. The young women Miller (2002) interviewed from street gangs in St. Louis consciously adopted 'masculine' toughness as opposed to girlishness as means of being taken seriously. Grundetjern (2015) found a similar strategy among girls involved in street crime in Oslo, Norway, as did Henriksen (2017) with girls in Copenhagen, Denmark. In *The Wire* (2002–2008), genderqueer character Snoop embodies a masculine style consistent with the need to enact violence in her role as a hit woman employed by a drug lord. Lopez and Bucholtz (2017) argue she is a less complex and well-drawn figure than other queer characters in the show, such as Omar Little, and this ultimately means the representation of Snoop re-inscribes stereotypes of the masculinity and criminality of Black women.

Jones (2008) research with Black girls in Philadelphia similarly found that some girls eschewed normative femininity and exhibited toughness—frequently out of necessity in order to protect themselves. Such a gender performance is not necessarily a form of conscious gender crossing. Whether actions and reactions are perceived as feminine or masculine depends on gender ideology more than it does on the intent of individuals when they act. Girls and young women may engage in fighting for reasons that have nothing to do with how they wish to be seen in terms of gender, or the way they perceive gender identity. However, their actions may be interpreted by others as masculine. Jones (2008) draws on Collins's (2005) analysis of intersections of race and gender to highlight how in the United States stereotypes about 'strong Black women' mean they are viewed as more independent and resilient than white women—which comes at a cost. Black women are more likely to be criminalised and imprisoned. McCall (1992) argues that where women gain gendered capital in one respect, they lose it in others. Perceived masculinity might help them to accrue street capital, but they may be formally or informally punished for lacking femininity.

Criminologists have identified gendered differences in violence and street crime, even where women and girls adopt actions perceived as masculine. A key difference is that women and girls do not see violence as gendered accomplishment—they do not fight to be feminine, or to achieve being a girl (De Coster & Heimer, 2017; Jones, 2008; Miller, 2002). In 'proving' masculinity, men and boys use violence to disavow femininity and distinguish themselves from women and girls (Jones, 2008). Women rarely escalate violence and can use femininity as a resource to minimise violence, especially in terms of fatal violence, which they for the most part avoid (Jones, 2008; Miller & Decker, 2001). Women and girls might consciously avoid a 'feminine' appearance, which risks connoting weakness, or instead place value on conventionally feminine beauty in terms of hair, clothes and make-up—or move tactically between these gendered appearances depending on the context (Henriksen, 2017; Jones, 2008).

Horrex (2020) analyses the depiction of gang girl style in LA set film *Mi Vida Loca* (1994), which cast gang members alongside professional actors. She argues style is more complex than either resistance or capitulation to norms of femininity but rather clears space for girls in hypermasculine gang culture. The film's characters adopt the Chicana associated Chola style in relation to hair and makeup and hip hop style clothing suitable for street-based drug dealing. Like *La Haine, Girlhood* (2015) is set in a Parisian banlieue but focuses on gang involved Black girls rather than young men. Marieme dresses in a hyperfeminine fashion to sell drugs in social gatherings but binds her breasts and adopts masculine clothing to sell on the streets, exhibiting the tactical deployment of gendered appearance (Wilson, 2017).

Feminine habitus is strategically deployed in a variety of ways in relation to street crime. Sexuality and the projection of (hetero)sexual availability can be a means for women to successfully carry out or be accomplices to street robbery (Contreras, 2008; Miller, 1998). Female drug dealers can be successful through exhibiting a conventional gender performance of niceness and politeness (Grundetjern, 2015). Some of the women involved in small-scale meth production in Alabama interviewed by Deitzer et al. (2019) believed men were better at, and more suited to, drug dealing and became sexually involved with partners as a means of gaining access to meth. Some women in lead roles in meth manufacturing emphasised the superiority of their emotional capital in terms of caretaking and interpersonal skills compared with men, and suggested this gave them the potential to be better meth cooks. Documentaries such as *Louis Theroux: The City Addicted to Crystal Meth* (BBC 2009) and *Meth Storm* (HBO 2017) examine methamphetamine addiction and dealing in relation to women and men in the United States.

Grundetjern (2015) describes a 'feminine business model' in the Norwegian drug economy where women similarly articulated how traditionally feminine attributes such as having good social skills and being able to show care enabled success. They also discussed the importance of their choice of business-like clothing to demonstrate professionalism. Caputo and King's (2011) interviews with female shoplifters revealed that many women treated shoplifting like a job and dressed for this work in business-like attire that would allow them to pass unnoticed in targeted outlets. The feminine business model resonates with the 'empowered' new femininities of the early twenty-first century, according to which women participate in public life, have career aspirations and utilise their 'soft skills' in order to be successful (Gill & Scharff, 2011). Grundetjern (2015) argues that in the Norwegian context, the feminine business model is consistent with prevailing norms of gender equality, which are stronger than in the United States. Women criticised the male domination of the drug economy but emphasised their ability to nevertheless thrive within it.

Involvement in street crime is contrary to appropriate or respectable femininity. The examples of adopting a 'professional' appearance for shoplifting or drug dealing demonstrate that a strategic performance of respectable femininity can be a resource for women. The female crack dealers in a small town England interviewed by Fleetwood (2014b) were unobtrusive in their communities and fitted selling crack around their children's school schedules. They adopted a friendly and professional habitus that enabled them to deal successfully and to avoid unwanted attention from authorities and family.

Fleetwood (2014a) argues that when women narrate their involvement in crime, they face the problem of fitting the inconsistency between crime and femininity into gendered narratives that preserve a valuable sense of self. Many women emphasise their motivations in terms of conventional scripts of femininity. Miller and Carbone-Lopez (2015) interviewed women who stated they took meth to aid weight loss and stay skinny, and to have increased energy for mothering and housework, rather than for recreational reasons. In this way, they could construct a moral account of their involvement in drug manufacturing. Miller and Carbone-Lopez (2015) interpret these mid-Western white women's narratives as reflecting understandings of respectable white womanhood particularly. This resonates with the wider American cultural imagination in which white women who use meth have not been demonised in the way that racialised women who used crack were in the 1980s and 90s (Linnemann, 2010).

Narratives of female victimhood have high cultural recognition as explanations for women's participation in crime, appearing in media, political and academic discourse (Maher, 1997). Ciesla et al.'s (2019) analysis of women's narratives of criminal experience revealed that 'choiceless victim' was by far the most prevalent narrative, which communicated negative emotions of helplessness, fear and sadness. Fleetwood (2014a) found that imprisoned female drug mules and prison staff supported narratives of victimisation over other explanations that might put more emphasis on agency or self-interest. Caribbean women imprisoned for drug smuggling in Barbados narrated their actions in relation to poverty, abuse and coercion and manipulation by male partners (Bailey, 2013). The significance of social and economic constraints and the exigencies of survival are relevant to women and men's crime, but are more culturally explicable through narratives of female victimhood.

Family roles and relationships, particularly motherhood, feature more strongly in women's narratives of criminality than men's (Fleetwood, 2014a). The female drug mules in Fleetwood's study rarely framed their actions in terms of wanting money for themselves, but as in order to improve their children's lives. Men drew instead on discourses of autonomy and entrepreneurship. Mullins and Wright (2003) noted that women were likely to stress that they used the proceeds from burglaries to buy necessities for their children, whereas men talked about guaranteeing independence. Ajzenstadt (2009) found Israeli women imprisoned for street crimes such as drug dealing and theft narrated their experiences through pro-natalist discourses that reflected dominant Israeli gender ideology. They gave needing to pay bills, or buy their children birthday presents, as reasons for stealing or drug dealing, in the context of limited employment opportunities. They also described such activities as more acceptable to maintain alongside motherhood than sex work.

In television drama *Weeds* (2005–2012), white, respectable suburban mother Nancy Botwin begins selling marijuana in order to support her children after her husband dies suddenly. Initially, Nancy's drug dealing identity is subordinate to her mothering identity—and adopted out of necessity. However, she becomes more deeply involved in the drug trade as the series progress, marrying a drug lord and inducting her sons into the drug trade (Walters & Harrison, 2014).

Fleetwood (2014a) argues it is difficult for people to depart from dominant cultural scripts, which for women are other rather than self-oriented. In relation to drug muling and much street crime, the commission is similar for women and men, as is the motivation in terms of a source of money. However, the stories they tell are different reflecting both different gendered lives, but also different norms and expectations and differences in habitus. Interpreting this is complicated. It could be that people feel unable to narrate their experiences in ways that radically depart from appropriate gender norms. For women this pressure is more intense as 'masculine' aspirations to freedom and self-determination are inconsistent with good motherhood. It could also be that there are cultural differences in how women and men perceive fulfilment and agency. Fleetwood (2014a) highlights that gendered narratives were remarkably consistent across her participants, despite the fact they came from a range of countries in both the Global North and South.

Fear and Victimisation

Young men are the most likely targets of street crimes such as assault and robbery (Spalek, 2016). Paradoxically, much criminological research has found that young heterosexual men are also the least likely social group to express fear of crime or to curtail their movement in public space. Goodey (1997) interprets unwillingness to admit to fear as related to aspects of hegemonic masculinity, which require discipline in terms of how, when and to whom vulnerability is expressed. Her research with adolescent boys revealed they admitted fearing 'folk devils' such as drug addicts and street drunks, but that such admissions involved complex negotiation of gender identity.

Managing the appearance of fear and vulnerability is an important component of avoiding victimisation on the streets and therefore a survival tactic. Day (2001) interviewed male students resident in the 'safe' Californian city of Irvine. Not showing fear in public space was a means to confirm masculinity and reject femininity, which was associated with vulnerability. The adoption of a 'badass' masculine performance in public was chosen in order to attain dominance and status, but also to induce fear in others. This was aimed mainly at other men, but not exclusively. The badass persona could be a resource to intimidate women who rejected sexual advances, for example. Chivalrous masculinity was a performance enacted for women, and consisted of offering them protection in public space through escorting them. Day (2001) argues contemporary masculine gender identity relies on a construction of femininity as vulnerability.

Perceived vulnerability to victimisation is gendered, but is also understood culturally in terms of race and class. Carlson (2014) examines the perception of gun carriers in Michigan that arming women was a way to 'equalise' their ability to fight back on the streets and reduce vulnerability. She argues that this demonstrates how they constructed crime as something violent and 'warlike' that happened on the streets—a masculine interpretation of crime. However, white men interviewed for the study were ready to cite their vulnerability to the violence of other men, a threat constructed as pervasive and sometimes understood in racialised terms, as a reason for carrying guns. In doing so, they leveraged vulnerability politics as a way to uphold the privilege and social power of white masculinity. Carlson's (2014) argument adds nuance to gendered understandings of fear of crime in public space, where fear of 'dangerous' others—constructed along gender, race and class lines—legitimates and politicises privileged men's expression of vulnerability.

Fear of victimisation is spatialised. Day's (2001) male student participants in Irvine regarded the city as a safe, if not boring, place. They symbolically contrasted it with Los Angeles, a feared urban area populated with 'hostile others' such as 'gangsters' and 'bad guys'. De Welde (2003) conducted ethnographic research in a women's self-defence course in a mid-sized city in the United States. This was predominantly attended by white women, for whom fear of crime was mainly fear of rape. These racialised anxieties were not directly expressed as fear of Black men, but of dangerous urban spaces associated with Black masculinity. Women usually did not feel afraid in familiar 'white safety zones'—the predominantly white middle-class areas in which they lived. The inner city was an imagined space of danger, but also of fetishised excitement (De Welde, 2003; McCarthy et al., 2004).

Doan and Higgins (2009) surveyed gay men and lesbian women in Tallahassee, Florida about their navigational strategies in urban space. These strategies were influenced by anxiety and concerns about safety that became embodied in gendered habitus. This was especially the case for participants whose gender identity and appearance was non-normative. Wattis et al. (2011) interviewed women students at a university in northeast England about fear of crime. They found that fears coalesced around places and local people. The town centre was viewed as crime prone, and the women associated this with social problems such as unemployment. However, they also discussed their positive experiences of living there. Although much research on women's fear of crime stresses rape and, by association, fear of men, the main crime women students were concerned about was street robbery. They also discussed confrontations with local women and children, rather than referring only to men as possible aggressors. Wattis et al. (2011) argue that differences of class and region were significant to student fears, although it was not as simple as all students being middle class, or from outside the town.

The construction of the feared subject is significant to the construction of crime. The imagined perpetrator of violence and theft in public space is the archetypal imagined criminal. In Western countries Black men, and other racialised men, have been portrayed as 'typical' criminals, as dangerous and to be feared (Lee, 2007). Day (2006) found that men of colour were aware of their status as feared subjects, particularly in areas where they stood out because of their race. White men tended not to perceive themselves as feared and were unaware that they might be seen as a threat by people of colour. Day (2006) argues these men benefited from the privilege of being 'unmarked' in terms of race, and less subject to suspicion. They were also perhaps unaware of when they were feared, for example in public spaces by women, as they were not culturally stigmatised as dangerous.

Dichotomising the feared and the fearing into separate groups is a simplification. Kinsella (2012) argues that rough sleepers are feared as potentially violent and criminal, and criminalised through legislation that controls 'anti-social' or uncivil behaviour. The need to improve safety justifies their removal from public spaces. However, homeless people are fearful of violent victimisation from the general public and from each other, while finding access to safe and secure spaces limited. Kinsella (2012) argues homeless people's fear is overlooked because the street is gendered as masculine space and most rough sleepers are men. They are only seen through the prism of threat rather than as fearful.

True crime podcasts, books, documentaries and television shows both evoke and reflect on fear of crime, frequently accompanied by gendered and racialised stereotypes about typical victims and likely criminals. As a genre, true crime is more heavily consumed by women. It is a source of entertainment and satisfies voyeurism, as well as offering an outlet for women's imagined fears of violent crime (Browder 2006; Boling & Hull, 2018). Listeners of podcast *My Favorite Murder* can also join online communities that bring fans together to discuss the show and their experiences, or fear, of crime. Journalist DenHoed (2019) argues the podcast promotes true crime as both a type of self-care via the expiation of anxiety and a form of feminist empowerment in hearing about violent criminals who get their come-uppance. However, this framing perpetuates notions of white femininity as fragile and the justice system as protective—a carceral feminist interpretation.

Stereotypes about who poses a threat are related to increased surveillance of certain groups and greater likelihood of their victimisation by the police. Hall et al.'s (1978) classic study of how a moral panic over mugging, a crime associated by the police and in the press with young Black men, in early 1970s Britain justified increased social control. Brunson and Miller (2006) interviewed young Black men and women in St. Louis about their experiences of aggressive policing strategies and how these were shaped by gender. Young men were disproportionate targets for strategies such as 'stop and search', which was related to a presumption of guilt influenced by the image of young Black men as symbolic criminals. They were treated as 'out of place'—and a threat—in public space. Young women were more likely to be stopped for curfew and truancy violations. Ritchie (2017) argues the racial profiling and police brutality experienced by Black women and women of colour in the United States has been invisible in comparison with the state violence perpetrated against Black men. However, such violence is endemic and interwoven with the disproportionate criminalisation and incarceration of Black women and women of colour.

As symbols of disorder, street crimes are intertwined with perceptions of gender, race, class and age. This symbolism affects who is most visible to authorities on the streets. The street is a site of mundane activity, pleasure and fear. It is also a potent imaginary space, existing in cultural representations and global flows of fashion, music, television and computer games.

References

Ajzenstadt, M. (2009). The relative autonomy of women offenders' decision making. *Theoretical Criminology, 13*(2), 201–225.

Anderson E. (1999). *Code of the street*. W. W. Norton.

Anderson, T. L. (2005). Dimensions of women's power in the illicit drug economy. *Theoretical Criminology, 9*(4), 371–400.

Bailey, C. (2013). Exploring female motivations for drug smuggling on the Island of Barbados: Evidence from her Majesty's prison, Barbados. *Feminist Criminology, 8*(2), 117–141.

Baird, A. (2012). The violent gang and the construction of masculinity amongst socially excluded young men. *Safer Communities, 11*(4), 179–190.

Baker, L. (1999). Screening race: Responses to theatre violence at "New Jack City" and "Boyz N the Hood." *The Velvet Light Trap, 44*, 4.

Bakkali, Y. (2019). Dying to live: Youth violence and the munpain. *The Sociological Review*. https://doi.org/10.1177/0038026119842012

Barlow, C., & Weare, S. (2019). Women as co-offenders: Pathways into crime and offending motivations. *The Howard Journal of Crime and Justice, 58*(1), 86–103.

Becker, S., & McCorkel, J. A. (2011). The gender of criminal opportunity: The impact of male co-offenders on women's crime. *Feminist Criminology, 6*(2), 79–110.

Boling, K. S., & Hull, K. (2018). Undisclosed information—Serial Is my favorite murder: Examining motivations in the true crime podcast audience. *Journal of Radio & Audio Media, 25*(1), 92–108.

Bourgois, P. (2003). *In search of respect: Selling crack in El Barrio.* Cambridge University Press.

Brookman, F., Mullins, C., Bennett, T., & Wright, R. (2007). Gender, motivation and the accomplishment of street robbery in the United Kingdom. *The British Journal of Criminology, 47*(6), 861–884.

Brotherton, D. C. (2015). *Youth street gangs: A critical appraisal.* Routledge.

Browder, L. (2006). Dystopian romance: True crime and the female reader. *The Journal of Popular Culture, 39*(6), 928–953.

Brunson, R. K., & Miller, J. (2006). Gender, race, and urban policing: The experience of African American youths. *Gender & Society, 20*(4), 531–552.

Burnett, C. (1999). Gang violence as survival strategy in the context of poverty in Davidsonville. *Society in Transition, 30*(1), 1–12.

Caputo, G. A., & King, A. (2011). Shoplifting: Work, agency, and gender. *Feminist Criminology, 6*(3), 159–177.

Carlson, J. (2014). The equalizer? Crime, vulnerability, and gender in pro-gun discourse. *Feminist Criminology, 9*(1), 59–83.

Ciesla, K., Ioannou, M., & Hammond, L. (2019). Women offenders' criminal narrative experience. *Journal of Criminal Psychology, 9*, 23–43.

Collins, P. H. (2005). *Black sexual politics: African Americans, gender, and the new racism.* Routledge.

Connell, R. (2005). *Masculinities.* Routledge.

Contreras, R. (2008). "Damn, Yo—Who's that girl?": An ethnographic analysis of masculinity in drug robberies. *Journal of Contemporary Ethnography, 38*(4), 465–492.

Copeland, K. J. (2018). *Moonlight,* Directed by Barry Jenkins. *Journal of Homosexuality, 65*(5), 687–689.

Copes, H., & Hochstetler, A. (2003). Situational construction of masculinity among male street thieves. *Journal of Contemporary Ethnography, 32*(3), 279–304.

Davies, A. (1998). Youth gangs, masculinity and violence in late Victorian Manchester and Salford. *Journal of Social History, 32*(2), 349–369.

Davies, A. (2006). Youth, violence, and courtship in late-Victorian Birmingham: The case of James Harper and Emily Pimm. *The History of the Family, 11*(2), 107–120.

Day, K. (2001). Constructing masculinity and women's fear in public space in Irvine, California. *Gender, Place & Culture, 8*(2), 109–127.

Day, K. (2006). Being feared: Masculinity and race in public space. *Environment and Planning A: Economy and Space, 38*(3), 569–586.

De Coster, S., & Heimer, K. (2017). Choice within constraint: An explanation of crime at the intersections. *Theoretical Criminology, 21*(1), 11–22.

de la Tierra, A. L. (2016). Essentializing manhood in "the street": Perilous masculinity and popular criminological ethnographies. *Feminist Criminology, 11*(4), 375–397.

De Welde, K. (2003). White women beware! Whiteness, fear of crime, and self-defense. *Race, Gender & Class, 10*(4), 75–91.

Deitzer, J. R., Leban, L., & Copes, H. (2019). "The times have changed, the dope has changed": Women's cooking roles and gender performances in shake methamphetamine markets*. *Criminology, 57*(2), 268–288.

DenHoed, A. (2019). The my favorite murder problem. *New Republic*.

Dhaenens, F., & Van Bauwel, S. (2012). The good, the bad or the queer: Articulations of queer resistance in The Wire. *Sexualities, 15*(5–6), 702–717.

Dikeç, M. (2011). *Badlands of the republic: Space, politics and urban policy*. Wiley.

Doan, P., & Higgins, H. (2009). Cognitive dimensions of way-finding: The implications of habitus, safety, and gender dissonance among gay and lesbian populations. *Environment and Planning A: Economy and Space, 41*(7), 1745–1762.

Dunn, J. C., & Ibarra, R. L. (2015). Becoming "Boss" in La Reina del Sur: Negotiating gender in a Narcotelenovela. *The Popular Cultural Studies Journal, 3*(1/2), 113–138.

Dziewanski, D. (2020). Femme fatales: Girl gangsters and violent street culture in Cape Town. *Feminist Criminology, 15*(4), 438–463.

Fatsis, L. (2019). Policing the beats: The criminalisation of UK drill and grime music by the London Metropolitan Police. *The Sociological Review, 67*(6), 1300–1316.

Fleetwood, J. (2014a). *Drug mules: Women in the international cocaine trade*. Palgrave.

Fleetwood, J. (2014b). Keeping out of trouble: Female crack cocaine dealers in England. *European Journal of Criminology, 11*(1), 91–109.

Fleury-Steiner, B. D., Dunn, K., & Fleury-Steiner, R. (2009). Governing through crime as commonsense racism: Race, space, and death penalty 'reform' in Delaware. *Punishment & Society, 11*(1), 5–24.

Freire-Medeiros, B. (2011). 'I went to the City of God': Gringos, guns and the touristic favela. *Journal of Latin American Cultural Studies, 20*(1), 21–34.

Gill, R., & Scharff, C. (2011). Introduction. In R. Gill & C. Scharff (Eds.), *New femininities: Postfeminism, neoliberalism and subjectivity* (pp. 1–20). Palgrave.

Goodey, J. (1997). Boys don't cry: Masculinities, fear of crime and fearlessness. *The British Journal of Criminology, 37*(3), 401–418.

Grundetjern, H. (2015). Women's gender performances and cultural heterogeneity in the illegal drug economy. *Criminology, 53*(2), 253–279.

Grundetjern, H., & Sandberg, S. (2012). Dealing with a gendered economy: Female drug dealers and street capital. *European Journal of Criminology, 9*(6), 621–635.

Hall, S., Critcher, C., Jefferson, T., Clarke, J., Roberts, B., Holmes, I., Meier Publishers, & United States of America. (1978). *Policing the crisis-mugging, the state, and law and order*. Macmillan.

Hallsworth, S. (2005). *Street crime*. Willan.

Hallsworth, S. (2013). *The gang and beyond: Interpreting violent street worlds*. Palgrave.

Heinonen, P. (2011). *Youth gangs and street children: Culture, nurture and masculinity in Ethiopia*. Berghahn.

Heitmeyer, W., Howell, S., Kurtenbach, S., Rauf, A., Zaman, M., & Zdun, S. (2019). *The codes of the street in risky neighborhoods*. Springer.

Henriksen, A.-K. (2017). Navigating hypermasculine terrains: Female tactics for safety and social mastery. *Feminist Criminology, 12*(4), 319–340.

Holligan, C. (2015). Breaking the code of the street: Extending Elijah Anderson's encryption of violent street governance to retaliation in Scotland. *Journal of Youth Studies, 18*(5), 634–648.

Holligan, C., Mclean, R., Irvine, A., & Brick, C. (2019). Keeping it in the family: Intersectionality and 'Class A' drug dealing by females in the West of Scotland. *Societies, 9*(1), 22.

Horrex, E. (2020). From teen angels to vogue: The subcultural styles of the girl gang in *Mi Vida Loca*. *Film, Fashion & Consumption, 9*(1), 43–63.

Ilan, J. (2015). *Understanding street culture: Poverty, crime, youth and cool*. Macmillan International Higher Education.

Ilan, J. (2020). Digital street culture decoded: Why criminalizing drill music is street illiterate and counterproductive. *The British Journal of Criminology, 60*(4), 994–1013.

Ilan, J. & Sandberg, S. (2019). How 'gangsters' become jihadists: Bourdieu, criminology and the crime–terrorism nexus. *European Journal of Criminology, 16*(3), 278–294.

Jones, N. (2008). Working 'the code': On girls, gender, and inner-city violence. *Australian & New Zealand Journal of Criminology, 41*(1), 63–83.

Kannan, M., Hall, R., & Hughey, M. W. (2017). Watching Moonlight in the twilight of Obama. *Humanity & Society, 41*(3), 287–298.

Kinsella, C. (2012). Re-locating fear on the streets: Homelessness, victimisation and fear of crime. *European Journal of Homelessness, 6*(2), 121–136.

Kruttschnitt, C., & Carbone-Lopez, K. (2006). Moving beyond the stereotypes: Women's subjective accounts of their violent crime*. *Criminology, 44*(2), 321–352.

Kubrin, C. E. (2005). Gangstas, thugs, and hustlas: Identity and the code of the street in rap music. *Social Problems, 52*(3), 360–378.

Laidler, K. J., & Hunt, G. (2001). Accomplishing femininity among the girls in the gang. *The British Journal of Criminology, 41*(4), 656–678.

Larke-Walsh, G. S. (2019). 'The King's shilling': How Peaky Blinders uses the experience of war to justify and celebrate toxic masculinity. *The Journal of Popular Television, 7*(1), 39–56.

Lee, M. (2007). *Inventing fear of crime: Criminology and the politics of anxiety*. Willan.

Linnemann, T. (2010). Mad men, meth moms, moral panic: Gendering meth crimes in the Midwest. *Critical Criminology, 18*(2), 95–110.

Long, P. (2017). Class, place and history in the imaginative landscapes of Peaky Blinders. In *Social class and television drama in contemporary Britain* (pp. 165–179). Springer.

Lopez, Q., & Bucholtz, M. (2017). "How my hair look?": Linguistic authenticity and racialized gender and sexuality on The Wire. *Journal of Language and Sexuality, 6*(1), 1–29.

Maher, L. (1997). *Sexed work: Gender, race and resistance in a Brooklyn drug market*. Oxford University Press.

Massood, P. J. (1996). Mapping the hood: The genealogy of city space in "Boyz N the Hood" and "Menace II Society." *Cinema Journal, 35*(2), 85–97.

McCall, L. (1992). Does gender fit? Bourdieu, feminism, and conceptions of social order. *Theory and Society, 21*(6), 837–867.

McCarthy, C., Rodriquez, A., Meecham, S., David, S., Wilson-Brown, C., Godina, H., Supryia, K., & Buendia, E. (2004). *Race, suburban resentment, and the representation of the inner city in contemporary film and television.* Routledge.

Miller, J. (1998). Up it up: Gender and the accomplishment of street robbery*. *Criminology, 36*(1), 37–66.

Miller, J. (2002). The strengths and limits of 'doing gender' for understanding street crime. *Theoretical Criminology, 6*(4), 433–460.

Miller, J., & Carbone-Lopez, K. (2015). Beyond 'doing gender': Incorporating race, class, place, and life transitions into feminist drug research. *Substance Use & Misuse, 50*(6), 693–707.

Miller, J., & Decker, S. H. (2001). Young women and gang violence: Gender, street offending, and violent victimization in gangs. *Justice Quarterly, 18*(1), 115–140.

Miller, T., Barrios, M. M., & Arroyave, J. (2019). Prime-time narcos: The Mafia and gender in Colombian television. *Feminist Media Studies, 19*(3), 348–363.

Mullins, C. W., & Cherbonneau, M. G. (2011). Establishing connections: Gender, motor vehicle theft, and disposal networks. *Justice Quarterly, 28*(2), 278–302.

Mullins, C. W., & Wright, R. (2003). Gender, social networks, and residential burglary*. *Criminology, 41*(3), 813–840.

Mullins, C. W., Wright, R., & Jacobs, B. A. (2004). Gender, streetlife and criminal retaliation*. *Criminology, 42*(4), 911–940.

O'Grady, B., & Gaetz, S. (2009). Street survival: A gendered analysis of youth homelessness in Toronto. In *Finding home: Policy options for addressing homelessness in Canada* (p. 7). Cities Centre Press.

Özer, L. (2019). Marginalised tower blocks: Crime and community on the council estate in Top Boy (2011–2013). In C. Lusin & R. Haekel (Eds.), *Community, seriality, and the state of the nation: British and Irish television series in the 21st century* (Vol. 83, pp. 193–212). Narr Francke Attempto Verlag.

Pain, R. (2001). Gender, race, age and fear in the city. *Urban Studies, 38*(5–6), 899–913.

Panfil, V. R. (2017). *The gang's all queer: The lives of gay gang members.* New York University Press.

Panfil, V. R., & Peterson, D. (2015). Gender, sexuality, and gangs. In S. H. Decker & D. C. Pyrooz (Eds.), *The handbook of gangs* (pp. 208–234). Wiley Blackwell.

Penglase, R. B. (2014). *Living with insecurity in a Brazilian favela: Urban violence and daily life*. Rutgers University Press.

Ritchie, A. J. (2017). *Invisible no more: Police violence against Black women and women of color*. Beacon Press.

Ross, J. I. (2018). Reframing urban street culture: Towards a dynamic and heuristic process model. *City, Culture and Society, 15*, 7–13.

Sandberg, S. (2008). Street capital: Ethnicity and violence on the streets of Oslo. *Theoretical Criminology, 12*(2), 153–171.

Sharma, S., & Sharma, A. (2000). 'So far so good...': La Haine and the poetics of the everyday. *Theory, Culture & Society, 17*(3), 103–116.

Simon, R. J. (1975). *Women and crime*. Rowman and Littlefield.

Spain, D. (2014). Gender and urban space. *Annual Review of Sociology, 40*, 581–598.

Spalek, B. (2016). *Crime victims: Theory, policy and practice*. Macmillan International Higher Education.

Spohrer, M. (2018). Menace II Society (1993). In S. J. Murguia (Ed.), *The encyclopedia of racism in American films* (pp. 379–381). Rowman and Littlefield.

Stapleton, S., & Terrio, S. (2012). Le Parkour: Urban street culture and the commoditization of male youth expression. *International Migration, 50*(6), 18–27.

Van Hellemont, E., & Densley, J. A. (2019). Gang glocalization: How the global mediascape creates and shapes local gang realities. *Crime, Media, Culture, 15*(1), 169–189.

Walters, S. D., & Harrison, L. (2014). Not ready to make nice: Aberrant mothers in contemporary culture. *Feminist Media Studies, 14*(1), 38–55.

Wattis, L., Green, E., & Radford, J. (2011). Women students' perceptions of crime and safety: Negotiating fear and risk in an English post-industrial landscape. *Gender, Place & Culture, 18*(6), 749–767.

Williams, J. P., & Kamaludeen, M. N. (2017). Muslim girl culture and social control in Southeast Asia: Exploring the hijabista and hijabster phenomena. *Crime, Media, Culture, 13*(2), 199–216.

Wilson, E. (2017). Scenes of Hurt and Rapture: Céline Sciamma's Girlhood. *Film Quarterly, 70*(3), 10–22.

Witherspoon, D. (2013). Bastards of the Party directed by Cle "Bone" Sloan. *Film & History: An Interdisciplinary Journal, 43*(1), 74–77.

Zubillaga, V. (2009). "Gaining respect": The logic of violence among young men in the Barrios of Caracas, Venezuela. In G. A. Jones & D. Rodgers (Eds.), *Youth violence in Latin America: Gangs and juvenile justice in perspective* (pp. 83–103). Palgrave.

6

Crimes of the Powerful

Crime and harm are not synonymous. Some of the most harmful phenomena do not result from crimes or illegal activity. Maldistribution of wealth and life chances is integral to global capitalism and causes great harm to those living in poverty. The climate emergency threatens all forms of life but is a consequence of economic systems not illegality. This chapter examines gender and the crimes of the powerful, although 'crimes' does not necessarily imply activities that are against the law. Rather, 'crimes of the powerful' are harmful acts perpetrated by states and corporations (Rothe & Kauzlarich, 2016). It focuses on three examples: corporate crime, green crime and genocide. Unlike street crime, crimes of the powerful are not necessarily committed by an identifiable individual or group of individuals, but by the functioning of governments, institutions, organisations and entire political and economic systems.

Crimes of the powerful are gendered, both in terms of perpetration and victimisation. It remains the case that around the world, men disproportionately occupy positions of power. Perhaps more significantly, norms and cultures of masculinity predominate in corporate and political institutions and systems. This does not mean women do not participate in the crimes of the powerful, or that men are not victimised by them.

© The Author(s), under exclusive license to Springer Nature
Switzerland AG 2022
L. Seal, *Gender, Crime and Justice*,
https://doi.org/10.1007/978-3-030-87488-9_6

However, it is important to recognise that power itself is gendered as masculine and the exercise of power is central to hegemonic masculinity (Connell, 2005). The distribution of harms is also affected by race, class, sexuality and geographical location, among other factors, meaning that an intersectional approach to analysis of crimes of the powerful is essential.

Corporate Crime

Corporate crimes are harms committed on behalf of and for the gain of corporations, which frequently also entail self-gain or benefits to highly placed individuals within them (Rothe & Kauzlarich, 2016). Most occupational crimes committed by individuals are petty and minor (Daly, 1989). Corporate crime refers to more seriously harmful acts that involve collaboration between collectivities and aggregates (Gottschalk, 2012). Corporate cultures are male dominated and masculinist, often prizing aggression, competitiveness and risk-taking as routes to success (Cavender & Jurik, 2017). Workplaces encourage competition and practise surveillance of workers' productivity. The context for these cultures is the deregulated markets of neoliberal capitalism, in which the individual is a self-maximising market agent. Film *In the Company of Men* (1997) portrays how corporate masculinities entail misogynistic behaviour. Two management consultants resolve to seduce and then humiliate a woman they perceive as vulnerable to enact revenge on womanhood. They bond through misogynistic and homophobic jokes. Their performance of masculinity is toxic, but also imbued with anxiety about being usurped by women, or deemed unworthy by other men (Boudreau, 2011).

Masculinities and femininities are constructed within organisations, both in terms of gendered norms and occupations. Corporate workplaces are transnational spaces, contributing to the creation of globalised masculinities and gender regimes (Connell, 2009). Connell's (2012) research on the construction of managerial masculinities in Australian financial companies identified that occupations were divided by gender. Most senior managers were men; women were concentrated in customer service and human resources roles. Managerial masculinities were for the most part performed as controlled and orderly rather than aggressive—although this was different in the dealing rooms, where aggression and overt competitiveness were required. Connell's (2012) research considered gendered occupational culture rather than crime or harm. However, appreciating the construction of corporate masculinities is necessary in order to contextualise corporate crime. Aggression and risk-taking are linked to harmful behaviour, although risk-taking is not dependent on the display of aggression. Levi (1994) observes that the connection between masculinity and corporate crime can result from a sense of entitlement as much as from prizing aggression.

Two classic examples of fictional representations of risk-taking as central to corporate masculinities, *Wall Street* (Stone, 1987) and *American Psycho* (Ellis, 1991), depict the entrenchment of neoliberal capitalism in the United States in the 1980s. *Wall Street's* Gordon Gekko, who notoriously proclaims 'Greed is Good', is the ultimate corporate villain—aggressive, amoral and reckless. Risk, over-confidence and competition are portrayed as integral to masculinist corporate culture (Reichardt, 2017). Patrick Bateman, the financier protagonist of *American Psycho*, is obsessed with money, status and power. He narrates acts of increasing violence, including a disturbing and intensely misogynistic murder, which may or may not be fantasies. Bateman is a ridiculous character, strongly emphasised in the film adaptation (2000), who exemplifies the imbrication of toxic masculinity and finance (La Berge, 2010; Reichardt, 2017).

Case study:

Challenger Space Shuttle Disaster. On 28 January 1986, the Challenger Space Shuttle exploded shortly after taking off, killing the seven astronauts on board. The explosion was caused by launching the shuttle in unfavourably cold weather conditions. The O ring, part of the seal in the rocket booster, only worked properly above a certain temperature, and the launch happened in conditions much colder than this safe level. Engineers at MTI, the company that made Challenger's propulsion system, had argued against the launch due to safety concerns but were overridden by managers, who were concerned about losing a lucrative government contract (Messerschmidt, 2017). Messerschmidt (2017) argues that managers at MTI prioritised growth over safety, consistent with a managerial masculinity that valorised risk-taking and suppressed fear. The engineers, on the other hand, valued expertise and technical knowledge above risk-taking and were willing to recommend caution. Messer-schmidt's (2017) argument highlights how organisationally constructed masculinities vary within corporate settings, and that risk-taking is not always a valued masculine attribute. However, where it is dominant it can have disastrous effects.

Organisational ideals of masculinity are not monolithic and vary according to a range of factors including type of organisation and geographical location. Although the performance of hypermasculinity might be acceptable or expected for financial traders, in other managerial roles it would be inappropriate as Connell (2012) highlights. In tech companies, intellectual bravado might be respected more than a domineering persona. Raesch et al. (2015) characterise this as 'geek masculinity', embodied by billionaires of the tech industry such as Bill Gates and Mark Zuckerberg. The latter's rise to success is depicted in *The Social Network* (2010), in which he prevails over Ivy League jocks (Salter & Blodgett, 2017). The Western normative versions of financial, managerial and geek masculinities are all based on whiteness, but this is not the case in Asian tech companies, for example. Zaidi and Poster (2017) examine how in South Asian knowledge work organisations and call centres, 'fusion masculinities' that incorporate local and transnational norms have reshaped hegemonic masculinity.

In Western countries, serious corporate crimes are disproportionately committed by middle-aged white men. The average age for such crimes is mid-40s, considerably older than for street crimes (Ruhland & Selzer, 2020). Studies from the United States and Norway find that women account for less than 10% of corporate criminals, here defined as people found guilty of crimes such as deceptive accounting, running Ponzi schemes and insider trading involving large sums of money (Benson & Gottschalk, 2015; Steffensmeier et al., 2013). These crimes can be motivated by certain norms of masculinity, including risk-taking and entitlement, but the overrepresentation of middle-aged white men is also related to opportunity as they disproportionately account for senior managers.

> **Case study:**
>
> The Enron Corporation was a phenomenally successful and well regarded energy company based in Texas. In 2001, it emerged that Enron and its auditor Arthur Andersen had misrepresented Enron's financial position through large-scale accounting fraud. Enron filed for bankruptcy, at the time the largest in American history, meaning employees and shareholders lost billions in pensions and stock prices. *Enron: The Smartest Guys in the Room* (2005) conveys a masculinist corporate culture based on aggression and risk-taking (Cavender & Jurik, 2017). In particular, this is shown through the in-house use of language such as 'rank and yank' to mean annually firing 15% of employees and 'pump and dump' for inflating stock prices and then selling shares. Fraudulent activities were given nicknames such as 'Death Star' and 'Fat Boy'.

High level corporate crime requires a degree of organisational power and autonomy that few women attain (Gottschalk & Smith, 2015; Holtfreter, 2015). Klenowski et al. (2011) found that women and men convicted of white-collar crimes made sense of their behaviour through different gendered scripts, with men emphasising the desire to fulfil their breadwinner role, and women their caregiving responsibilities. However, their participants were not high level corporate criminals.

> **Case study:**
>
> There are few examples of high-profile female corporate criminals. Martha Stewart, an American celebrity, had her own television show and related business empire based on cookery and lifestyle. In 2004, she was found guilty of conspiracy and obstruction of justice in an insider trading scandal and sentenced to prison. Stewart sold shares in ImClone, a biopharmaceutical company, after being tipped off that a new drug was not going to be approved. Liu and Miller (2019) compare the media coverage of Stewart's involvement with that of Sam Waksal, ImClone's CEO. Waksal was central to the scandal and convicted of more serious crimes than Stewart, whose involvement was peripheral. He was the

subject of far fewer news reports and, unlike Stewart, was not ridiculed by the press.

Stabile (2004) argues the fall of a powerful women elicits more derision than the fall of a powerful man. Martha Stewart was perceived as cold and masculine in demeanour, and portrayed as getting what she deserved. Kenneth Lay, former CEO and Chairman of Enron, made billions at the expense of his customers and shareholders. In selling her ImClone shares, Martha Stewart made around $50,000. Stabile (2004) notes there were far more articles on Stewart than there were about Lay, a major corporate criminal, during the Enron scandal. The fascination with Stewart demonstrated the newsworthiness of celebrity combined with gendered transgression. The relative lack of interest in Sam Waksal and Kenneth Lay shows the naturalisation of white masculinity in relation to corporate crime. Although more harmful, their actions were not transgressive in terms of gender. Cohn and Enloe (2003) argue that Lay's 'blandness' meant he could evade interest. The invisibility of his masculine power was part of his privilege (Cohn & Enloe, 2003). Walenta (2020) argues that during the 2006 trial, Jeffrey Skilling, former CEO of Enron, embodied the white masculine culture of the corporation.

The global financial crisis of 2008 is an example of large scale, incredibly harmful corporate crime. Much of the activity that led to the crash was not illegal and, in fact, upheld rather than subverted the values inculcated by neoliberal capitalism and held by the elite masculine business class (Knights & Tullberg, 2012). The willingness of American banks to lend to irresponsible mortgage companies and of pension funds and financial institutions to buy risky assets led to major banks facing bankruptcy. Government bailouts of banks in the United States and other countries took place in order to prevent their collapse and resulting economic catastrophe. Despite the bailouts and other measures to rescue the economy, the financial crisis triggered the worst worldwide recession since 1929. As Knights and Tullberg (2012) explain, of the major institutions that caused the crisis, only Lehmann Brothers, an investment bank, had falsified accounts. The others had not behaved illegally but within the parameters of deregulated financial markets. Documentaries *Capitalism: A Love Story* (2009) and *Inside Job* (2010) explain the causes of the 2008 financial crash and relate them to wider structures. *Inside Lehman Brothers: The Whistle Blowers* (2018) tells the story of the collapse of Lehman Brothers via interviews with whistleblowers who exposed fraudulent practices.

Deregulation created the economic context for the 2008 financial crisis. A gendered perspective enables an analysis of the significance of managerial masculinities to corporate crime and financial disaster (Knights & Tullberg, 2012). The global political economy, and Western financial capitalism in particular, is masculinised (Griffin, 2013). Griffin (2013) highlights the pervasive culture of privilege and emphasis on competitive success and masculine prowess in the finance industry. This masculinist culture privileges the experiences of white, Western, upper middle-class men (which does not mean they are the only people employed in such organisations).

Western masculinist capitalism derives from histories of colonialism, evident in business-speak tropes of invasion and occupation. Transnational corporations, global markets and electronic media perpetuate colonial power, operating through a 'metropole apparatus' bequeathed by colonialism (Connell, 2016). Managerial masculinity is shaped by a discourse of superiority valorising conquest, competition and control (Knights & Tullberg, 2012). Griffin (2013) notes that in financial industries, colonialist tropes exist alongside a discourse of risk, realised in risky financial operations. Despite constructions of domination, Knights and Tullberg (2012) argue that managerial masculinities are precarious and dependent on chasing success. This precarity helped to fuel the widespread risky behaviour that led to the financial crisis.

The practices in the US housing market that led to the financial crash are dramatised in *The Big Short* (2015), which depicts three groups of short sellers—investors who bet against the market—who recognise the fragility of the American economy ahead of the crash. Based on Michael Lewis's (2010) book, the film offers a critique of reckless capitalism. Benke (2018) argues its portrayal of masculinity, however, reaffirms belief in the superiority of rich white men. The short sellers embody the same social demographics as typical Wall Street financiers. They are distinguished by their perspicacity in seeing that an economy based on the sale subprime mortgages is unsustainable, not by departing from the norms of masculinised financial culture.

Margin Call (2011), a fictionalised version of the fall of Lehmann Brothers, shows crisis unfolding at an investment bank over a twenty-four-hour period. It portrays the centrality of risk to the bank's operations, which conditions the characters' relationship with masculinity and success. The management of risk is initially represented as feminine and therefore weak, but its necessity becomes clear as the damage wrought by risky financial behaviour emerges (Maclean, 2016). The Head of Risk Management is the only female character and is scapegoated for the crisis and forced to resign. The technical management of risk is reasserted as an aspect of 'Alpha Male' financial masculinity in contrast with recklessness—but as dependent on the suppression of femininity (Maclean, 2016).

Green Crime

Major environmental harms, such as the climate emergency, can be understood as state-corporate crimes because the interrelationship between governments and corporations creates these harms. Kramer and Michalowski (2012) argue business and political actors both work to prevent environmental regulation. Wonders and Danner (2015) describe the climate emergency as a state-corporate crime of omission as it cannot be mitigated without action from governments and corporations. Green harms affect all forms of life and threaten global catastrophe. Communities of colour, people living in poverty and people in the Global South are disproportionately affected by environmental harm (Gaarder, 2013). Documentaries such as *This Changes Everything* (2014) and *Before the Flood* (2016) examine the effects of the climate emergency and extend the public conversation about it, as does the David Attenborough series *Our Planet* (2019).

Globally, women constitute the majority of people living in poverty and are victimised by environmental harms to a greater degree than men (Wonders & Danner, 2015). Women and girls account for 70% of the world's poorest people, and their poverty means they are more affected by the climate emergency as access to food and water becomes more precarious. Women are particularly affected by food shortages as they often go hungry in order to feed their families (Gaard, 2015). Women are also more likely to die as a result of natural disasters due to factors such as not receiving warnings, being more likely to be at home when disaster strikes and discrimination in relief policies (Gaard, 2015; Neumayer & Plümper, 2007). Women were 90% of fatalities in the Bangladesh cyclone of 1991 and 75% of fatalities after the Tsunami in Aceh, Indonesia in 2004 (Gaard, 2015). Other forms of green victimisation impact disproportionately on marginalised women; for example, female migrant farm workers are over-exposed to pesticides (Lynch, 2018). *Circle of Poison* (2015) exposes how pesticides banned in the United States are exported to countries in the Global South, and are used on crops imported back into the US.

Case study:

Hurricane Katrina struck New Orleans in the United States in August 2005. Around 1500 people died (and there were further deaths in other regions) and thousands were made homeless. Belkhir and Charlemaine (2007) outline the social factors that made the hurricane such a disaster: poorly maintained levees (embankments), no evacuation plans for people without the resources to leave, slow official response and environmental damage that hastened the frequency and force of hurricanes. Residents who were poor and Black bore the brunt of the disaster, as they were unable to leave the city and had no alternative accommodation. Black women, especially if they had children, were particularly badly affected but this gendered aspect of the disaster was little commented on in media coverage or public discussion. *When the Levees Broke* (2006) and *Trouble the Water* (2008) detail the human tragedy of Hurricane Katrina in New Orleans, as well as its disproportionate impact on poor Black people. *Trouble the Water* reconstructs events from footage taken by Kimberly Roberts, a Black woman and resident of the Lower Ninth Ward, who is also the subject of the documentary.

Ecofeminism highlights the links between the oppression of women and of nature, and the twin gendered and environmental harms wrought by capitalist growth (Lane, 1998; Lynch & Stretsky, 2003). It recognises non-humans as victims. Women, children and animals are devalued, objectified and exploited by masculinist, capitalist norms (Sollund, 2017). Ecofeminism highlights environmental harm as gendered, although in celebrating the association of women with nature, risks essentialising femininity and reinforcing sexist stereotypes about women's maternal nature and special capacity for care (Kings, 2017; Lane, 1998). Naturalising women's vulnerability to green harm can obscure its social production. It is important to acknowledge the intersectionality of green victimisation along lines of race, poverty and geographical location (Lane, 1998; Lynch & Stretsky, 2003). Wealthy women can better insulate themselves from green harm and also reap many of the benefits of environmental exploitation.

Mad Max: Fury Road (2015) represents an example of a big budget Hollywood film influenced by ecofeminist principles. Set in a postapocalyptic future, it explicitly connects environmental destruction to patriarchal capitalism. The landscape is barren and fuel and water are in short supply as a consequence of oil wars. In the Citadel authority resides with armed cult leader, Immortan Joe. The film's hero is Furiosa, one of Joe's lieutenants, who turns against him and liberates the five wives that he has imprisoned as 'breeders'. The question 'Who Killed the World?' appears in the film twice: once as graffiti and once as a line voiced by one of Joe's wives. The question highlights how *Fury Road* attributes environmental destruction to capitalist overconsumption and masculinist militarism, with hope represented by a maternalist women's culture. As such, it has a strong ecofeminist message (Boulware, 2016; Seal & O'Neill, 2017), although one that exhibits some of the pitfalls of ecofeminism. While *Fury Road's* portrayal of Furiosa as warrior-hero transcends the association between women and nature as connoting passivity, the film lays the blame for environmental destruction with capitalist patriarchy without acknowledging the significance of the distinction between the Global North and South, and how wealthier women are complicit with environmental harm (Seal & O'Neill, 2017; Yates, 2017).

The domination of nature as masculinist, and the connection between globalised hegemonic masculinity and the environmentally harmful prioritisation of growth and profit, can be emphasised without essentialising women and men (Gaard, 2015; Wonders & Danner, 2015). As with the managerial masculinities discussed in the previous section, the valorisation of conquest in the domination and exploitation of nature is related to legacies of colonialism (Wonders & Danner, 2015). Kings (2017) emphasises the need for intersectional ecofeminism that does not focus solely on gender. She illustrates this necessity through a discussion of menstrual hygiene in India, where caste and gender combine to limit the ability of young women to manage their menstrual hygiene. Lack of access to running water or means of disposing of sanitary products are not problems faced by middle-class Indian women. Gaard (2015) advocates a posthumanist queer ecofeminism that recognises the impact of environmental harm on non-humans, and which incorporates attention to queer and transgendered people.

Posthumanism and ecofeminism appear as themes in contemporary science fiction films such as *Arrival* (2016) and *Annihilation* (2019), which deploy the intrusion of alien life on Earth as means to explore the relationship between humans, non-humans and the environment. In *Arrival*, a female linguist manages to decode the language of aliens whose spaceships hover over different locations above Earth. She averts an attack on the aliens by working out that when they refer to a 'weapon', they mean their language and not something harmful. In *Annihilation*, five women with different areas of expertise are selected to enter the Shimmer, a mysterious, alien area that appeared after a meteor landed at the site. Inside the Shimmer, the boundaries between human, animal and plant life are porous; humans merge with animals, plants grow in the shape of the women. Both films centre female characters as best able to comprehend alien life and connect this to motherhood—explicitly in *Arrival* and as subtext in *Annihilation*. Potentially, this draws on an essentialist ecofeminism that identifies women with nature and nurturance—but the active female protagonists in these films complicate this portrayal, as does the examination of the limits of the human.

There is a strong global tradition of feminist activism for environmental justice. In 1970s India, women in the Chipko movement encircled trees to prevent them from being cut down (Kings, 2017). Sami feminist activists in Scandinavia campaign for land and water rights, as well as LGBTQ and Indigenous rights. In the 1980s, Sami feminists protested against the construction of the Alta river dam in Norway and in the present Sami feminists have used art and music to highlight the gendered and environmental impact of mining in traditional lands (Bladow, 2019). In Latin America, feminist women in the La Via Campesina international peasant movement oppose agro-business in favour of sustainable agriculture using sit ins, demonstrations and performance. They centre Indigenous knowledge and build alliances across species and cultures. Specific actions have included occupying sugar mills and water processing factories to protest the environmental damage caused by agribusiness and water privatisation (Imperial, 2019).

Genocide

State crime does not exist as a concept in international law (Balint, 2011). As Balint (2011) argues, the law can be a companion to state crime when governments make laws that enable the perpetration of vast human rights violations. State crime encompasses large-scale harms, such as genocide, state-mandated murder and apartheid, carried out 'in the name of the state', frequently as part of nation building and nationalist projects (Balint, 2011: 3). This section discusses genocide as an example of a gendered state crime. The United Nations Convention on Prevention and Punishment of Genocide 1948 defines genocide as the 'intent to destroy, in whole or in part, a national, ethnical, racial or religious group' (Jamieson, 1999: 132). This Convention established genocide as a crime under international law. It does not include political or social groups within its definition, although broader understandings of genocide do extend to such groups (Randall, 2015).

As a crime aimed at the destruction of a group, genocide is intensely gendered (von Joeden-Forgey, 2012). Gendered patterns of violence and murder are integral to genocidal strategies (Randall, 2015; von Joeden-Forgey, 2010). Gender specific genocidal practices include the separation and massacre of men, and the mass rape of women. Derderian (2005) analyses how during the Armenian genocide of 1915, men were viewed as the bearers of Armenian ethnicity and were massacred, whereas women and children were perceived as transformable into Turkishness. When women are perceived as the bearers of ethnicity, rape and sexual violence are targeted at preventing the reproduction of the group (Randall, 2015).

> **Case study:**
>
> The Armenian genocide refers to the massacres, individual killings and deportation via death march of Armenian people living in the Ottoman Empire 1915–1916, with further massacres taking place up until 1923. Up to 1.5 million Armenian people died. Armenians were accused of siding with Russia in the First World War against the Ottoman-Turkish government, which was allied with Germany. To this day, Turkey does not recognise what happened as genocide and it is a crime in Turkey to describe it as such (Suny, 2015).

Civilian men are the primary targets of genocidal murder. This was demonstrated by the horrific Srebrenica massacre in Bosnia in 1995, when Bosnian Serb soldiers killed eight thousand Muslim men (Randall, 2015). Several films and documentaries about the Srebrenica massacre are told from the perspective of Bosnian women who endured what happened to their male relatives. *Srebrenica: Women Who Refuse to Die* (2012) comprises interviews with Bosnian Muslim women whose husbands and relatives were killed in the Srebrenican massacre and *Halima's Path* (2012) is the fictional story of a woman attempting to recover the bones of her son who died in a massacre in the Bosnian War. *Quo Vadis, Aida?* (2020) concerns a female UN translator who attempts to avert the massacre and save her husband and sons. From the perspective of British journalists, *Welcome to Sarajevo* (1997) portrays the persecution and murder of Muslims, including children, in the Bosnian War. There have been historical variations to the pattern of men as primary targets. Jewish women were killed at higher rates than men when they arrived at extermination camps during the Holocaust (von Joeden-Forgey, 2010).

Discourses of femininity and masculinity shape the perpetration and experience of genocide (Jones, 2002; Randall, 2015). Jones (2002) argues that in Rwanda, propaganda aimed at young Hutu men framed genocidal killing as a type of work. This had appeal because of high unemployment at the time, which compromised young men's masculine identities. Hutu men who refused to participate in the genocide were scapegoated as cowards. The injunction for men to do their job, or do their duty, in relation to genocide implicitly appeals to notions of masculinity (Myrttinen, 2018).

The Act of Killing (2012) focuses on perpetrators of the mass killings of Indonesian Communist Party members in the mid-1960s. These killings were not genocide according to the UN definition as they targeted a political group. However, they were planned and strategic and are frequently described as genocide. Not only are the killers interviewed in the documentary, they also re-enact some of the murders they carried out. These men perform an aggressive masculinity, which in the 1960s was constructed as under threat from the Communist Party and its association with Gerwani, a progressive women's organisation. This threat was perceived as destabilising the gender order and, by association, showed the Communist Party to be unmanly. The military dictatorship believed that the Communist Party needed to be destroyed to save the nation, and part of this was the necessity of preserving the gender order (Wieringa, 2014). Chaudhary (2018: 75) notes that the men's re-enactments of violence perform 'the fantasy of a masculinist will to power' and self-consciously exhibit the influence of gangster films. When not acting, they make misogynistic jokes and recall the 'excitement' of raping a girl.

The perpetrators of genocide are usually men, but women do participate in the planning and implementation of genocide, notably in Rwanda and Cambodia. However, whether or not women participate in genocide directly, or occupy senior positions in a genocidal regime, it is a masculinist crime (von Joeden-Forgey, 2010). Genocidal ideologies such as Nazism were explicitly masculinist, suturing the purity and superiority of the nation with German masculinity. The persecution and subsequent genocide of LGBTQ people in extermination camps was intended to eliminate sexual identity and gender expression deemed polluting of normative masculinity and femininity (Myrttinen, 2018). Documentary *Paragraph 175* (2000) features interviews with gay and lesbian survivors of the Holocaust, including a man who helped refugees escape the regime.

The mass rape of women is a recurrent aspect of genocide and war. The International Tribunals on Rwanda and Yugoslavia recognised rape as a crime of genocide (Randall, 2015). *The Uncondemned* (2015) depicts how activists and lawyers successfully campaigned to get mass rape committed during the Rwandan genocide recognised as an international war crime. Women are frequently constructed as symbolic representatives of collectivities—of ethnic, racial and national identities—and of the boundaries of the collective (Lentin, 1999). Mass rape as a genocidal strategy breaches these boundaries and symbolically attacks the whole group's identity. Sometimes enforced pregnancy is part of the intention in the belief that the children will belong to the perpetrator's ethnic group (von Joeden-Forgey, 2010). *Esma's Secret* (2006) is the story of a single mother whose daughter was conceived through a wartime rape during the Bosnian genocide, but whom she has raised to believe that her father was a war hero, representing the buried grief and stigma of wartime rape.

Women's symbolic representation of the collective means rape is perpetrated to humiliate the wider group, as well as attack the victims (von Joeden-Forgey, 2012). In the Armenian genocide, rapes were perpetrated in public and in front of women's family members to dehumanise Armenian people and to quash potential resistance (Derderian, 2005). Rape in genocide is also accompanied by the torture, evisceration and murder of women (von Joeden-Forgey, 2010). Women are less likely to be targeted for mass killing than men, but more likely to die in murders involving sexual violence (von Joeden-Forgey, 2012). Mass rape in Rwanda, Bosnia and Darfur was a systematic part of genocide, although rape can also occur as part of the genocidal violence without being planned.

Von Joeden-Forgey (2012) argues that understanding sexual violence as integral to genocide, and highlighting how it is carried out in a ritualised way, is important as an early warning that genocide is underway and for formulating prevention. Smith (2015) contends the definition of genocide, and the global attention paid to some instances of mass rape at the expense of others, occludes the mass sexual violence perpetrated as part of colonial conquest. Mass rapes of Indigenous women in Guatemala and Chiapas have not been defined as genocide but were carried out to subjugate and humiliate the wider group.

Men are also victims of sexual violence during genocide. There were mass rapes of women in Darfur by the Janjaweed militia, as well as rapes of Darfuri men. The rape of men was intended to emasculate them by contravening their role as protectors and demonstrating their powerlessness. The rapes were also a tool of humiliation as they connoted homosexuality, a devalued identity in Sudan (Ferrales et al., 2016). Muslim men were raped, sexually assaulted and forced to perform sex acts on one another as a form of humiliation in Bosnia in the 1990s (Sivakumaran, 2007).

Overwhelmingly, men are the main perpetrators of genocidal violence (Nyseth Brehm et al., 2016). However, women do participate in genocide—something which can be obscured by regarding women as 'universal victims' (Lentin, 1999). It is necessary to understand women's violent agency, rather than seeing female perpetrators as anomalies (Brown, 2014). In the Rwandan genocide, Hutu women in the political elite helped orchestrate the violence through making propaganda radio broadcasts calling for Tutsis to be murdered and by ordering soldiers to rape women (Sharlach, 1999). Propaganda lauded Hutu women as superior to Tutsi women and urged Hutu women to act. Women's role in the violence was predominantly through indirect means, such as exposing Tutsis in hiding, but women also committed murder and participated in gang rapes (Brown, 2014). *Keepers of Memory* (2004) is constructed from survivors' accounts of the Rwandan genocide and includes testimony of the complicity of nuns with murder squads. Brown (2014) argues that the mobilisation of Hutu women drew on discourses of femininity, such as the duty of motherhood. Women's violent agency was complicit with genocidal patriarchy.

Case study:

Pauline Nyiramasuhuko was Minister for the Family and Women's Affairs in the Rwandan Government. She took part in planning the genocide of Tutsis, and ordered and supervised massacres and rapes, as well as abductions and detention. Nyiramasuhuko was convicted in 2011 by the International Criminal Tribunal of Rwanda of crimes including conspiracy to commit genocide, genocide, extermination and rape, and was sentenced to life imprisonment. Sjoberg (2010) argues that expla-nations for Nyiramasuhuko's involvement have sought to distinguish her from 'normal' women who are supposedly incapable of such crimes, and have interpreted her behaviour as stemming from motherhood 'gone wrong'. Nyiramasuhuko mobilised her supposed incapability of commit-ting violence as a mother—unsuccessfully—to protest her innocence. Discourses of femininity shaped perceptions of Nyiramasuhuko, whether to condemn or defend her.

The memorialisation of genocide, and its place in collective memory, is gendered. This is exemplified by which stories are remembered and retold—whether they communicate men's victimisation predominantly, whether they rely on gendered stereotyping, and whether they erase certain experiences, such as sexual abuse or the persecution of LGBTQ people (Randall, 2015). The most memorialised genocide is the Holo-caust. Collective memory of the Holocaust has been created through museums, films, novels and televisions programmes. An initial focus on men was modified by attention to women's experiences such as of preg-nancy, motherhood and sexual abuse—but Horowitz (2000) argues this relegated women to one category of experience. Portraying a range of women's experiences of the Holocaust is no longer unusual as films such as *Nina's Journey* (2005), *Sarah's Key* (2010) and *Remembrance* (2011) attest. Brown and Rafter (2013) examine *Katyn* (2007) as an example of a cinematic contribution to the collective memory of genocide told from the point of view of women, who remember the Polish victims of a massacre carried out by Russians in 1940, and learn more about what happened to their husbands, fathers and brothers.

Jacobs (2008) analyses the representation of gender at Auschwitz-Birkenau Memorial and Museum, arguing women were represented as mothers or as embodied victims of suffering. Men were represented through the stereotype of emasculation—as unable to protect women and children. Images of resistance were not as frequent as those of helplessness and suffering. Jacobs (2008) argues there is a danger that gendered memorialisation sensationalises genocide and exploits the dead. Mannergren Selimovic (2020) scrutinises the commemoration of women victims of the Rwandan genocide in official memorials, arguing they are either figured as passive rape victims or as moral mothers. Women are not depicted as active agents with a range of experiences. These state-funded memorials represent an elite and top down creation of gendered memory, which constructs a marginalised role for women in the contemporary nation. Beyond official memorials, there is a multiplicity of stories in Rwanda about women and genocide, but these do not get told at official sites of remembrance.

Crimes of the powerful refer to a diverse range of harms perpetrated by states and corporations, and/or dominant social and political groups. Both who commits these crimes, and who is affected by them, is shaped by intersectional gender identities. This assertion is not an argument for essentialist interpretations of gender, but is intended instead to focus analysis on how gender is relevant to inequalities of power in political and economic systems.

References

Balint, J. (2011). *Genocide, state crime and the law: In the name of the state.* Routledge.

Belkhir, J. A., & Charlemaine, C. (2007). Race, gender and class lessons from Hurricane Katrina. *Race, Gender & Class, 14*(1/2), 120–152.

Benke, G. (2018). Humor and heuristics: Culture, genre, and economic thought in The Big Short. *Journal of Cultural Economy, 11*(4), 303–314.

Benson, M. L., & Gottschalk, P. (2015). Gender and white-collar crime in Norway: An empirical study of media reports. *International Journal of Law, Crime and Justice, 43*(4), 535–552.

Bladow, K. (2019). "Never shut up my native": Indigenous feminist protest art in Sápmi. *Feminist Studies, 45*(2–3), 312–332.

Boudreau, B. (2011). Sexually suspect: Masculine anxiety in the films of Neil LaBute. In E. Watson & M. Shaw (Eds.), *Performing American masculinities: The 21st-century man in popular culture* (pp. 37–57). Indiana University Press.

Boulware, T. (2016). 'Who killed the world': Building a feminist utopia from the ashes of toxic masculinity in Mad Max: Fury Road. *Mise-en-scène|The Journal of Film & Visual Narration, 1*(1), 1–17.

Brown, S. E. (2014). Female perpetrators of the Rwandan genocide. *International Feminist Journal of Politics, 16*(3), 448–469.

Brown, M., & Rafter, N. (2013). Genocide films, public criminology, collective memory. *The British Journal of Criminology, 53*(6), 1017–1032.

Cavender, G., & Jurik, N. C. (2017). Risky business: Visual representations in corporate crime films. In M. Brown & E. Carrabine (Eds.), *Routledge international handbook of visual criminology* (pp. 215–228). Routledge.

Chaudhary, Z. R. (2018). This time with feeling: Impunity and the play of fantasy in the Act of Killing. *Boundary 2, 45*(4), 65–101.

Cohn, C., & Enloe, C. (2003). A conversation with Cynthia Enloe: Feminists look at masculinity and the men who wage war. *Signs: Journal of Women in Culture and Society, 28*(4): 1187–1107.

Connell, R. (2005). *Masculinities*. Routledge.

Connell, R. (2009). A thousand miles from kind: Men, masculinities and modern institutions. *The Journal of Men's Studies, 16*(3), 237–252.

Connell, R. (2012). Inside the glass tower: The construction of masculinities in finance capital. In P. McDonald & E. Jeanes (Eds.), *Men, wage work and family* (pp. 75–89). Routledge.

Connell, R. (2016). Masculinities in global perspective: Hegemony, contestation, and changing structures of power. *Theory and Society, 45*(4), 303–318.

Daly, K. (1989). Gender and varieties of white-collar crime*. *Criminology, 27*(4), 769–794.

Derderian, K. (2005). Common fate, different experience: Gender-specific aspects of the Armenian Genocide, 1915–1917. *Holocaust and Genocide Studies, 19*(1), 1–25.

Ferrales, G., Nyseth Brehm, H., & Mcelrath, S. (2016). Gender-based violence against men and boys in Darfur: The gender-genocide nexus. *Gender & Society, 30*(4), 565–589.

Gaard, G. (2015). Ecofeminism and climate change. *Women's Studies International Forum, 49*, 20–33.

Gaarder, E. (2013). Evading responsibility for green harm. In A. Brisman & N. South (Eds.), *Routledge international handbook of green criminology* (pp. 272–281). London.

Gottschalk, P. (2012). Gender and white-collar crime: Only four percent female criminals. *Journal of Money Laundering Control, 15*(3), 362–373.

Gottschalk, P., & Smith, R. (2015). Gender and white-collar crime: Examining representations of women in media? *Journal of Gender Studies, 24*(3), 310–325.

Griffin, P. (2013). Gendering global finance: Crisis, masculinity, and responsibility. *Men and Masculinities, 16*(1), 9–34.

Holtfreter, K. (2015). General theory, gender-specific theory, and white-collar crime. *Journal of Financial Crime, 22*(4), 422–431.

Horowitz, S. R. (2000). Gender, genocide, and Jewish memory. *Prooftexts, 20*(1–2), 158–190.

Imperial, M. (2019). New materialist feminist ecological practices: La via campesina and activist environmental work. *Social Sciences, 8*(8), 235.

Jacobs, J. (2008). Gender and collective memory: Women and representation at Auschwitz. *Memory Studies, 1*(2), 211–225.

Jamieson, R. (1999). Genocide and the social production of immorality. *Theoretical Criminology, 3*(2), 131–146.

Jones, A. (2002). Gender and genocide in Rwanda. *Journal of Genocide Research, 4*(1), 65–94.

Kings, A. E. (2017). Intersectionality and the changing face of ecofeminism. *Ethics and the Environment, 22*(1), 63–87.

Klenowski, P. M., Copes, H., & Mullins, C. W. (2011). Gender, identity, and accounts: How white collar offenders do gender when making sense of their crimes. *Justice Quarterly, 28*(1), 46–69.

Knights, D., & Tullberg, M. (2012). Managing masculinity/mismanaging the corporation. *Organization, 19*(4), 385–404.

Kramer, R. C., & Michalowski, R. J. (2012). Is global warming a state-corporate crime? *Climate change from a criminological perspective* (pp. 71–88). Springer.

La Berge, L. C. (2010). The men who make the killings: American Psycho, financial masculinity, and 1980s financial print culture. *Studies in American Fiction, 37*(2), 273–296.

Lane, P. (1998). Ecofeminism meets criminology. *Theoretical Criminology*, 2(2): 235–248.

Lentin, R. (1999). The rape of the nation: Women narrativising genocide. *Sociological Research Online, 4*(2), 75–83.

Levi, M. (1994). Masculinities and white-collar crime. In T. Newburn & E. A. Stanko (Eds.), *Just boys doing business* (pp. 234–252). Routledge.

Lewis, M. (2010). *The Big Short: Inside the doomsday machine.* Penguin.

Liu, L., & Miller, S. L. (2019). Intersectional approach to top executive white-collar offenders' discourses: A case study of the Martha Stewart and Sam Waksal insider trading scandal. *Sociological Inquiry, 89*(4), 600–623.

Lynch, M. J. (2018). Acknowledging female victims of green crimes: Environmental exposure of women to industrial pollutants. *Feminist Criminology, 13*(4), 404–427.

Lynch, M. J., & Stretsky, P. B. (2003). The meaning of green: Contrasting criminological perspectives. *Theoretical Criminology, 7*(2), 217–238.

Maclean, K. (2016). Gender, risk and the Wall Street alpha male. *Journal of Gender Studies, 25*(4), 427–444.

Mannergren Selimovic, J. (2020). Gender, narrative and affect: Top-down politics of commemoration in post-genocide Rwanda. *Memory Studies, 13*(2), 131–145.

Messerschmidt, J. W. (2017). Managing to kill: Masculinities and the space shuttle Challenger explosion. In S. Tomsen (Ed.), *Crime, criminal justice and masculinities* (pp. 191–212). Routledge.

Myrttinen, H. (2018). Men, masculinities and genocide. In M. M. Connellan & C. Fröhlich (Eds.), *A gendered lens for genocide prevention* (pp. 27–47). Springer.

Neumayer, E., & Plümper, T. (2007). The gendered nature of natural disasters: The impact of catastrophic events on the gender gap in life expectancy, 1981–2002. *Annals of the Association of American Geographers, 97*(3), 551–566.

Nyseth Brehm, H., Uggen, C., & Gasanabo, J.-D. (2016). Age, gender, and the crime of crimes: Toward a life-course theory of genocide participation*. *Criminology, 54*(4), 713–743.

Raesch, M., Lee, M., & Cooper, F. R. (2015). From lonesome cowboys to geek masculinities: A study of documentary films on the financial crisis. *Interactions: Studies in Communication & Culture, 6*(3), 287–301.

Randall, A. E. (2015). Gendering genocide studies. In A. E. Randall (Ed.), *Genocide and gender in the twentieth century: A comparative survey*. Bloomsbury Publishing.

Reichardt, U. (2017). Wall Street and representations of masculinity in contemporary American film and fiction. In S. Horlacher & K. Floyd (Eds.), *Contemporary masculinities in the UK and the US* (pp. 219–232). Springer.

Rothe, D., & Kauzlarich, D. (2016). *Crimes of the powerful: An introduction*. Routledge.

Ruhland, E. L., & Selzer, N. (2020). Gender differences in white-collar offending and supervision. *Criminal Justice Studies, 33*(1), 13–30.

Salter, A., & Blodgett, B. (2017). *Toxic geek masculinity in media: Sexism, trolling, and identity policing*. Springer.

Seal, L., & M. O'Neill (2017). Transgressive imaginations. In S. Tombs & D. Whyte (Eds.), *Oxford research encyclopedia of criminology and criminal justice*. Oxford University Press.

Sharlach, L. (1999). Gender and genocide in Rwanda: Women as agents and objects of Genocide. *Journal of Genocide Research, 1*(3), 387–399.

Sivakumaran, S. (2007). Sexual violence against men in armed conflict. *European Journal of International Law, 18*(2), 253–276.

Sjoberg, L. (2010). Women and the genocidal rape of women: The gender dynamics of gendered war crimes. In D. Bergoffen, P. R. Gilbert, T. Harvey, & C. L. McNeely (Eds.), *Confronting global gender justice* (pp. 39–52). Routledge.

Smith, A. (2015). *Conquest: Sexual violence and American Indian genocide*. Duke University Press.

Sollund, R. (2017). Doing green, critical criminology with an auto-ethnographic, feminist approach. *Critical Criminology, 25*(2), 245–260.

Stabile, C. A. (2004). Getting what she deserved: The news media, Martha Stewart, and masculine domination. *Feminist Media Studies, 4*(3), 315–332.

Steffensmeier, D. J., Schwartz, J., & Roche, M. (2013). Gender and twenty-first-century corporate crime: Female involvement and the gender gap in enron-era corporate frauds. *American Sociological Review, 78*(3), 448–476.

Suny, F. G. (2015). *"They can live in the desert but nowhere else": A history of the Armenian genocide*. Princeton University Press.

von Joeden-Forgey, E. (2010). Gender and genocide. In D. Bloxham & A. D. Moses (Eds.), *The Oxford handbook of genocide studies*. Oxford University Press.

von Joeden-Forgey, E. (2012). Gender and the future of genocide studies and prevention. *Genocide Studies and Prevention, 7*(1), 89–107.

Walenta, J. (2020). Courtroom ethnography: Researching the intersection of law, space, and everyday practices. *The Professional Geographer, 72*(1), 131–138.

Wieringa, S. E. (2014). Persisting silence: Sexual slander, mass murder, and the Act of Killing. *Asian Journal of Women's Studies, 20*(3), 50–76.

Wonders, N. A., & Danner, M. J. E. (2015). Gendering climate change: A feminist criminological perspective. *Critical Criminology, 23*(4), 401–416.

Yates, M. (2017). Re-casting nature as feminist space in Mad Max: Fury Road. *Science Fiction Film & Television, 10*(3), 353–370.

Zaidi, Y., & Poster, W. R. (2017). Shifting masculinities in the South Asian outsourcing industry. In H. Peterson (Ed.), *Gender in transnational knowledge work* (pp. 119–140). Springer.

7

Policing and the Courts

The maintenance of order and the exercise of authority and control are deeply gendered. Order, control and authority are socially and culturally coded as masculine. The social institutions that are responsible for upholding order and keeping control, such as the police and the courts, represent masculine authority and derive their legitimacy from this authority (Heidensohn, 1992). Such institutions uphold different kinds of control depending on the place and time in which they are located. Authoritarian forms of governance rely on 'hard' masculine authority, whereas liberal democratic governance is underpinned by norms of masculine rationality and paternalism—with recent shifts towards women and men working in partnership (Klatzer & Schlager, 2020; Marx Ferree, 2020). The coding of institutions of order, control and authority as masculine does not mean that only men work within them (although historically women were excluded from the police and legal professions). However, it does mean that cis heterosexual white men more closely fit the notion of ideal police officers, lawyers and judges. As gendered institutions, policing and the courts have masculine working cultures that shape how women and LGBTQ people fare within them. The masculinity of policing and the courts also affects how individuals

© The Author(s), under exclusive license to Springer Nature Switzerland AG 2022
L. Seal, *Gender, Crime and Justice*,
https://doi.org/10.1007/978-3-030-87488-9_7

from different social groups are treated when they come into contact with them. This chapter examines gender in relation to the police and legal professions, as well as how different groups are policed and sentenced.

Certain forms of authority and control are culturally understood as feminine and typically relate to notions of maternalism. Agencies of social welfare have historically been more hospitable for women as workers and exert a different kind of social control from policing; one that is based on shaping normative behaviour rather than using physical force. Privileged women's social welfare work provided them with roles in the public domain specialising in the welfare of women and children (Heidensohn, 1992; Martin & Jurik, 2006). Heidensohn (1992) argues women's social control of women and children is understood as legitimate, but their social control of men has less legitimacy. This has implications for women's involvement—and progression—in policing and the legal professions.

There are two different justifications for increasing women's representation in policing and the legal professions. The first is formal equality. If women are to be equal citizens, they need to be full participants in all areas of society and to play a role in upholding order and keeping control. Formal equality demands not just entry into different agencies and professions, but also representation at senior levels. The second justification relates to the notion that women have particular attributes and skills to bring to professional work, which enrich and improve different fields. Arguments made on this basis stress women's greater capacity for collaborative working and evincing care. Such capacities are not necessarily deemed to be natural, but as resulting from women's social positioning and lived experiences (Daly, 1989; Martin & Jurik, 2006).

These two justifications do not have to exist in tension with one another; it is possible to argue that both formal equality and the representation of special skills are important. However, the formal equality justification by itself does not imply that women transform policing, lawyering or judging simply by their inclusion, whereas the justification based on women's difference from men does. An intersectional feminist perspective complicates both of these justifications. An equal gender balance can be achieved while leaving other inequalities, for example of race and class, in place. Women do not constitute a homogenous group so identifying their particular skills and attributes as women is difficult, if not impossible.

The gendering of power, control and authority as masculine poses important political questions. If agencies of social control have an equal gender balance but perpetuate inequality and masculinist oppression, what has been gained? If social control is 'feminised' but inequality and oppression remain, what has been gained? These questions relate to how authority should be exercised, and on whose behalf.

Policing Culture

Policing culture refers to the values, beliefs and attitudes that underpin the working lives and occupational identities of police officers, of which masculinity is a central component (Atkinson, 2017). Reiner (2010) characterises policing culture as a mix of conservatism, machismo, racism and pragmatism and Brown (2007) argues that it is deeply gendered and suffused with masculine imagery. Brough et al. (2016) conceptualise the 'cultural web' of policing as a combination of control, masculinity, a sense of the police as a family and a mentality of 'us vs. them'. The police force is a 'masculine frontier' and working as a police officer is an occupation that confers masculine identity (Aiello, 2014). Being a police officer is understood as an enduring identity (du Plessis et al., 2021). From a historical perspective, Barrie and Broomhall (2012) argue that policing offers a case study in how masculinity has been constructed and applied over the last three hundred years. This has encompassed multiple understandings and expressions of masculinity but the embedding of policing within masculinity is a strong continuity across this period. The mutual reinforcement of the masculinity of the police with the masculinity of those who are policed is another continuity—in other words, policing largely entails interactions between men.

Proving masculinity is a consistent theme of policing culture (Rawski & Workman-Stark, 2018). Masculine ideals of displaying physical strength and exhibiting violence and heroism form part of the values of and attitudes of policing culture (Kurtz & Upton, 2018). Masculine contest culture entails putting work first, demonstrating strength and stamina and refusing to show weakness (Rawski & Workman-Stark, 2018). The masculinity of policing culture has been resistant to change, with formal attempts to modernise the police by increasing officer diversity and shifting attitudes leading to a backlash from within (Loftus, 2009, 2010). Atkinson (2017) describes the Scottish police as a patriarchal institution, in which police officers are mainly men and women are concentrated in other roles such as intelligence analysis.

The gender order in policing subordinates femininity and certain masculinities, prizing a construction of hegemonic masculinity as authoritative and paternal. Kurtz and Upton (2018) identify 'war stories' as an important part of masculine policing culture and a way of doing masculinity. War stories feature tales of heroism on the job and are told with humour. Kurtz and Upton (2018) highlight an apocryphal 'core story' of a woman officer who finds herself unable to deal with a large, physically aggressive male suspect as creating a gendered narrative of women officers as less competent. They suggest police storytelling is influenced by media portrayals of policing as well as experiences on the job.

The masculinity of policing culture and of police officers is portrayed and reinforced by popular culture. Scharrer (2012) analysed representations of masculinity in policing and detective television shows over four decades. Displays of aggression by male officers were a constant over time. By the 1980s, emotionalism was represented as a component part of police masculinity, although this receded in the shows of the 1990s. Overall, Scharrer (2012) found police shows shifted to portrayals of conflicted masculinity, where police officers were both aggressive and to some degree sensitive. Conflicted masculinity remains a staple of male police officers and detectives in television. *Southland*'s (2009–2013) John Cooper is heroic, paternal with more junior officers and a professional role model. He is also addicted to painkillers and tortured by his sexuality as a gay man (Weissmann, 2016). Lead characters such as Harry Bosch (*Bosch*, 2014–2021) and Raylan Givens (*Justified*, 2010–2015) are heroic but also possess emotional depth. *The Shield*'s (2002–2008) Vic Mackey is a troubled, violent man—an antihero rather than a hero—but also an example of conflicted masculinity (Hagelin & Silverman, 2017).

Aiello (2014) assessed the gendered performance of policing in Hollywood films, finding the ideal officer was a 'hotshot' man, who succeeded in cracking the case or catching the bad guy. The hotshot is emotionally expressive, ignores the rules and is sexually attractive to women. He traces this ideal in Hollywood films over time, including *Lethal Weapon* (1987), *Rush Hour* (1998) and *The Other Guys* (2010). Aiello (2014) notes that this portrayal is counter to the ideal officer of police recruitment materials, which are gender neutral. However, cultural images of the excessive masculinity of policing create a feedback loop of policing as a masculine occupation.

The 'cult of masculinity' has been central to analyses of policing culture, but Silvestri (2017) argues conceptualising the relevance of masculinity to policing requires more nuance. The construction of the ideal officer as male extends beyond gendered performances of heroism and physical strength. Revising this image would not change the underlying masculinity of policing as an institution. Instead of physical strength, Silvestri (2017) focuses on the significance of time to policing. To be viewed as an ideal police officer requires working full-time, being willing and able to put in long hours and having an uninterrupted career. In particular, a commitment to being always available is at a premium in terms of progressing to senior management. This analysis of time and its relationship with a successful policing career can be conceptualised as a form of hegemonic masculinity, which is achieved via professional success, assuredness and authority rather than physical strength and heroism (Connell & Messerschmidt, 2005). Surface-level gender neutrality in the police as an organisation leaves the deeper masculinity of policing culture intact as the 'ideal' police officer or manager remains an able-bodied man unencumbered by care responsibilities (Murray, 2021; Silvestri, 2017).

British drama *Prime Suspect* (1991–2006) was ground-breaking in portraying Jane Tennison, a complex woman, as a senior police detective who contends with masculine police culture, including the sexism she experiences as part of undertaking her day-to-day duties (Cavender & Jurik, 2007; Creeber, 2001). The tension between mothering responsibilities and performing police work is a frequent theme of crime dramas with female leads or main characters, such as *Spiral*'s (2005–2020) Laure

Berthaud and *The Killing*'s (2007–2012) Sarah Lund. Wilton (2018) analyses the representation of the politics of family and changing gender roles in *Broadchurch* (2013–2017) and *Happy Valley* (2014 ongoing). In *Broadchurch* Ellie Miller struggles to balance the demands of home and work, particularly in relation to motherhood. *Happy Valley*'s Catherine Cawood is a grandmother and the main carer of her grandson. She has accepted a demotion in an attempt to gain a better work/life balance. Wilton (2018) notes Miller and Cawood do not keep their professional and public lives separate and show the challenges of combining care responsibilities with a policing career.

Intersectionality in Policing

The justification that women could bring particular skills to policing was significant to their entry into the police force, which was made on the basis of difference in terms of gender identity. In the UK, women were first included in the police in 1915 and did not gain the same employment terms as men until 1975 (Jackson, 2006). Women officers were deemed specialists in preventing child abuse and neglect, policing families, domestic violence and juvenile justice. Their occupational identity was distinct from male officers and organisationally women officers had separate branches and departments until the 1970s (Jackson, 2006).

Globally, women are underrepresented in policing. They account for around a quarter of officers in most developed democracies, with lower representation in authoritarian systems and emergent democracies (Prenzler & Sinclair, 2013). This paints the picture with a broad brush, however. In the United States, 13.5% of officers are women, whereas in South Africa they are 23.5% and in Ghana 19.7% (Prenzler & Sinclair, 2013; Swan, 2016). Women's representation at senior levels is even more disproportionate than at the officer level with only around half of the percentage of representation women achieve at that level (Haake, 2018; Swan, 2016). Women's inclusion in policing as officers has plateaued in recent years, although there is variation internationally (Rossler et al., 2020). Women are often concentrated in alternative roles in policing from sworn officers. Women are 30% of officers in Sweden, representation well above the global average, but employment in the police remains gender segregated with women more commonly working in administrative roles or as in-house investigators (Haake, 2018). Boogaard and Roggeband (2010) highlight gender segregation in the Dutch police force, with women of colour overrepresented as administrative staff.

Specific barriers and limitations for female officers have been identified in studies from different countries. Women police officers in Turkey felt they did not have the same progression opportunities as men and battled with too few childcare options combined with too many duties (Gültekin et al., 2010). In the Tamil Nadu police force in India women had more household duties than male officers, which was perceived by women and men as meaning men were able to perform better professionally (Natarajan, 2014). Swan (2016) identified family commitments as a major barrier to women's progression in the police in the United States. These findings confirm Silvestri's (2017) analysis of time as significant to the enduring masculinity of policing. Martin and Jurik (2006) argue the criminal justice system reflects society's wider inequalities and gender ideologies. Women's greater responsibility for unpaid care and domestic labour reflects the gender order.

Other factors than care responsibilities can limit women's progression. In Liberia, there were concerted efforts to increase women's representation in the police after the 2003 peace agreement that ended the civil war. However, women remained concentrated at the patrol officer level due to having restricted educational backgrounds (Bacon, 2015). For women police officers in Tamil Nadu, the paramilitary model of policing was a burden as they did not see themselves as matching a militaristic style (Natarajan, 2014). Where people from different social groups are under-represented in policing, they experience tokenism. This entails isolation, feeling hypervisible and having fewer opportunities to advance. In the Milwaukee Police Department in the United States, women officers and Black and Latinx officers experienced tokenism, with Black women and men experiencing the most negative effects (Stroshine & Brandl, 2011).

Women officers' views on whether they have distinct or different skills by virtue of their gender vary. From their interviews with American officers, Morash and Haarr (2011) found some women perceived women as more capable of doing the compassionate side of police work than men. They saw women as equally suited to policing as men, but with different abilities. Other participants saw their gender as a background identity irrelevant to their professional life. However, women felt they were more scrutinised in their roles than men and were judged according to their gender in a way men were not (Morash & Haarr, 2011). The notion of women and people of colour as having special competencies can create opportunities as well as limitations. Boogaard and Roggeband (2010) argue that in the Dutch police, women's perceived aptitude for working relationally and the culturally specific knowledge held by officers of colour were viewed positively and could be a basis to challenge inequalities in the force. However, there was also a risk that 'special competencies' reinforced gendered and racialised stereotypes. Murray (2021) interprets women taking roles consistent with 'women's work', such as community liaison, as an adaptive strategy to masculinist police culture. The perceived distinctive abilities possessed by women officers finds some portrayal in popular culture. Weissmann (2016) argues *Southland* (2009–2013) represents officer Lydia Adams as exercising her 'affective knowledge' to the benefit of her policing competence, rather than attempting to suppress emotion as the male characters do to negative effect.

Greater inclusion of women as police officers has been suggested as a remedy to police brutality, which is argued to result from male dominance in policing and the prizing of aggression and heroism in masculine policing culture (Porter & Prenzler, 2017). Women are argued to be more respectful in their interactions and better at defusing conflict. Porter and Prenzler (2017) assessed excessive force complaints against police officers in Queensland, Australia. Women had fewer complaints made against them and where they did a male officer was usually involved as well. Porter and Prenzler (2017) argue these findings support the case for the positive effect of increasing the representation of women police officers, although they caution that justifications should not be made on grounds of gender essentialism.

In majority white countries, white men disproportionately occupy senior management roles. White women are more likely to be promoted through the ranks than women of colour (Morash & Haarr, 2011; Pren-zler & Sinclair, 2013). Despite relatively higher levels of representation in the Swedish police force, women and men officers saw masculinist policing culture as inhibiting women's progression to seniority (Haake, 2018). Silvestri et al. (2013) argue greater inclusion of women at senior levels improves the quality of leadership as women's management approaches are typically more consultative and transformative. Initiatives to increase senior representation are limited in places like England and Wales where leaders must be recruited from within the police as there are fewer possible women candidates. This potentially damages the legitimacy of the police as they do not reflect the population they serve (Silvestri et al., 2013).

The masculinity and machismo of policing culture traditionally excluded LGBTQ officers, who often hid their identities and risked experiencing discrimination and homophobia at work if they did not. This culture of exclusion has shifted in recent years, with police forces actively seeking to recruit LGBTQ officers and the development of professional support networks (Pickles, 2020; Rennstam & Sullivan, 2018). From their interviews with gay male police officers in the UK, Rumens and Broomfield (2012) found their participants were comfortable with being out and believed their identity as gay men could be an asset within the police. However, the 'traditional' masculinity of policing culture could limit the integration of gay men and a perceived 'feminine' identity was undesirable as it was deemed unsuitable for certain aspects of the job.

Impression management in relation to gender performance was discussed by American gay and lesbian police officers in Mennicke et al.'s (2018) research. Gay men perceived the need to be hypermasculine to evade presumptions of incompetence. Lesbian women were more comfortable with being out at work as their sexuality was not viewed as incompatible with policing. However, they were still passed over for promotion. Rennstam and Sullivan (2018) describe the current position of LGBTQ officers in the Swedish police force as one of 'peripheral inclusion'. Although policing culture has shifted, homophobia and discrimination have not disappeared. Acceptance co-exists with exclusion. Transgender police officers in Britain and the United States experience transphobia at work, for example through punishing, and therefore misgendering, them for uniform violations or being excluded from the bathroom consistent with their gender identity (Panter, 2018). Panter (2018) emphasises that policing is structured in relation to the traditional gender binary and this disadvantages trans officers, making them 'out of place'.

There is a plethora of non-heterosexual police characters in popular culture. *Instinct* (2018–2019) is notable for having a gay man as the main character. Colvin and Moton (2021) argue the representation of lesbian women as police officers on television is aspirational, in that it is positive beyond the actual experiences of lesbian women in the police. Lesbian officers are portrayed as competent, serious, racially diverse and achieving senior management positions. Colvin and Moton (2021) cite *The Wire*'s (2002–2008) Kima Greggs and *Bosch*'s (2014–2021) Grace Billets as examples (although Season 7 of Bosch features a storyline about Billets experiencing co-ordinated homophobic abuse from male officers).

Police sitcom *Brooklyn Nine-Nine* (2013–2021) features a diverse cast of characters that includes Raymond Holt, a gay Black man, as the station's captain and a bisexual Latinx woman officer, Rosa Diaz. Season 5 depicts Rosa's decision to come out as bisexual at work and to her family. Brooklyn Nine-Nine is consistent with Colvin and Moton's (2021) notion of aspirational portrayals and largely places experiences of racism and homophobia in the police force in the past, although addresses issues such as sexual harassment and racial profiling in later seasons. Screen representations of transgender police officers are rare, although *Queen Sugar*'s (2016 ongoing) Toine Wilkins, a trans man and police officer, is an exception.

Policing Intersectionality

Race, Racism and Gender

Experiences of being policed relate to intersectional social positioning. In New York, Black and Latinx women account for 81% of women who are stopped by the police, and Black and Latinx men make up 85% of those stopped (Crenshaw et al., 2015). Traffic stops are one of the most frequent ways that individuals encounter the police. Evidence from the United States shows they are racially disproportionate. Christiani (2020) analysed police data on traffic stops in Illinois to explore the significance of stereotypes. White people were stereotyped positively, with white women being perceived as in need of protection. Black and Latinx men were the most likely to be searched during a stop. Christiani (2020) argues the police act according to 'scripts of suspicion', which link Black people to crime and violence and stereotype Black people and people of colour as drug involved. Suspicion is higher of people located in poor neighbourhoods. Black and Latinx young people in New York experienced microaggressions from the police, which included being stopped too often, the presumption of criminality and being treated as inferior (Rengifo & Pater, 2017).

Cobbina et al. (2019) researched how Black residents in Ferguson, Missouri who were involved in community action after the police shooting of Michael Brown managed involuntary police encounters. Women and men both adopted strategies of resisting the police or capitulating by being co-operative. They were however treated differently according to gender—men were more likely to be arrested and women discussed experiences of disrespectful treatment. Certain policies and approaches by the police have implications for the policing of women's bodies. Women of colour experience profiling by being stereotyped as drug involved and undergoing invasive body searches. Seizing condoms is used as evidence of involvement in sex work and disproportionately affects women of colour and LBGTQ people (Ritchie & Jones-Brown, 2017).

Police use of force and police brutality is racially disproportionate. White officers are more likely to use force in interactions with Black people and men are more likely to experience the use of force from the police than women (Wright & Headley, 2020). In Germany, people of colour face higher levels of police violence and higher rates of death in custody than white people (Bruce-Jones, 2015). Bruce-Jones (2015) argues police officers rely on defences of greater perceived threat from people of colour, which mobilise racialised stereotypes of dangerousness, to excuse use of excessive force. Thompson (2021) argues in European countries racist policing is a form of intersectional violence;

racialised people categorised as neurodiverse or mentally ill are particularly vulnerable to police harassment and violence. Negative stereotypes about 'madness' intersect with racist stereotypes about Black people as aggressive and assumptions that racialised people are criminals not victims.

The issue of racist police killings of Black Americans has been urgent in recent years. The shooting of 18 year old Michael Brown by a white police officer in 2014 in Ferguson, Missouri led to protests against racist police brutality, which were met with a military style police response. Documentary *Ferguson Rises* (2021) conveys the resistance mounted by community members. The murder of George Floyd by police officer Derek Chauvin in Minneapolis in 2020 gained worldwide attention and expressions of solidarity. The killing of Breonna Taylor during a house raid in Louisville, Kentucky in the same year also caused outrage. Gilbert and Ray (2016) describe racist police killings in the United States as a public health issue that is shaped by the legacy of the policing of enslaved people by white overseers on plantations and of lynchings. They argue racist perceptions of Black men as violent predators with superhuman strength influences and acts as a justification for police brutality.

The persistence of the police killings of Black men as a social problem is illustrated by *Do the Right Thing* (1989), which shows a white police officer killing the character Radio Raheem by keeping him in a chokehold, a scene resonant with the murder of George Floyd in 2020. *Fruitvale Station* (2013) dramatises the police shooting of Oscar Grant, a young Black man, on New Year's Eve in Oakland in 2009. As Munby (2015) argues, the film's realistic style and location of Grant in ordinary domesticity highlights the tragedy and police shootings as a political issue.

Police killings of Black women in the United States have not received the same level of attention as the killing of Black men and women's cases have not become symbols of the effects of systemic racism to the same degree—although the killing of Breonna Taylor was significant to mobilising Black Lives Matter demonstrations against police brutality (Crenshaw et al., 2015). Crenshaw et al. (2015) argue the public conversation on police killing needs to be expanded to include women. Like Black men, Black women experience stereotyping by the police and wider mainstream culture as superhuman and menacing. Police violence towards women is more likely to be in the context of their domestic lives than it is for men. The African American Policy Forum, established by Kimberle Crenshaw and Luke Charles Harris, began the #SayHerName campaign to raise awareness of women and girls who are victims of police killings and in the process to raise awareness of how state violence entails violence against women (Crenshaw et al., 2015; Williams, 2016).

Case studies:

Breonna Taylor was shot dead in March 2020 by police officers during a 'no knock' raid on her apartment in Louisville, Kentucky made in order to look for someone else. No knock warrants enable the police to forcibly enter a home without warning or identifying themselves. Not knowing what was happening, Taylor's boyfriend Kenneth Walker shot a police officer in the leg when they raided, and the police killed Taylor in the indiscriminate return of fire. She received no medical attention until 20 minutes after being shot. George Floyd was arrested in Minneapolis in May 2020 after a convenience store owner reported him to the police for paying with a counterfeit $20 bill. After the arrest, Floyd was pinned down by the police and officer Derek Chauvin knelt on his neck for nine minutes, killing him. Chauvin was sentenced to over 22 years in prison in June 2021 for the murder of George Floyd.

LGBTQ People

LGBTQ people have a fraught history with policing. The police had a significant role in 'policing perversion' in places and times where certain sexual practices or forms of gender expression were against the law (Dwyer, 2014). This policing involved targeting LGBTQ people in public and carrying out sting operations in which the police used deception to apprehend people. This historical context means LGBTQ people often have a negative view of the police as symbolising repression, which affects their likelihood of engaging with the police (Pickles, 2020). Pickles (2020) surveyed LGBTQ people in the northeast of

England, finding while over 70% had experienced hate crime, only 4% had reported it to the police.

In many places, police forces have attempted to change their image of 'policing perversion' and perpetuating homophobia. Russell (2016) analyses this 'image work' through a case study of the Chief Commissioner of police in Victoria, Australia joining the Sydney Pride March in 2002. Taking part in Pride offered a counter story to queer histories of repressive policing and provided a replacement narrative of the police as modern, adaptive and inclusive. Crucially, it placed homophobia in the past. The origins of Pride lie in protests against police homophobia and violence. Participation aimed to increase police legitimacy—among LGBTQ people and more widely. It is now routine for the police in many countries to join Pride marches, although this is controversial as it can be interpreted as compromising Pride's radical political roots (Russell, 2016). Police forces have adopted measures beyond the symbolic to counter homophobia, such as LGBTQ liaison officers and establishing partnerships with LGBTQ services and organisations (Dwyer, 2014).

Biopics *Breaking the Code* (1996) and *The Imitation Game* (2014) about mathematician and computer scientist Alan Turing, who was instrumental in enabling intelligence services' codebreaking through the work he did at Bletchley Park in England during the Second World War, represent the human impact of policing perversion. Turing was prosecuted for 'gross indecency' in 1952 for having a sexual relationship with a man. He accepted undergoing chemical castration rather than a custodial sentence. As a result of his conviction, Turing lost his security clearance and could not do further work for Bletchley Park. He died by suicide in 1954. Following a campaign, he received a royal pardon in 2013 and legislation was enacted in 2017 to allow historical convictions for consensual sex between men to be pardoned.

Negative interactions between LGBTQ people the police are not only a legacy of the past. Dwyer (2015) interviewed young people in Australia about their experiences with the police. Participants felt they gained attention from the police in public space due to 'looking queer' and therefore out of place in heterosexual spaces. In particular, expressions of intimacy were policed. Some participants had also been subjected to homophobic language from police officers. In relation to experiences of reporting crime, Javaid (2021) argues when non-heterosexual men report sexual violence to the police they are subordinated in relation to hegemonic masculinity and sometimes mocked as a result.

Trans people's positivity and trust of the police is lower than cis people's (Serpe & Nadal, 2017). Lanham et al. (2019) interviewed trans women from Barbados, Trinidad, Haiti and El Salvador about their experiences of the police. Some women reported positive interactions in which they were treated with respect. However, participants discussed numerous negative experiences such as being treated rudely and being blamed for crimes they had experienced. In El Salvador, women had been robbed and sexually abused by police and soldiers, and in El Salvador and Haiti women had been arrested and detained for their gender expression.

Analyses of the police as inevitably repressive and violent towards marginalised communities in order to shore up the existing social order underpin calls to reduce, or abolish, the police. 'Defunding' the police refers to cutting police budgets and functions and reallocating funds to welfare-based services and/or community-based alternatives instead. This reduction of the purview of the police can be understood as a step towards abolition (Fleetwood & Lea, 2020). Feminist and queer abolitionism argues for abolition of the police and prisons in favour of different models and practices of justice and is discussed further in Chapter 9.

Gender and Legal Professions

As with professional policing, women were historically excluded from joining the legal professions. In Britain—and across the British Empire—the Sex Disqualification (Removal) Act 1919 changed this, meaning women could enter the legal professions, act as magistrates and sit on juries. In 1922, Helena Normanton became the first woman in Britain to be admitted to the Inns of Court as a barrister. To practice law anywhere in the British Empire, barristers had to join an Inn and be located in London for three years (Bourne, 2016; Pepitone, 2016). Normanton campaigned for admission, using press publicity to establish her reputation and to become a public figure. After Normanton, women could be admitted but remained concentrated in crime and family work rather than the more lucrative commercial work. They also had to contend with misogyny and a prevailing masculine culture that excluded women (Bourne, 2016; Pepitone, 2016). For a long time, women barristers were the exception rather than the rule (Pepitone, 2016).

The imperial context meant it was not only British women who were admitted to Inns of Court in the 1920s. Chen and Li (2021) examine the careers of the first four women barristers from colonial Burma, who undertook their legal education and training in Britain before returning home The women were from privileged families in Burma but in Britain were portrayed as cultural and racial 'others'. After returning to Rangoon, they worked to advance women's rights. Chen and Li (2021) argue these women were part of contemporary global modernity, connecting the imperial metropole to the periphery. Like Helena Normanton, however, they were exceptional not usual.

The Sex Disqualification (Removal) Act 1919 brought women into the magistracy, the first time women had held formal roles in the law courts in Britain. By the 1940s, 20% of Justices of the Peace were women, representing a higher proportion of women than any other civic or public activity apart from voting (Logan, 2007). The Act also enabled women to sit on juries but levels of representation remained lower. In the 1920s, women were a minority of jurors and many trials had no women on the jury (Crosby, 2017). Women could be excluded from juries due to property disqualification (the main barrier), peremptory challenge or the power of the judge to order a men-only jury (Logan, 2013). There was a perception women were needed as jurors for trials involving women or children, but that women's greater emotionality made them unsuited for certain trials (Crosby, 2017). Logan (2013) argues male lawyers objected to the presence of women in what they perceived as masculine space and attitudes did not change significantly until the 1960s. Women did not achieve parity on juries until 1974 (Logan, 2013).

In the United States, prior to the 1970s, women performed specialist work in the criminal justice system related to juvenile justice, supervising women and working as family lawyers. They were rarely judges. The Equal Employment Opportunity Act 1972 and Crime Control Act

1973 increased women's representation in criminal justice-related occupations. The expansion of the criminal justice system from the 1970s onwards also increased the numbers of women employed as there were more roles to fill (Martin & Jurik, 2006). Women are no longer confined to 'specialist' spheres and constitute half of the enrolments in American law schools but face barriers to progression to senior levels, for reasons such as a lack of flexible working and childcare (Lee, 2015; Martin & Jurik, 2006). Sheffield (1993) assesses the portrayal of women lawyers on screen 1930–1990. He identifies *Hill Street Blues*'s (1981–1987) depiction of Assistant Public Defender Joyce Davenport as influential in terms of departing from portrayals of women as secondary to men. Davenport is tough, independent and not defined by men.

Research on women trial attorneys and litigators in the United States reveals experiences of gender bias, such as being mistaken for a paralegal or criticised for having a 'shrill' voice (Lee, 2015). Jurors hold implicit biases against female attorneys, rating the expression of anger positively for men but negatively for women. More widely, adherence to normative gender performance is viewed favourably by juries, which disadvantages women as men gain approval for seeming authoritative, whereas women must seem caring (Goodman, 2017; Lee, 2015). Goodman (2017) argues stock stories in the media influence juror perceptions of women and men attorneys. Contemporary media representations of women lawyers can be negative, evincing stereotypes of them as neurotic, over-ambitious and failed mothers (Schulz & Youn, 2020). Chronopoulou (2020) compares portrayals of women lawyers in American film *My Days of Mercy* (2017) and Israeli film *In Between* (2016), which is about Palestinian characters. She argues the films resist heteronormativity by depicting queer relationships and do not reduce women's lifestyle to nuclear family life. In this sense, the films transcend representations of traditional femininity. However, they advance an aestheticised, consumer-based lifestyle, consistent with neoliberal 'new femininities'.

Black women and women of colour legal professionals negotiate a white male setting, in which they are rendered out of place and experience racist harassment. Negative perceptions are shaped by gendered and racialised stereotypes such the 'angry Black woman' and the 'dragon lady' (Lee, 2015). Ragusa and Groves (2012) found senior women barristers in Australia embraced an ideology of meritocracy, which they substituted for the stereotypical portrayal of the 'successful barrister' as a man. However, notions of meritocratic competency were grounded in masculinism and were ultimately more beneficial for men. Mason and Vaughan (2017) surveyed and interviewed LGBTQ barristers in England and Wales finding work-related experiences of homophobia, biphobia and transphobia. Although usually out to colleagues, only a quarter of barristers were out to their clients.

Women are underrepresented as judges, particularly in the higher courts and do not fit the default image of the judge as an older white man (Rackley, 2012; Schultz & Shaw, 2013; Treanor, 2020). Masculinity is inscribed into the judicial script, and as with other criminal justice and legal professions, the attribution of authority as masculine means that women and men who are perceived as 'feminine' have less legitimacy (Schultz & Shaw, 2013). Treanor (2020) addresses gendered barriers to women entering the judiciary in Northern Ireland. Judges are more likely to have followed a career as a barrister than a solicitor, and women are underrepresented as barristers, restricting the pool. Maternity leave is damaging for women barristers' careers and there is a 'motherhood penalty' for barristers and judges due to lack of work flexibility.

Arguments for greater inclusion of women as judges are sometimes made on the basis they diversify decision-making, strengthening the judiciary. Rackley (2012) finds that judges in the UK make a difference to decision-making, whereas Kenney (2012) argues this is not borne out in the United States, where there are no significant differences between women and men's decisions, apart from in sex discrimination cases. Kenney (2012) states women judges tend to reject the view that they are different from men in terms of how they do their job. The structure of the legal system is significant to gender difference. Wei and Xiong (2020) found there was no difference in the length of sentences awarded by women and men judges in China and there was little scope for difference to manifest. Sentencing guidelines limited judicial discretion, as did the 'Iron Triangle' of police, prosecution and court. Judges were largely bound by the decisions of the police and prosecution.

Olson (2013) analyses the gendered habitus of two reality television judges: American *Judge Judy* and German *Richterin Barbara Salesch*. She argues both shows promote women judges as a positive force and portray women in charge of courtrooms as normal and beneficial. The two shows diverge according to the prevailing penal cultures of the countries in which they are made. *Judge Judy* espouses a neoliberal ethos of self-reliance and responsibility, with an emphasis on retributive justice. She shames marginalised women in her courtroom. *Richterin Barbara Salesch* expresses empathy for people experiencing difficulties and reflects the social democratic principles prevalent in Germany.

Intersectionality in the Courtroom

In the United States, the courtroom is constructed as a white space and legal narratives and legal truth are racially coded as white. Disproportionately, the work of the court is administered and presided over by white actors, which makes whiteness invisible as dominant in the racial order. Historically, Black witnesses were excluded from the court and could not testify against white people. When formal exclusion ended, Black people's inclusion as witnesses was undermined through other means, such as the use of peremptory challenge (Carlin, 2016). Carlin (2016) assesses the reception of Rachel Jeantel's testimony as a witness in the 2013 trial of George Zimmerman for the murder of Trayvon Martin in Florida. Jeantel was Martin's best friend and the last person to see him alive before Zimmerman shot and killed him. As a working class Black girl, Jeantel was unintelligible in the white courtroom and subject to the 'demeanour gap', whereby she was perceived as lacking credibility and respectability. Docuseries *Rest in Power: The Trayvon Martin Story* (2018) takes an in depth look at the circumstances of Martin's shooting, the legal context surrounding Zimmerman's case, the trial and the case's role in galvanising Black Lives Matter protests.

Gathings and Parrotta (2013) conducted courtroom observation in North Carolina to analyse the significance of gendered narratives to lenient outcomes. Leniency was related to defendants showing they fit appropriate gender norms in a way that could be matched to mitigation in the sentencing guidelines. For men, mitigation included being in stable employment and being a good worker and, if they were supporting their family, being able to demonstrate being a good provider. Women were not held to the same expectations of fulfilling paid employment and could be economically dependent and still viewed favourably. For women, providing support could interpreted as caring for children. Gathings and Parrotta (2013) emphasise that guilt was rarely contested in the cases they observed so meeting normative gender expectations that chimed with reasons for mitigation was necessary to negotiate a light sentence.

Discourses of gender and race are significant in probation reviews. Romain Dagenhardt (2020) observed probation reviews in domestic violence courts in the American Midwest in relation to how judges, attorneys and probation officers understood probationers' non-compliance. There were recurrent discourses of mental health and responsibility, which were framed differently according to the gender and race of defendants. Women and men were both judged to have responsibility to provide for their children financially, but more emphasis was placed on judging women's caregiving. Women were more likely to be interpreted as having depression and problems related to trauma, whereas men were viewed as having 'anger issues'. Mental health was a more prevalent discourse for white defendants. Black probationers were framed as not taking responsibility for meeting the conditions of their probation, rather than benefitting from explanations based on mental health. Romain Dagenhardt (2020) notes Black and Latinx men were constructed through racialised stereotypes as hypersexed and aggressive.

High-profile crimes become venues for the public working through of salient and contested social and cultural issues and this includes the construction of intersectional identities (Chancer, 2005). Widely reported trials of high-profile crimes can become global media sensations, especially if they are televised as in the United States. The O J Simpson trial in 1995, for the murder of his ex-wife Nicole Brown Simpson and of Ronald Goodman, was a landmark example—at the time it was dubbed 'the trial of the century'. The defence team expressed concern about racism in the criminal justice system and the media, and invoked the racist history of the LAPD as significant to whether Simpson could be tried fairly. The racism of the LAPD was particularly salient in the 1990s due to the police beating of Rodney King in 1991 and the subsequent unrest it provoked. Chancer (2005) argues issues of race and gender were polarised in reactions to the trial. There were concerns that as a Black man, Simpson was being unfairly blamed for the murder of white victims and tried in a system rigged against him. There were also concerns that the case represented how men's violence towards women could escalate to murder. Series *The People v O J Simpson: American Crime Story* (2016) dramatises the trial in relation to the contemporary context of race, crime and policing—and Simpson's celebrity. Longform documentary *O J: Made in America* (2016) examines Simpson's rise to fame, success, the crime and his life afterwards. Episode four focuses on the trial.

Intersectionality and Sentencing

American studies of sentencing consistently find that women receive lighter sentences than men and are less likely to be sentenced to custody. This disparity does not necessarily mean judgement of gender itself is a factor in sentencing; legal factors such as the severity of the crime or number of previous convictions are relevant to sentencing. Women tend to commit less serious crimes than men and are less likely to have a significant criminal history (Doerner & Demuth, 2014). Doerner and Demuth (2014) argue that American sentencing data reveals women are sentenced more leniently than men even when legal factors are accounted for. Certain 'focal concerns' are argued to influence sentencing; these are level of blameworthiness, the need to protect the community and practical constraints (Steffensmeier, 1980; Steffensmeier et al., 2017). These can be shaped by gender, such as the practical constraint that women are more likely than men to be primary carers for children, meaning women's incarceration has a greater social cost (Bontrager et al., 2013).

Steffensmeier et al.'s (2017) analysis of sentencing in Pennsylvania found legal factors had the biggest effect on sentencing but that extralegal factors related to gender, race and age also had an effect. Men were sentenced more harshly than women, Black and Latinx people more severely than white people and young adults more harshly than teenagers or older adults. Gender-related disparities are mediated by race. In the

United States, Black and Latinx women receive shorter sentences than Black and Latinx men, but longer sentences than white women (Farrell et al., 2010). Farrell et al. (2010) argue paternalism is significant to women's lighter sentencing, which benefits white women especially.

Where gender, or more specifically women's femininity, becomes significant in sentencing, it is argued to either reflect paternalistic views, leading to lighter sentences, or perceptions of 'evil' womanhood, which lead to harsher sentencing (Bontrager et al., 2013). Studies of sentencing in England and Wales find recurrent gendered themes of pathology, domesticity, respectability and sexuality, which shape both understandings of women's behaviour and what is deemed to be best for them (Gelsthorpe & Sharpe, 2015). Women are often seen as troubled rather than troublesome. This does not always connect to lenient treatment. In England and Wales twice as many women without previous convictions are imprisoned than men, suggesting imprisonment is viewed as being for their own good (Gelsthorpe & Sharpe, 2015). This approach is paternalistic, but not lenient.

Lightowlers (2018) analysed sentencing data from the Crown Courts in England and Wales and discovered that although women are sentenced more leniently than men, intoxication at the time of their crime increased the harshness of their punishment more than it did for men. Perceived gender inappropriate behaviour—being seen as troublesome rather than troubled—reduced leniency. Pina Sanchez and Harris (2020) analysed gendered sentencing disparities in relation to assault, burglary and drugs offences. They found that even controlling for mitigating factors, men were twice as likely to be imprisoned as women and received longer sentences than women. They argue this difference can be justified— imprisonment is more harmful to women, women are more open to rehabilitation and also pose less of a public threat. However, while the sentencing guidelines for England and Wales are gender neutral, sentencing itself is gendered. The role of focal concerns in sentencing is not always advantageous to women. In Germany, women are more likely to receive penalty fees for minor thefts than men, who are more likely to receive dismissal. Leuschner (2021) argues this harsher treatment of women reflects a stereotype that they are more likely to pay fees on time and in full; therefore, prosecutors see the imposition of penalty fees on women as more efficient and financially attractive.

Gender disparities are not always an aspect of sentencing. Kruttschnitt and Savolainen (2009) did not find preferential treatment for women in terms of sentencing in Finland, a country deemed to have greater gender equality than the United States or UK. Pluskota's (2018) historical research into the sentencing of petty offences in lower courts in nineteenth-century Bologna, Amsterdam and Le Havre revealed sentencing was not gendered. The trial process was rapid and of low public interest. Consequently, trials for petty crimes were not venues for the performance of gendered identities or for the reinforcement of gender norms. These findings are a useful point of comparison with contemporary American research on gender disparities as they highlight the importance of context and variation to the relevance of gender to sentencing practice.

The gendering of order, authority and control as masculine has implications for the constitution of agencies of social control such as the police and courts, the work they do and the experiences of the individuals who work within them. The default 'white maleness' of the ideal police officer, lawyer or judge is disadvantageous to the progression of those who depart from whiteness or masculinity. As agencies of power, the police and courts uphold the dominant social order, which is reflected in patterns of policing and sentencing.

References

Aiello, M. F. (2014). Policing the masculine frontier: Cultural criminological analysis of the gendered performance of policing. *Crime, Media, Culture, 10*(1), 59–79.

Atkinson, C. (2017). Patriarchy, gender, infantilisation: A cultural account of police intelligence work in Scotland. *Australian & New Zealand Journal of Criminology, 50*(2), 234–251.

Bacon, L. (2015). Liberia's gender-sensitive police reform: Improving representation and responsiveness in a post-conflict setting. *International Peacekeeping, 22*(4), 372–397.

Barrie, D. G., & Broomhall, S. (2012). *A history of police and masculinities, 1700–2010*. Routledge.

Bontrager, S., Barrick, K., & Stupi, E. (2013). Gender and sentencing: A meta-analysis of contemporary research. *Journal of Gender, Race & Justice, 16*(2), 349–372.

Boogaard, B., & Roggeband, C. (2010). Paradoxes of intersectionality: Theorizing inequality in the Dutch police force through structure and agency. *Organization, 17*(1), 53–75.

Bourne, J. (2016). *Helena Normanton and the opening of the bar to women*. Waterside Press.

Brough, P., Chataway, S., & Biggs, A. (2016). 'You don't want people knowing you're a copper!' A contemporary assessment of police organisational culture. *International Journal of Police Science & Management, 18*(1), 28–36.

Brown, J. (2007). From cult of masculinity to smart macho: Gender perspectives on police occupational culture. *Sociology of Crime, Law and Deviance, 8*, 205–226.

Bruce-Jones, E. (2015). German policing at the intersection: Race, gender, migrant status and mental health. *Race & Class, 56*(3), 36–49.

Carlin, A. (2016). The courtroom as white space: Racial performance as noncredibility. *UCLA Law Review, 63*(2), 449–484.

Cavender, G., & Jurik, N. (2007). Scene composition and justice for women: An analysis of the portrayal of Detective Tennison in the British television program Prime Suspect. *Feminist Criminology, 2*(4), 277–303.

Chancer, L. S. (2005). *High-profile crimes*. University of Chicago Press.

Chen, L., & Li, Y. (2021). Seeking 'A fair field' for women in the legal profession: Pioneering women lawyers from Burma of 1924–1935. *Britain and the World, 14*(2), 105–127.

Christiani, L. (2020). Intersectional stereotyping in policing: An analysis of traffic stop outcomes. *Politics, Groups, and Identities*, 1–23.

Chronopoulou, A. (2020). My Days of Mercy and In Between: Echoing changes in cinematic representations of women lawyers. *Athens Journal of Law, 6*, 391.

Cobbina, J. E., Conteh, M., & Emrich, C. (2019). Race, gender, and responses to the police among Ferguson residents and protesters. *Race and Justice, 9*(3), 276–303.

Colvin, R., & Moton, L. (2021). Lesbian police officers: A review of television portrayals and their lived experiences. *Public Integrity, 23*(3), 253–268.

Connell, R. W., & Messerschmidt, J. W. (2005). Hegemonic masculinity: Rethinking the concept. *Gender & Society, 19*(6), 829–859.

Creeber, G. (2001). Cigarettes and alcohol: Investigating gender, genre, and gratification in Prime Suspect. *Television & New Media, 2*(2), 149–166.

Crenshaw, K., Ritchie, A., Anspach, R., Gilmer, R., & Harris, L. (2015). *Say her name: Resisting police brutality against black women*. African American Policy Forum.

Crosby, K. (2017). Keeping women off the jury in 1920s England and Wales. *Legal Studies, 37*(4), 695–717.

Daly, K. (1989). Criminal justice ideologies and practices in different voices: Some feminist questions about justice' (1989). *International Journal of the Sociology of Law, 17*(1), 1–18.

Doerner, J. K., & Demuth, S. (2014). Gender and sentencing in the federal courts: Are women treated more leniently?". *Criminal Justice Policy Review, 25*(2), 242–269.

du Plessis, C., Winterbotham, S., Fein, E. C., Brownlow, C., du Preez, J., McKenna, B., Chen, P., Beel, N., & du Plessis, G. (2021). I'm still in the blue family: Gender and professional identity construction in police officers. *Journal of Police and Criminal Psychology, 36*(3), 386–396.

Dwyer, A. (2014). Pleasures, perversities, and partnerships: The historical emergence of LGBT-police relationships. In *Handbook of LGBT communities, crime, and justice* (pp. 149–164). Springer.

Dwyer, A. (2015). Teaching young queers a lesson: How police teach lessons about non-heteronormativity in public spaces. *Sexuality & Culture, 19*(3), 493–512.

Farrell, A., Ward, G., & Rousseau, D. (2010). Intersections of gender and race in federal sentencing: Examining court contexts and effects of representative court authorities criminal sentencing guidelines conference. *Journal of Gender, Race & Justice, 14*, 85.

Fleetwood, J., & Lea, J. (2020). De-funding the police in the UK. *British Society of Criminology Newsletter, 85*(Summer), 25–35.

Gathings, M. J., & Parrotta, K. (2013). The use of gendered narratives in the courtroom: Constructing an identity worthy of leniency. *Journal of Contemporary Ethnography, 42*(6), 668–689.

Gelsthorpe, L., & Sharpe, G. (2015). Women and sentencing: Challenges and choices. *Exploring sentencing practice in England and Wales* (pp. 118–136), Springer.

Gilbert, K. L., & Ray, R. (2016). Why police kill black males with impunity: Applying public health critical race praxis (PHCRP) to address the determinants of policing behaviors and "justifiable" homicides in the USA. *Journal of Urban Health, 93*(1), 122–140.

Goodman, C. C. (2017). Nevertheless she persisted: From Mrs. Bradwell to Annalise Keating, gender bias in the courtroom 2017 special issue: Enhancing women's effect on law enforcement in the age of police and protest. *Wm. & Mary J. Women & L., 24*(1), 167–198.

Gültekin, K., Leichtman, E. C., & Garrison, C. G. (2010). Gender issues and the women of the Turkish National Police. *Police Practice and Research, 11*(5), 423–436.

Haake, U. (2018). Conditions for gender equality in police leadership—Making way for senior police women. *Police Practice and Research, 19*(3), 241–252.

Hagelin, S., & Silverman, G. (2017). The female antihero and police power in FX's Justified. *Feminist Media Studies, 17*(5), 851–865.

Heidensohn, F. (1992). *Women in control?: The role of women in law enforcement*. Clarendon Press.

Jackson, L. A. (2006). *Women police: Gender, welfare and surveillance in the twentieth century*. Manchester University Press.

Javaid, A. (2021). A hierarchy of masculinity and sexuality: Gendering the police, and the obfuscation of policing sexual violence against non-heterosexual victims. In *Sexual Violence on Trial* (pp. 133–145). Routledge.

Kenney, S. (2012). *Gender and justice: Why women in the judiciary really matter*. Routledge.

Klatzer, E., & Schlager, C. (2020). Losing grounds: Masculine-authoritarian reconfigurations of power structures in the European Union. In S. Wohl, E. Springler, M. Pachel, & B. Zeilinger (Eds.), *The State of the European Union* (pp. 45–75). Springer.

Kruttschnitt, C., & Savolainen, J. (2009). Ages of chivalry, places of paternalism: Gender and criminal sentencing in Finland. *European Journal of Criminology, 6*(3), 225–247.

Kurtz, D. L., & Upton, L. L. (2018). The gender in stories: How war stories and police narratives shape masculine police culture. *Women & Criminal Justice, 28*(4), 282–300.

Lanham, M., Ridgeway, K., Dayton, R., Castillo, B. M., Brennan, C., Davis, D. A., Emmanuel, D., Morales, G. J., Cheririser, C., Rodriguez, B., Cooke, J., Santi, K., & Evens, E. (2019). "We're going to leave you to last, because of how you are": Transgender women's experiences of gender-based violence in healthcare, education and police encounters in Latin America and the Caribbean. *Violence and Gender, 6*, 37–46.

Lee, C. (2015). Gender bias in the courtroom: Combating implicit bias against women trial attorneys and litigators. *Cardozo Journal of Law & Gender, 22*(2), 229–252.

Leuschner, F. (2021). Exploring gender disparities in the prosecution of theft cases: Propensity score matching on data from German court files. *European Journal of Criminology*. https://doi.org/10.1177/14773708211003011

Lightowlers, C. (2018). Drunk and doubly deviant? The role of gender and intoxication in sentencing assault offences. *The British Journal of Criminology, 59*(3), 693–717.

Loftus, B. (2009). *Police culture in a changing world*. Oxford University Press.

Loftus, B. (2010). Police occupational culture: Classic themes, altered times. *Policing and Society, 20*(1), 1–20.

Logan, A. (2007). In search of equal citizenship: The campaign for women magistrates in England and Wales, 1910–1939. *Women's History Review, 16*(4), 501–518.

Logan, A. (2013). 'Building a new and better order'? Women and jury service in England and Wales, c.1920–70. *Women's History Review, 22*(5), 701–716.

Martin, S. E., & Jurik, N. C. (2006). *Doing justice, doing gender: Women in legal and criminal justice occupations*. Sage.

Marx Ferree, M. (2020). The crisis of masculinity for gendered democracies: Before, during, and after Trump. *Sociological Forum, 35*(S1), 898–917.

Mason, M., & Vaughan, S. (2017). *Sexuality at the bar: An empirical exploration into the experiences of LGBT+ Barristers in England & Wales* (University of Westminster School of Law Research Paper).

Mennicke, A., Gromer, J., Oehme, K., & MacConnie, L. (2018). Workplace experiences of gay and lesbian criminal justice officers in the United States: A qualitative investigation of officers attending a LGBT law enforcement conference. *Policing and Society, 28*(6), 712–729.

Morash, M., & Haarr, R. N. (2011). Doing, redoing, and undoing gender: Variation in gender identities of women working as police officers. *Feminist Criminology, 7*(1), 3–23.

Munby, J. (2015). Art in the age of "New Jim Crow": Delimiting the scope of racial justice and Black film production since Rodney King. In J. Metcalf & C. Spaulding (Eds.), *African American culture and society after Rodney King: Provocations and protests, progression and "post-racialism"*. Ashgate.

Murray, S. E. (2021). Seeing and doing gender at work: A qualitative analysis of Canadian male and female police officers. *Feminist Criminology, 16*(1), 91–109.

Natarajan, M. (2014). Police culture and the integration of women officers in India. *International Journal of Police Science & Management, 16*(2), 124–139.

Olson, G. (2013). Intersections of gender and legal culture in two women judge shows: Judge Judy and Richterin Barbara Salesch. In H. Petersen, J. M. L. Villaverde, & I. Lund-Andersen (Eds.), *Contemporary Gender Relations and Changes in Legal Cultures* (pp. 29–58). DJOF. Forthcoming.

Panter, H. (2018). *Transgender cops: The intersection of gender and sexuality expectations in police cultures*. Routledge.

Pepitone, R. (2016). Gender, space, and ritual: Women barristers, the inns of court, and the interwar press. *Journal of Women's History, 28*(1), 60–83.

Pickles, J. (2020). Policing hate and bridging communities: A qualitative evaluation of relations between LGBT+ people and the police within the North East of England. *Policing and Society, 30*(7), 741–759.

Pina Sanchez, J., & Harris, L. (2020). Sentencing gender? Investigating the presence of gender disparities in Crown Court sentences. *Criminal Law Review, 2020*(1), 3–28.

Pluskota, M. (2018). Petty criminality, gender bias, and judicial practice in nineteenth-century Europe. *Journal of Social History, 51*(4), 717–735.

Porter, L. E., & Prenzler, T. (2017). Police officer gender and excessive force complaints: An Australian study. *Policing and Society, 27*(8), 865–883.

Prenzler, T., & Sinclair, G. (2013). The status of women police officers: An international review. *International Journal of Law, Crime and Justice, 41*(2), 115–131.

Rackley, E. (2012). *Women, judging and the judiciary: From difference to diversity*. Routledge-Cavendish.

Ragusa, A. T., & Groves, P. (2012). Gendered meritocracy? Women senior counsels in Australia's legal profession. *Australian Journal of Gender and Law, 1*, 1–17.

Rawski, S. L., & Workman-Stark, A. L. (2018). Masculinity contest cultures in policing organizations and recommendations for training interventions. *Journal of Social Issues, 74*(3), 607–627.

Reiner, R. (2010). *The politics of the police*. Oxford University Press.

Rengifo, A. F., & Pater, M. (2017). Close call: Race and gender in encounters with the police by Black and Latino/a youth in New York City. *Sociological Inquiry, 87*(2), 337–361.

Rennstam, J., & Sullivan, K. R. (2018). Peripheral inclusion through informal silencing and voice—A Study of LGB officers in the Swedish Police. *Gender, Work & Organization, 25*(2), 177–194.

Ritchie, A. J., & Jones-Brown, D. (2017). Policing race, gender, and sex: A review of law enforcement policies. *Women & Criminal Justice, 27*(1), 21–50.

Romain Dagenhardt, D. M. (2020). Observing gender and race discourses in probation review hearings. *Feminist Criminology, 15*(4), 492–515.

Rossler, M. T., Rabe-Hemp, C. E., Peuterbaugh, M., & Scheer, C. (2020). Influence of gender on perceptions of barriers to a police patrol career. *Police Quarterly, 23*(3), 368–395.

Rumens, N., & Broomfield, J. (2012). Gay men in the police: Identity disclosure and management issues. *Human Resource Management Journal, 22*(3), 283–298.

Russell, E. K. (2016). A 'fair cop': Queer histories, affect and police image work in Pride March. *Crime, Media, Culture, 13*(3), 277–293.

Scharrer, E. (2012). More than "Just the facts"?: Portrayals of masculinity in police and detective programs over time. *Howard Journal of Communications, 23*(1), 88–109.

Schultz, U., & Shaw, G. (2013). *Gender and judging*. Bloomsbury Publishing.

Schulz, J. L., & Youn, J. (2020). Monsters and madwomen? Neurosis, ambition and mothering in women lawyers in film. *Law, Culture and the Humanities, 16*(3), 411–431.

Serpe, C. R., & Nadal, K. L. (2017). Perceptions of police: Experiences in the trans* community. *Journal of Gay & Lesbian Social Services, 29*(3), 280–299.

Sheffield, R. (1993). On film: A social history of women lawyers in popular culture 1930–1990. *Loyola of Los Angeles Entertainment Law Review, 14*, 73.

Silvestri, M. (2017). Police culture and gender: Revisiting the 'cult of masculinity'. *Policing: A Journal of Policy and Practice, 11*(3), 289–300.

Silvestri, M., Tong, S., & Brown, J. (2013). Gender and police leadership: Time for a paradigm shift? *International Journal of Police Science & Management, 15*(1), 61–73.

Steffensmeier, D., Painter-Davis, N., & Ulmer, J. (2017). Intersectionality of race, ethnicity, gender, and age on criminal punishment. *Sociological Perspectives, 60*(4), 810–833.

Steffensmeier, D. J. (1980). Assessing the impact of the women's movement on sex-based differences in the handling of adult criminal defendants. *Crime & Delinquency, 26*(3), 344–357.

Stroshine, M. S., & Brandl, S. G. (2011). Race, gender, and tokenism in policing: An empirical elaboration. *Police Quarterly, 14*(4), 344–365.

Swan, A. A. (2016). Masculine, feminine, or androgynous: The influence of gender identity on job satisfaction among female police officers. *Women & Criminal Justice, 26*(1), 1–19.

Thompson, V. E. (2021). Policing in Europe: Disability justice and abolitionist intersectional care. *Race & Class, 62*(3), 61–76.

Treanor, L. (2020). Problems in the pathways to judicial success: Women in the legal profession in Northern Ireland. *International Journal of the Legal Profession, 27*(2), 203–216.

Wei, S., & Xiong, M. (2020). Judges' gender and sentencing in China: An empirical inquiry. *Feminist Criminology, 15*(2), 217–250.

Weissmann, E. (2016). Women, television and feelings: Theorising emotional difference of gender in SouthLAnd and Mad Men. In *Emotions in Contemporary TV Series* (pp. 87–101). Springer.

Williams, S. (2016). #SayHerName: Using digital activism to document violence against black women. *Feminist Media Studies, 16*(5), 922–925.

Wilton, S. (2018). Mothers hunting murderers: Representations of motherhood in Broadchurch and Happy Valley. *Clues, 36*(1), 101–110.

Wright, J. E., & Headley, A. M. (2020). Police use of force interactions: Is race relevant or gender germane? *The American Review of Public Administration, 50*(8), 851–864.

8

Prison and Community Penalties

Social control in the form of enacting punishment is one of the primary emblems of state power. As well as affecting the individuals who experience it, punishment sends a message to the wider community and demonstrates the authority of the state. 'Grand theorising' about the role punishment, particularly imprisonment, in the late twentieth and early twenty-first centuries has emphasised the connection between the political and economic order and the way social control is enacted. Frequently, this grand theorising has ignored or underplayed the significance of gender (Bosworth & Kaufman, 2012). Race has been better integrated into 'grand theories', although its intersections with gender have not (Baldry & Cunneen, 2014). Gender is central to understanding punishment in two ways: the politics that underpin punishment are gendered; and the practice of punishment is a form of gendered governance.

Strategies of punishment based on control and containment exemplify a masculinist vision of 'tough' state power, which dismisses alternative approaches as soft and effeminate (Kohler-Hausmann, 2017). Kohler-Hausmann argues that in the context of the United States, this gendered politics has drawn on racialised and gendered tropes of dangerous Black

© The Author(s), under exclusive license to Springer Nature
Switzerland AG 2022
L. Seal, *Gender, Crime and Justice*,
https://doi.org/10.1007/978-3-030-87488-9_8

masculinity and Black women as a drain on state resources to justify a tough approach. Masculinist politics have underpinned the expansion of incarceration but also welfare retrenchment. Attention to strategies of punishment as one aspect of gendered governance among others helps to contextualise punishment and further highlights the centrality of gender to social control. Gelsthorpe (2010) emphasises the need to pay attention to wider discourses of 'moral tutelage' beyond punishment, which guide political approaches to punishment and welfare and also do work on a micro level in families and institutional settings.

The historical development of punishment has been intertwined with the maintenance of gendered and racialised hierarchies (Haley, 2016). Ideologies of gender and race have a 'carceral life' and punishment is one element of entrenching the gendered racial order. Haley (2016) examines the state of Georgia to argue the treatment of imprisoned Black women was important to the history of white supremacy and the development of the southern penal regime. Black women were othered as being outside of the gender binary, which solidified white womanhood as a coherent identity. Gross (2015) highlights that in nineteenth-century America, Black women were subject to the law's punishment but were not entitled to its protection. Black women made a highly disproportionate share of the female prison population. In 1904, 90% of female prisoners in the American South were Black. Unlike white women, Black women worked on prison chain gangs alongside men.

Representations of slavery depict the use of cruel punishment, implicitly connecting past and present. *12 Years a Slave* (2014), based on a memoir by Solomon Northrup, depicts slavery as a system of racialised terror and as a disciplinary system upholding the racial order of white supremacy. Solomon endures physical beating and a near lynching, and is forced to whip Patsey, an enslaved woman. Physical violence perpetrated by white owners and overseers against Black enslaved people, both incidental and life-threatening, is shown to be integral to slavery as a system (Ball, 2016). These scenes of physical violence are shocking and brutal, but the film portrays how they exist alongside the 'everyday' experiences of slavery such as being taken to market and examined by potential buyers (Thaggert, 2014). Ball (2016) argues the film trenchantly demonstrates how slavery itself was an act of violence.

Men frequently account for the majority of those subjected to state punishment but there is historical variation. More women than men were committed to penal custody in Barbados 1873–1917, which was a consequence of high rates of male migration. Women made up 60% of the workforce, mainly as plantation labourers and domestic servants. Penal practice was shaped by the planter elite's labour concerns—the need to control a large and seasonally employed workforce, and gender-based concerns—the social control of Black women in the context of a lack of patriarchal control (Green, 2012). Murdocca (2013) argues that Canadian white settler society enacted racial governance through a particular construction of racialised difference as cultural difference. This construction was bound together with forms of rule, which justified differential treatment of Indigenous people on the grounds of cultural difference. This approach has disadvantaged Indigenous people, and Indigenous women especially.

Theorisations of the expansion of mass incarceration, the new penology and the culture of control need to be nuanced to incorporate intersections of gender and race. In Australia and New Zealand, the application of punishment is highly racialised, with Indigenous people experiencing imprisonment at a rate of many times that of white people. In New Zealand, Maori men form over half of the sentenced male prison population but only 15% of the general population (McIntosh & Workman, 2017). As a group, Maori women had the fastest growing incarceration rate in New Zealand in the 2010s (Deckert, 2020). Indigenous women constitute 34% of the Australian women's prison population but make up 2% of the general population (Baldry & Cunneen, 2014). This disparity means Indigenous women are incarcerated at 1.6 times the rate of non-Indigenous men (Stubbs, 2020). Documentary *Prison Songs* (2015) portrays the day-to-day lives of inmates in Berrimah prison in Darwin, Australia, where more than 80% of prisoners are Indigenous. It explores the lives of participants before they came to prison and the process of writing songs based on their experiences. Analyses of the punitive turn in Western countries in late modernity overlook the continuity in harsh punishment experienced by Indigenous people under white settler colonialism, and how they have been subject to distinct forms of racialised and gendered control (Baldry & Cunneen, 2014; Stubbs, 2020). Baldry and Cunneen (2014) argue Indigenous Australians were never the recipients of penal welfarism, an approach to punishment based on rehabilitation and treatment, but have experienced a harsh colonial mode of penality.

Gendered Imprisonment

All forms of punishment, social control and 'moral tutelage' are gendered but prison demonstrates the gendering of punishment, and its role in gendered governance, particularly starkly. Prison reinforces wider normative values, and one of these is the masculine/feminine gender binary (Bosworth & Kaufman, 2012; Richie, 2012). Bosworth and Kaufman (2012) argue prison does not just reflect this binary, it is also an important site for solidifying and propagating it. Prison reform in mid-nineteenth-century Jamaica was integral to wider attempts by colonial authorities to refashion gender relations after slavery ended. Gender segregation in prison was instituted in order to enact the gender binary; for example, women did domestic labour such as washing and cooking, men broke stones and did agricultural work (Paton, 2004). This gendered division was a colonial introduction and instantiated colonial power (Lugones, 2007).

Gendered differences in prison regimes uphold the wider gender order. Carlen (1983) connects the non-penal disciplining of women via domesticity with disciplinary regimes in women's prisons that aimed to cultivate domesticity. Her findings from studying a Scottish prison in the early 1980s demonstrated the historical continuity of gendered discipline. In Victorian England, women criminals were judged against the middle-class standard of the 'ideal' woman and prison regimes developed in order to restore the imprisoned woman to appropriate femininity (Zedner, 1991). These middle-class standards of femininity were directly related to the coloniality of gender, perceived to be a marker of British superiority. *Affinity* (2008) adapts a novel by Sarah Waters about Margaret, an upper middle-class woman in the 1870s who becomes a prison visitor to a women's prison and enters a romantic relationship with

Selina, one of the inmates. It draws parallels between the surveillance and gender regulation of Victorian families and medicine, and imprisonment. Margaret and Selina do not conform to appropriate femininity and experience different, but related, forms of confinement (Millbank, 2004).

In the twentieth century, perceptions of women criminals as mentally unstable to an extent displaced moralistic views, but the notion that women and men required differential treatment in prison remained (Zedner, 1991). McCorkel (2013) argues in California in the 1990s the women's prison regime shifted from emphasising rehabilitation to individual responsibilisation and self-regulation. However, the notion that women and men were different, and belonged in separate institutions, persisted. Russian prison regimes seek to 'refeminise' women prisoners, one aspect of which is to hold beauty pageants that judge women according to both feminine appearance and the demonstration of domestic skills (Moran et al., 2009). *Miss Gulag* (2007) explores the life stories of three participants in the 'Miss Spring' beauty pageant in a Russian prison and *La Corona* (2008) depicts a prison beauty pageant in Bogota, Colombia. Both documentaries use the pageants as a means to examine gender discipline in women's prisons (Matthews, 2015).

Prisons as institutions are gendered and racialised projects (Britton, 2003). The generic prisoner is male and notions of 'dangerous' masculinity are embedded in the disciplinary structure of prisons (Curtis, 2014). In the United States, understandings of dangerous masculinity are racialised, influenced by stereotypes about the putative hyperviolence and hypersexuality of Black men in particular. Shabazz (2015) traces the development of punitive techniques deployed by white American authorities against Black men from slave ships and plantations into prisons to argue Black masculinity has been shaped by carceral power. The farm system in Southern penitentiaries was based on hard agricultural labour, reproducing the conditions of chattel slavery. The system was justified by racist logic about the best way to discipline Black criminals and eschewed rehabilitation. *The Farm: Angola USA* (1998) depicts inmate experiences in Angola prison, Louisiana, which was built on a former slave plantation. At the time it was made, the prison population was three quarters Black with a white administration, mirroring the racialised repression of the plantation. As discussed, Black women were sometimes required to perform the same physical labour as men, reflecting a denial of their womanhood (Britton, 2003). Alves (2014) argues the Brazilian prison system is organised around 'racial knowledge' that reproduces the colonial order and represents a carceral continuum between slavery and the present-day penal regime. *Brazil: An Inconvenient History* (2008) examines Brazil's history as a Portuguese colony with a huge enslaved population. *13th* (2016) traces the links between chattel slavery and subsequent forms of institutionalised racism in the United States and mass incarceration. It is named after the Thirteenth Amendment to the American constitution, which abolished slavery and involuntary servitude, except as punishment for a crime.

The role of prison regimes in upholding and reproducing the gender binary has profound implications for trans and gender non-conforming people who may be prisoned in an institution that does not match their gender identity (Jenness & Fenstermaker, 2014; Pemberton, 2013). Prisons recognise people as either female or male (Jenness & Fenstermaker, 2014). Individuals who do not fit this binary exceed the limits of carceral gender. Imprisoned trans people face barriers in accessing appropriate healthcare, including hormones that enable gender expression (Hughto et al., 2018). Trans women incarcerated in men's prisons experience high levels of violence, including sexual violence (Hughto et al., 2018; Jenness & Fenstermaker, 2014). *Where Justice Ends* (2019) examines the experiences of trans people in American prisons, such as sexual violence from staff and inmates, inadequate medical care and disproportionate application of solitary confinement. Fundamentally, the organisation of the prison system around the gender binary stigmatises gender non-conformity and renders trans and gender non-conforming people abnormal (Hughto et al., 2018). This represents an urgent problem for trans and gender non-conforming people in prison and exemplifies the role of the penal system in upholding the wider gender order.

Case study:

CeCe McDonald, a Black trans woman, was charged with second degree murder in Minneapolis in 2011 after killing a white cisgender man who along with a group verbally abused her with racial and transphobic slurs. Although arguing she acted in self-defence, McDonald pled guilty to second degree manslaughter rather than face a murder trial. She served her sentence in two men's prisons (Johnson, 2013). A campaign for her release highlighted the violence trans women of colour experience in prison and after being released in 2014 McDonald became a prominent prison abolition campaigner (Fischer, 2016). *FREE CeCe* (2013), made while she was still incarcerated, relates her story and the wider issue of endemic violence against trans women of colour.

Case study:

Sophia Burset, Orange is the New Black. The most internationally viewed representation of women's imprisonment in recent years, *Orange is the New Black* (2013–2019) depicts a fictional women's prison in upstate New York. It was ground breaking in portraying a trans character, Sophia Burset, played by trans actor Laverne Cox, and in highlighting issues pertaining to trans prisoners such as the struggle to gain access to hormone therapies and experiences of transphobic abuse. Thomas (2019) argues *Orange is the New Black*'s portrayal of Sophia humanises trans people and advocates for the recognition of their rights and personhood but does not sufficiently address intersections of race and gender.

Experiences of Imprisonment: Women and Femininity

The global prison population is rising—it has grown by more than 20% since 2002, and in 2020 stood at over eleven million people (Penal Reform International & Thailand Institute of Justice, 2020). Sudbury

(2005) describes this expansion of imprisonment as 'global lockdown', which has disproportionately impacted women of colour, Indigenous women and women in the Global South. Since 2000, the women's prison population worldwide has grown by 50% (Penal Reform International & Thailand Institute of Justice, 2020). Increasingly harsh penalties for drugs-related crimes, the criminalisation of migration and lengthening prison sentences help to explain this growth (Harmon & Boppre, 2018; Sudbury, 2005). Women prison populations in Southeast Asia are comparatively large, with several countries in the region having twice the proportion of women prisoners as the global average. Punitive drug laws and policies have driven this situation (Chuenurah & Sornprohm, 2020). Documentary *Conviction* (2019) was made collaboratively between imprisoned women in Nova Scotia, Canada and filmmakers. It highlights that women are the fastest growing segment of the prison population. The three-part *Women in Prison* (2016) examines the distinct needs of incarcerated women in American prisons in the context of the dramatic increase in the number of women in prison.

Globally, women account for around 10% of the prison population (Penal Reform International & Thailand Institute of Justice, 2020). In most contexts, it is true to state that women are far less likely to be imprisoned than men although as discussed, Indigenous women in Australia have a higher rate of imprisonment than non-Indigenous men (Stubbs, 2020). Such intersectional variation is important to bear in mind. Women's comparative rarity in the prison system can mean they are a forgotten or ignored population (Pallot et al., 2012). Fewer institutions for women have the consequence that women may be incarcerated far from their homes, making visits from friends and relatives difficult and expensive. Pallot et al. (2012) highlight isolation and incarceration far from home as an extreme condition of women's imprisonment in Russia. *Babs: Russian Women in Prison* (2000) shows harsh conditions in a remote women's prison in Russia. Maria Alyokhina and Nadezhda Tolokonnikova, members of Russian feminist punk band, Pussy Riot, were imprisoned for a performance of one of their songs outside Moscow Cathedral in 2012. Granted amnesties in 2013, they have campaigned to highlight 'slave labour conditions' and abuse in women's prisons (Mescheryakov & Wesolowsky, 2019).

Most imprisoned women are convicted of non-violent crimes, and frequently these are crimes of survival related to poverty, such as welfare fraud, minor property crimes, sex work and drug offences (Balfour, 2013; Malloch & McIvor, 2013). Women in prison report experience of high levels of victimisation through gender-based violence, and disproportionately experience mental health and addiction-related problems. They have often lived lives of extreme economic precariousness (Frois, 2017; Russell et al., 2020). The trauma that imprisoned women have experienced in their lives is compounded by incarceration (Carlton & Segrave, 2011). The second series of *Prison* (2020) was filmed inside Foston Hall, an English women's prison. It highlights the impact of the women's prior experiences of physical, emotional and sexual abuse and issues related to addiction. Globally, women of colour are 'hyperpresent' in prison systems, including the stark overrepresentation of Indigenous women in prison populations (Balfour, 2013; Bell, 2017; Sudbury, 2005). Balfour (2013) argues that contemporary trends in imprisonment demonstrate that 'global lockdown' is a form of state violence against poor women, women of colour and Indigenous women.

Fictional portrayals of women's prisons in television shows are one of the key ways members of the public are exposed to issues related to women's imprisonment. This makes them consequential for how women prisoners and their lives are understood, and shapes attitudes to women's punishment (Cecil, 2007; DeCarvalho, 2021). Piper Kerman, the main character in *Orange is the New Black* (2013–2019), is white and upper middle class making her atypical in terms of the women's prison population. However, the novelty of her privileged social position acts as a device for bringing wider issues to the audience (Schwan, 2016). *Orange is the New Black*'s storylines depict sexual assault in prison, women's histories of abuse and addiction, attempted suicide, gender identity and racism (Terry, 2016). Schwan (2016) argues that in doing so, the show tacitly critiques the mass incarceration of women and supports prison reform. Similarly, the Mexican series *Capadocia* (2008–2012) and Australian series *Wentworth* (2013-present) portray social issues related to imprisonment and the complexity of imprisoned women's lives (DeCarvalho, 2021; Smith, 2018). In particular, *Wentworth* highlights indigeneity and imprisonment by having three Indigenous women as the main characters. DeCarvalho (2021) praises the nuanced performances of these characters and storylines that address the pervasiveness of racism and the role of prison in perpetuating oppression of Indigenous women. She notes, however, that the vast overrepresentation of Indigenous women in the Australian prison system is not portrayed.

Gender Responsiveness

Acknowledgement that women prisoners have different histories and different needs from men has influenced penal policy and practice across several jurisdictions, and to an extent represents the incorporation of certain feminist principles into the penal system (Hannah-Moffat, 2010). Bloom et al.'s (2003) gender responsive strategies for working with women who commit crime were developed to underpin and advance gendered justice, and recognise women's histories of abuse, trauma and addiction. Gender responsiveness entails focussing on women's practical needs through appropriate programming that is multidimensional across areas such as housing, education and healthcare, and includes women's children and families.

Hannah-Moffat (2010) argues that gender responsiveness contains normative assumptions about women's greater capacity for interpersonal relationships. Gender responsive programming conflicts with another imperative of contemporary penality—risk assessment. Gender sensitive risk assessment tools transform women's 'needs' into 'risks', with normative understandings of peer, intimate and parental relationships forming the basis of gendered governance. In the Canadian context, Indigenous women in particular are characterised as having 'high risk needs' that cast doubt on their perceived potential to rehabilitate (Hannah-Moffat, 2010). Player (2014) examines how in the United Kingdom prisons, and the criminal justice system more widely, are required by law to ensure gender equality. Coupled with this has been a policy approach that recognises differences between women and men, and emphasises the benefits for women of holistic community-based programmes rather than incarceration. However, this gender responsive trend has been contradicted by a risk assessment framework that does not fit with a holistic approach. Other sentencing imperatives, such as the 'need' for punishment if deserved, also undermine gender responsiveness.

The adoption of gender responsive strategies in women's prisons and other areas of the criminal justice system did not result in fewer women being sent to prison, with consequences for marginalised women who are most at risk from being imprisoned. Gendered reform can compound women's experiences of punishment by increasing its legitimacy (Segrave & Carlton, 2013). Carlen (2002) describes this enhanced legitimacy as 'carceral clawback', whereby the justification for women's prisons is presented as something other than punishment—for addiction treatment, parenting training, or providing 'life skills' and education. Gender responsive programming explicitly legitimises punishment by making it more 'suitable' for women and therefore consistent with notions of rights and gender equality. Segrave and Carlton (2010) argue prison can protect women from significant harms by providing access to addiction support and respite from a violent male partner. However, prison is not rehabilitative; it might offer a break from problems on the outside but not solutions. It deepens trauma and does not address long-term causes of social harms.

The majority of imprisoned women are mothers of children under the age of eighteen (Malloch & McIvor, 2013; McCorkel, 2013). Reflecting the gender order, women are more likely than men to have been living with their children prior to incarceration (Barnes & Stringer, 2014; Freitas et al., 2016). In England and Wales, only 5% of the children of imprisoned women remain in their family home, the others are mainly taken care of by other relatives. Booth (2017) describes women's imprisonment as a 'family sentence' because of its disruptiveness to family life. Imprisonment is an assault on women's mothering identities. 'Doing motherhood', in the form of activities such as cooking meals, reading bedtime stories and helping with homework becomes impossible (Booth, 2017). If women are incarcerated a long distance from their families, maintaining contact can be difficult. Visits from children to prison entail a whirl of emotions for mothers, from joy at spending time with their children to feelings of loss and grief when the visit ends (Baldwin, 2018).

Imprisonment connotes 'bad' motherhood and having failed as a mother (Baldwin, 2018; Booth, 2017). This negatively affects women's identities as 'successful' mothering is a constituent part of doing normative femininity and meeting cultural expectations of womanhood. Imprisoned mothers frequently feel stigmatised, their mothering identities are 'spoiled' and become a basis for stigma rather than approbation (Booth, 2017; Easterling & Feldmeyer, 2017). This stigma can be intensified by racism. Deckert's (2020) analysis of news media portrayals of criminalised women in New Zealand found negative portrayals of Maori women were compounded by more frequently mentioning they were mothers than in stories about Pakeha (white) women. 'Prisoner' is a master status so powerful it overrides other aspects of identity, including motherhood (Haney, 2013). Baldwin's (2018) interviews with English women who had experienced imprisonment revealed some of them did not tell their children they had been to prison if their sentence was prior to motherhood, or when their children were too young to remember. Johnston's (2019) historical analysis of mothers in Victorian English prisons shows imprisonment disrupted women's lives and identities, as well as their children's lives—who often ended up in institutional care. Prisons were not designed to sustain mothering, a finding which resonates in the twenty-first century.

Some prisons have mother and baby, or mother and child units, or allow young children to stay in prison with their mothers. Freitas et al. (2016) discuss practices in different countries, which range from not allowing children to stay in prisons at all, to allowing babies or children up to the age of six. In Portugal, children can remain in prison with their mothers up to the age of three and it is left to the woman's own decision as to whether to have her (small) children with her. Women experienced advantages and disadvantages; they were able to maintain closeness with their children but had to do so in an environment inimical to the 'usual' exercise of motherhood (Freitas et al., 2016). From her research in a mother and child unit in California, Haney (2013) argues that in prison, motherhood is undermined and subsumed by punishment. Constant surveillance, lack of privacy and lack of control over their daily routine undercut women's mothering. At the same time, the unit espoused a model of 'intensive mothering' against which women were heavily judged. Resonant with critiques of gender responsive punishment, motherhood was turned into a technique of penal control. Documentary *Mothers of Bedford* (2011) shows over a four-year period a Children's Centre mothering programme at a high security prison in New York state that provides parenting training and promotes sustaining ties between women and their children. The programme garners success in enabling women to have meaningful relationships with their children.

Men and Masculinity

Men's prisons are hypermasculine environments and a gendered performance of exaggerated masculinity, exhibiting a willingness to fight, is needed as a form of protection from violence and to survive within the dominant culture (Hefner, 2018; Jewkes, 2005b). Bodily performance of physical toughness through working out in the gym is a visual marker of hypermasculinity (Ricciardelli, 2015). Status hierarchies based on toughness and physical strength are important because the majority of imprisoned men have low economic and political power. The display of hypermasculinity assumes high symbolic importance as the means to achieve status (Michalski, 2015). Other routes to hegemonic masculinity are blocked by the experience of imprisonment: independence is removed, men cannot perform the breadwinner role for their families, influence they may have had on the outside is irrelevant (Bandyopadhyay, 2006). Incarceration in prison places men in a feminised position in which they lose control of their identities and hypermasculinity is a partial solution to this feminisation (Sloan, 2016).

Fighting is a means to achieve social status and to accomplish being a 'real' man—one who shows strength and conceals weakness (Michalski, 2015; Morse & Wright, 2019). Saving face and not backing down are at a premium in adult male prisons and secure institutions for boys (Phillips, 2012; Ricciardelli, 2015). In order to enhance status, violence must be consistent with the 'inmate code'—it should be in response to violence or to express grievance. Uncontrolled aggression is not consistent with the code, which Michalski (2015) compares to Anderson's (1999) code of the street. Status is also related to the perceived masculinity of the crimes men are convicted for. In Canadian prisons, Ricciardelli (2015) argues armed robbery and drug dealing are crimes with high status; in Indian prisons 'lifers' gain the most respect (Bandyopadhyay, 2006). Sex offenders, and men who have victimised women or children, are at the bottom of the hierarchy. Men who are unable to defend themselves from violence in prison are subordinate in the hierarchy, especially if they are victims of sexual violence (Michalski, 2015). Gear (2010) argues in South African prisons, sexual violence against another man confirms the masculinity and status of the perpetrator while 'unmanning' the victim.

Performing heterosexuality through expressing the desire to have sex with women and flirting with women prison staff is another aspect of the inmate code and necessary for safety. Being gay is associated with weakness and femininity, and men who are in sexual relationships with other men in prison usually seek to hide it (Hefner, 2018). Trans women and other gender non-conforming people incarcerated in men's prisons experience high levels of sexual and other violence. Their violation of heteronormativity and codes of masculinity means gender non-conforming people are understood by staff and inmates as having failed to 'man up' (Jenness & Fenstermaker, 2014).

The 'prison genre' in fictional portrayals was typically of men's prisons and represented a hypermasculine world where women, and femininity, were absent (Cuklanz & Erol, 2021). Television show *Oz* (1997–2003) is set in an experimental unit in a high security prison and was the first American series to focus on prison life—prior to that, the prison genre was confined to film (Yousman, 2009). The only women to appear are two medical staff, it otherwise depicts a homosocial environment (Foss, 2018). Violence is central to the inmate hierarchy and is a means for individuals to exert dominance and control over others (Cuklanz & Erol, 2021). The prisoners are shown lifting weights and boxing, which enable them to engage in the 'masculine masquerade' of a tough body. Depiction of spectacular violence in *Oz* drives the dramatic momentum of the show, rather than a more realistic portrayal of stasis and boredom (Jarvis, 2005). Murder is routine, as are baroque and sadistic violent acts (Yousman, 2009). Sexual assault and rape are also frequently depicted, with sexual predators targeting 'vulnerable' characters (Foss, 2018). Yousman (2009) highlights that *Oz* aired on television while the American prison population rapidly expanded. As such, it represents men at the bottom of the race and class hierarchy as resorting to their 'natural' behaviour of uncontrolled violence and tacitly justifies punitive criminal justice policies.

Documentaries about prison frequently exhibit fascination with hard masculinities and tough prison regimes, including titles such as *The Most Notorious Gangs in Prison* (2015) and *America's Toughest Prisons* (2006-present). *Inside the World's Toughest Prisons* (2016-present) features men's prisons from around the world, emphasising harsh conditions, violence and chaos. Other documentary series such as *Prison* (2019) and *Inside Prison: Britain Behind Bars* (2019) highlight issues such as drug use, mental health problems and violence between prisoners and prison staff while taking a less sensationalised approach.

While men's prisons internationally are sites of violence, status and hierarchy, prison masculinities are more complex, diverse and contradictory than hypermasculinity alone. Maguire (2021) argues the conceptualisation of prison masculinity needs to be broadened beyond hegemonic and hypermasculinity to incorporate vulnerable carceral masculinities and attention to low status prisoners. Crewe (2014) acknowledges that the environment of a men's prison requires suppression of emotion. However, men form 'homosocial' bonds with each other that provide a sense of fraternity and emotional support. Living together means engaging in mundane routines and rituals that foster intimacy, such as making tea and watching television. Prison life entails exhibiting a front of toughness but also experiences of special bonds with other men based on nurturance and closeness (Rymhs, 2012). Men's masculine identities are not fixed or monolithic, but rather are variable, context specific and in flux (Bartlett & Eriksson, 2019; Morse & Wright, 2019; Phillips, 2012). Fictional portrayals such as *Oz* do not focus on the mundane day-to-day of prison. 1970s British sitcom *Porridge* (1974–1977) is not a realistic dramatisation of prison life at the time; it is intentionally light-hearted and does not represent prison violence or the basic living conditions men in prison would have endured in the 1970s. However, as

Jewkes (2005a) highlights, like most sitcoms *Porridge* is primarily about relationships. The central father/son type relationship between old timer Fletcher and first timer Godber acknowledges the homosocial bonding between male prisoners that provides emotional support.

Prison life has an emotional geography, with certain 'intermediate zones' in which emotion can be more freely expressed than in other areas. These include spaces such as the visiting room, classrooms and the chaplaincy, where impression management in relation to hypermasculinity does not have to be as carefully managed as on the wings (Crewe et al., 2014). Documentaries *The Work* (2017), which is about a group therapy retreat for men incarcerated in Folsom State Prison, California and *College Behind Bars* (2019), which shows men and women prisoners undertaking college level education in two New York prisons, communicate the importance of these rehabilitative programmes but also the significance of intermediate zones in facilitating greater emotional expression. One such other intermediate, or ambiguous, space is the self-cook area found in some prisons (Earle & Phillips, 2012). Preparing and sharing food offers some relief from the prison regime. It also involves the negotiation of identity in relation to gender, race and ethnicity. In addition to enabling the expression of a wider range of masculinities, self-cook areas act as a contact zone between men of different ethnicities and one in which the privilege of whiteness is destabilised (Earle & Phillips, 2012).

Visiting rooms are intermediate zones in which men interact with their families and, for some, perform fathering selves (Bartlett & Eriksson, 2019). Bartlett and Eriksson (2019) describe the father identity as a 'backstage' persona for imprisoned men. The performance of active fathering is denied and maintaining bonds with children is difficult. However, men's 'hidden selves' as fathers can be important in the maintenance of a coherent sense of self. A fathering self can exist alongside a tough persona and willingness to use violence, demonstrating the multifaceted nature of masculine gender performance (Phillips, 2012). A self-perception of being a 'good father' is a means to resist the status of prisoner—a devalued identity (Ugelvik, 2014). Ugelvik (2014) notes that in Scandinavian countries, contemporary norms of fatherhood are not based on a breadwinner model, but an ideal of contributing equally to child-rearing and spending time with children. In his ethnographic research in a Norwegian men's prison, Ugelvik (2014) interviewed foreign nationals who viewed their understandings of fatherhood as culturally superior to the Scandinavian model and as a source of worth. Series *Prison Break* (2005–2017) portrays fatherhood as essential to masculine identity and commitment to being a good father as a core component of hegemonic masculinity. It does not show much interaction between the imprisoned men and their children but Lincoln, one of the two main characters, has a son and regards fatherhood as a key aspect of successful masculinity (Cuklanz & Erol, 2021). Documentary *Prison Dads* (2013) features the stories of incarcerated fathers in Glen Parva Young Offenders Institution, as well as their families on the outside. It explores the emotional toll of separation from their children and its impact on building and maintaining family relationships.

Community Penalties

Community penalties have received less attention from criminologists than imprisonment, although these sanctions are more widely experienced. Probation is the most frequently used form of correctional control in the United States and, in most countries, people under community supervision vastly outnumber those who are imprisoned (McNeill & Beyens, 2013; Phelps, 2020). As Robinson (2016) argues, the contemporary use of community penalties demonstrates penal shifts towards increased punitive control, with mass supervision expanding alongside mass incarceration. Community penalties are interrelated with imprisonment, however, as violating their conditions can lead to a custodial sentence. Therefore, mass supervision feeds mass incarceration (Phelps, 2020). In the context of the United States, Phelps (2020) notes that gender and racial disparities are not as wide in relation to probation as they are to imprisonment. Women account for 29% of people on probation and men 71%. Smaller racial disparities may reflect white people's privilege in being more likely to receive community over custodial sentences (Phelps, 2020).

The lack of attention given to community penalties in comparison with imprisonment is mirrored in the cultural penal imagination, in which community penalties are relatively invisible and do not induce fascination. There are, however, some notable portrayals. *Elysium* (2013) is a dystopian science fiction film in which environmentally damaged Earth is inhabited by the poor, while the rich have escaped to the Elysium space station. Those on Earth are monitored and controlled by security droids, who fulfil the functions of police and parole officers (Mirrlees & Pedersen, 2016). Fitzgibbon and Lea (2014) note that the depiction of protagonist Max interacting with his droid parole officer reflects the mass supervision approach to probation, which prioritises surveillance and control. British television series *Misfits* (2009–2013) follows a group of five young people serving Community Payback sentences, who acquire superpowers after a thunderstorm. Gonnermann (2019) argues the show portrays adults in authority as corrupt. The understanding of 'community' in community sentencing is a quid pro quo—people take from and give back to the community, rather than experiencing a collective built on mutual trust and solidarity.

Portrayals such as *Public Enemies* (2012) and *The Angel's Share* (2012) are grounded in realism rather than science fiction. *Public Enemies* is a three-part drama about a female probation officer working with a man released from prison after a ten-year sentence. It is primarily a story of wrongful conviction (and a romance) but does address the punitive shift in probation from welfare to the prioritisation of risk management (Nellis, 2012). Film *The Angel's Share* (2012) is a comedy depicting a group of young men brought together after being sentenced to community service who plot to steal some valuable old whisky. It features a positive portrayal of their probation officer, Harry, who introduces them to single malt whisky.

Life on Parole (2017) is an American documentary series following four people during their first year on parole and examines how they negotiate re-establishing their lives outside of prison. British series *Crime and Punishment* (2019) focuses on different aspects of the criminal justice system, including the Probation Service and Parole Board and *The Road from Crime* (2012) explores community-based interventions in Scotland that support desistance from crime.

Women have been perceived as especially suitable for community penalties. This is partly on practical grounds as avoiding imprisonment means they can remain with their children if they are mothers. Women's suitability for community penalties is also assumed on ideological grounds, exhibiting an entrenched belief that women who commit crime are more reformable, and more in need of supportive intervention, than men. These assumptions mean women receive community sentences at an earlier stage in their criminal career than men. Responsibilities in relation to domestic care work, such as childcare, make meeting the conditions of these sentences, such as meetings with probation officers, difficult (Malloch & McIvor, 2013). Violating conditions puts women in danger of receiving a prison sentence. Gelsthorpe (2010) argues the perception community penalties are suitable for women to provide them with support is a form of carceral clawback, whereby penal measures are justified on welfare grounds.

In Britain, the imperative for sanctions to be gender responsive was met via community-based women's centres, which brought together different services to offer criminalised women 'holistic' support with housing, employment and healthcare. By meeting women's needs, women's centres were expressly intended to reduce women's risk of imprisonment (Hedderman et al., 2011). In Scotland, the development of community justice centres for women emphasised therapeutic approaches and the use of intensive mentoring to provide practical and emotional support (Malloch et al., 2014). Women reported finding this support valuable and were included in the development of plans for their rehabilitation (Gelsthorpe, 2013; Malloch et al., 2014).

Community-based women's centres have legitimacy with the women who use them and more widely the notion that women in the criminal justice system should receive different treatment from men seems to be accepted by the public (Gelsthorpe, 2013). However, in Britain they have not been successful in reducing the size of the female prison population, and the proportion of women in England and Wales receiving community sentences against prison fell slightly during the last decade (Player, 2014). Player (2014) highlights tensions in sentencing policy between risk and gender responsiveness that work against diverting women from custody. Community-based services delivered via the voluntary sector are under-resourced, a problem that has deepened in Britain due to austerity in public spending. They also entail the complex navigation of multiple agencies. Malloch et al. (2014) argue that recourse to support in the community is likely to be ineffective if the community is under strain. Without transformative change to tackle entrenched inequalities, their effectiveness is limited.

In the United States, probation and parole frequently entail employment mandates, meaning people must attempt to find 'reliable' paid work, or face possible incarceration. This requirement places women at a disadvantage as the kind of work they are likely to find is concentrated in the service sector, which unlike the labouring jobs available to men, carry out background checks (Gurusami, 2017). Compulsory meetings with probation and parole officers conflict with work schedules. Gurusami (2017) analyses the labour market as a site of punishment and surveillance over Black women, who are disproportionately represented in community penalties and re-entry programmes, where carceral and welfare-based disciplinary practices intertwine.

Community penalties for women raise issues of gendered governance. Barton's (2005) historical work on 'semi-penal' institutions for women examines how institutions such as refuges, reformatories and homes represented a continuum of women's social control exercised through disciplinary discourses of femininity. Supervision in these institutions was provided by other women, headed by a 'matron' figure, and evinced a 'mother daughter' mode of control. Feminised governance is at play in contemporary semi-penal institutions such as bail and probation hostels, which emphasise personal responsibility and empowerment through developing life skills and domestic skills as routes to rehabilitation. This governance is underpinned by maternalistic power relations between staff and residents (Barton & Cooper, 2012).

Case study:

Magdalene laundries in Ireland were an example of women's semi-penal control. At their peak in the 1950s, there were around a thousand women confined in these institutions and the last one did not close until 1996 (O'Sullivan & O'Donnell, 2007). These institutions confined women and girls for a range of gendered reasons, such as having babies outside of marriage, if they had been sexually abused or were perceived to be at risk of sexualisation, as well as for other 'welfare-based' reasons or as a probation condition (Seal & O'Neill, 2019). *The Magdalene Sisters* (2002) dramatises the stories of four young women confined in a Magdelene laundry in the 1960s. It portrays the regime based on domestic labour and the maternalistic power relations between the nuns and 'penitents'. The nuns are rendered as somewhat one-dimensional, although the film represents the laundries as resulting ultimately from a patriarchal society (Seal & O'Neill, 2019).

Most people under community supervision are men. The gendered implications of community penalties in relation to men and masculinities have not been as well researched as they have in relation to women and femininities. Holland and Scourfield (2000) argue most men on probation occupy a position of marginalised masculinity; they cannot achieve ideals of masculinity through employment, property ownership, educational achievement or consumer spending. Effective practice with men serving community sentences involves creative engagement with men's subjective experiences of masculinity and how these are shaped by, and contribute to, social discourses of masculinity (Weaver & McNeill, 2010). In working with men, probation officers construct their knowledge about men through prevalent discourses of masculinity. These include common sense understandings of crime as typical male behaviour, and feminist influenced interpretations about the connection between norms of masculinity and violence (Holland & Scourfield, 2000).

Søgaard et al. (2016) examine the significance of discourses of masculinity in a Danish reformatory for young men. The reformatory sought to bring about transformation in service users through boxing, moving them on from criminal careers and illegal drug use. The narrative of transformation through boxing emphasised developing personal responsibility and willingness to struggle to succeed. This incorporated hypermasculine symbolism of boxing as masculine individualism, which drew on portrayals from popular culture such as *Rocky* (1976) and *Cinderella Man* (2005). In this sense, the reformatory redirected narratives of masculinity that were part of street cultures into normative, neoliberal understandings of masculine success. It did not challenge hypermasculinity. The gender dynamics of rehabilitation programmes that include boxing coaching are explored in documentary *Fighting for Life* (2018), which examines the work of a female coach Sharita van der Hulst working with men in a South African prison. It is unusual for a woman to take such a role, but the documentary shows van der Hulst's success in gaining their enthusiasm and trust.

One third of the people on probation or parole in the United States is Black. Miller and Stuart (2017) argue people who have been convicted of a crime experience a form of citizenship that is distinct from those who have not. They define this experience as 'carceral citizenship', a different legal and standing and separate social world. Carceral citizenship is a raced and classed form of citizenship disproportionately applied to poor Black people, and poor Black men particularly. *Free Meek* (2019) chronicles rapper Meek Mill's years long experiences with the American criminal justice system. After being imprisoned aged 19, he served a long sentence of probation during which he was returned to prison several times for violations. The series portrays how, as a carceral citizen, Mill struggles to break out of a cycle of racialised punishment and control through which he is sanctioned for elements of his music career, such as his touring schedule and lyrics. As a successful rapper, he has the resources to legally challenge his convictions but most Black men in a similar position do not.

Desistance and Restorative Justice

Analyses of desistance—the process through which people stop committing crime—are frequently unmarked by consideration of gender but have been developed from research about men and boys. Gendered differences and the gender inequality experienced by women must be incorporated into understandings of desistance, or desistance theories will reinforce this inequality (Barr, 2019). Österman (2018) explored criminalised women's subjective experiences of desistance in Sweden and England and Wales. The Swedish model was more conducive to women's desistance from crime because it provided better support for drug and alcohol addiction issues, better support in terms of finding employment and was characterised by less conflictual relations between the women and authorities, giving the system greater legitimacy.

Perceptions of masculinity are relevant to desistance for men. Independence and self-control are elements of normative masculinity, as is settling into a 'conventional' life of legitimate employment and a family, which can be woven into men's desistance narratives. These norms of masculinity also present a challenge to desistance as they are not always easy to attain (Carlsson, 2013). Fader and Traylor (2015) call for an intersectional approach to understanding desistance that pays attention to how gender, race, class and age interlock with one another. For example, they note the neoliberalisation of social policy in relation to welfare has especially adversely affected poor women of colour, which must be understood as a gendered, racialised and classed barrier to desistance through the structural imposition of economic strain.

Restorative justice practices seek to help reintegrate someone who has committed a crime back into the community. Restorative justice conferencing is a meeting between the person who committed the crime, the victim/s and, possibly, other affected people such as family or community members. Restorative justice can be effective with women and girls as it is based on communication, building relationships and empathy, arguably reflecting more feminine than masculine values (Elis, 2005; Österman & Masson, 2018). However, there is also a danger that assumptions about the suitability of women and girls for restorative justice reproduce gendered stereotypes about ideal femininity and entrench traditional gender roles (Elis, 2005). Österman and Masson (2018) highlight gendered risks of restorative justice conferencing for women, which include the perpetuation of stereotypes, adverse effects on mental health and the reinscription of guilt and shame. Cook (2006) argues that in restorative justice conferences inequalities of gender, race and class are not eliminated but become subtle means of reinforcing domination. Restorative justice aims to reintegrate the person who has caused harm—but Cook (2006) emphasises this premium on reintegration encourages conformity to conventional expectations of gender.

Punishment reflects and deepens intersectional inequalities and has been instrumental in creating these inequalities. Systems of punishment establish and reinforce the gender binary both by requiring gender segregation but also in relation to the normative behaviour they seek to inculcate. Social control and punishment are forms of gendered governance, which can be enacted starkly through imprisonment or more subtly through other forms of moral tutelage. Ultimately, punishment is emblematic of state power and upholds gendered and racialised hierarchies.

References

Alves, J. A. (2014). From necropolis to blackpolis: Necropolitical governance and black spatial praxis in São Paulo, Brazil. *Antipode, 46*(2), 323–339.

Anderson, E. (1999). *Code of the street*. W. W. Norton and Company.

Baldry, E., & Cunneen, C. (2014). Imprisoned Indigenous women and the shadow of colonial patriarchy. *Australian & New Zealand Journal of Criminology, 47*(2), 276–298.

Baldwin, L. (2018). Motherhood disrupted: Reflections of post-prison mothers. *Emotion, Space and Society, 26*, 49–56.

Balfour, G. (2013). Theorizing the intersectionality of victimization, criminalization, and punishment of women: An introduction to the special issue. *International Review of Victimology, 19*(1), 3–5.

Ball, E. L. (2016). The unbearable liminality of Blackness: Reconsidering violence in Steve McQueen's *12 Years a Slave. Transition, 119*, 175–186.

Bandyopadhyay, M. (2006). Competing masculinities in a prison. *Men and Masculinities, 9*(2), 186–203.

Barnes, S. L., & Stringer, E. C. (2014). Is motherhood important? Imprisoned women's maternal experiences before and during confinement and their postrelease expectations. *Feminist Criminology, 9*(1), 3–23.

Barr, Ú. (2019). *Desisting sisters: Gender, power and desistance in the criminal (In)justice system*. Springer.

Bartlett, T. S., & Eriksson, A. (2019). How fathers construct and perform masculinity in a liminal prison space. *Punishment & Society, 21*(3), 275–294.

Barton, A. (2005). *Fragile moralities and dangerous sexualities: Two centuries of semi-penal institutionalisation for women*. Ashgate.

Barton, A., & Cooper, V. (2012). Hostels and community justice for women. In M. Malloch & G. McIvor (Eds.), *Women, punishment and social justice: Human rights and penal practices* (pp. 136–151). Routledge.

Bell, K. E. (2017). Prison violence and the intersectionality of race/ethnicity and gender. *Criminology, Criminal Justice, Law & Society, 18*(1), i–121.

Bloom, B., Owen, B., & Covington, S. (2003). *Gender-responsive strategies*. National Institute of Corrections.

Booth, N. (2017). Maternal imprisonment: A family sentence. In J. Hudson & C. Needham (Eds.), *Social policy review* (Vol. 29, pp. 105–126). The Policy Press and Social Policy Association.

Bosworth, M., & Kaufman, E. (2012). Gender and punishment. In *Handbook of punishment and society* (pp. 186–204). Sage.

Britton, D. M. (2003). *At work in the iron cage: The prison as gendered organization*. NYU Press.

Carlen, P. (1983). *Women's imprisonment: A study in social control*. Routledge & Kegan Paul.

Carlen, P. (2002). Women's imprisonment: Models of reform and change. *Probation Journal, 49*(2), 76–87.

Carlsson, C. (2013). Masculinities, persistence, and desistance. *Criminology, 51*(3), 661–693.

Carlton, B., & Segrave, M. (2011). Women's survival post-imprisonment: Connecting imprisonment with pains past and present. *Punishment & Society, 13*(5), 551–570.

Cecil, D. K. (2007). Looking beyond caged heat: Media images of women in prison. *Feminist Criminology, 2*(4), 304–326.

Chuenurah, C., & Sornprohm, U. (2020). Drug policy and women prisoners in Southeast Asia. In J. Buxton, G. Margo, & L. Burger (Eds.), *The impact of global drug policy on women: Shifting the needle* (pp. 131–139). Emerald Publishing Limited.

Cook, K. J. (2006). Doing difference and accountability in restorative justice conferences. *Theoretical Criminology, 10*(1), 107–124.

Crewe, B. (2014). Not looking hard enough: Masculinity, emotion, and prison research. *Qualitative Inquiry, 20*(4), 392–403.

Crewe, B., Warr, J, Bennett, P., & Smith, A. (2014). The emotional geography of prison life. *Theoretical Criminology, 18*, 56–74.

Cuklanz, L., & Erol, A. (2021). New feminist studies in audiovisual industries| The shifting image of hegemonic masculinity in contemporary television series. *International Journal of Communication, 15*, 545–562.

Curtis, A. (2014). "You have to cut it off at the knee": Dangerous masculinity and security inside a men's prison. *Men and Masculinities, 17*(2), 120–146.

DeCarvalho, L. J. (2021). Visible only behind bars: How Indigenous Australian women reframe and reclaim their experiences on Wentworth. *Women's Studies in Communication, 44*(1), 65–80.

Deckert, A. (2020). Indigeneity matters: Portrayal of women offenders in New Zealand newspapers. *Crime, Media, Culture, 16*(3), 337–357.

Earle, R., & Phillips, C. (2012). Digesting men? Ethnicity, gender and food: Perspectives from a 'prison ethnography.' *Theoretical Criminology, 16*(2), 141–156.

Easterling, B. A., & Feldmeyer, B. (2017). Race, incarceration, and motherhood: Spoiled identity among rural white mothers in prison. *The Prison Journal, 97*(2), 143–165.

Elis, L. (2005). Restorative justice programs, gender, and recidivism. *Public Organization Review, 5*(4), 375–389.

Fader, J. J., & Traylor, L. L. (2015). Dealing with difference in desistance theory: The promise of intersectionality for new avenues of inquiry. *Sociology Compass, 9*(4), 247–260.

Fischer, M. (2016). #Free_CeCe: The material convergence of social media activism. *Feminist Media Studies, 16*(5), 755–771.

Fitzgibbon, W., & Lea, J. (2014). Defending probation: Beyond privatisation and security. *European Journal of Probation, 6*(1), 24–41.

Foss, K. A. (2018). Dominating the (female) incarcerated body: Gender and medical control in prison dramas. In K. A. Foss (Ed.), *Demystifying the big house: Exploring prison experience and media representations* (pp. 89–110). Southern Illinois University Press.

Freitas, A. M., Inácio, A. R., & Saavedra, L. (2016). Motherhood in prison: Reconciling the irreconcilable. *The Prison Journal, 96*(3), 415–436.

Frois, C. (2017). *Female imprisonment: An ethnography of everyday life in confinement.* Palgrave.

Gear, S. (2010). Imprisoning men in violence: Masculinity and sexual abuse: A view from South African prisons. *South African Crime Quarterly, 33*, 25–32.

Gelsthorpe, L. (2010). Women, crime and control. *Criminology & Criminal Justice, 10*(4), 375–386.

Gelsthorpe, L. (2013). Legitimacy, law and locality: Making the case for change. In M. Malloch & G. McIvor (Eds.), *Women, punishment and social justice* (pp. 13–25). Routledge.

Gonnermann, A. (2019). 'With great power comes'... nothing: Superheroes, teenage delinquents, and dysfunctional community structures in Misfits

(2009-2013). In C. Lustin & R. Haekel (Eds.), *Mannheimer Beiträge zur Literatur-und Kulturwissenschaft* (Vol. 83, pp. 213–238). Narr Francke Attempto Verlag.

Green, C. A. (2012). Local geographies of crime and punishment in a plantation colony: Gender and incarceration in Barbados, 1878–1928. *New West Indian Guide / Nieuwe West-Indische Gids, 86*(3–4), 263.

Gross, K. N. (2015). African American women, mass incarceration, and the politics of protection. *Journal of American History, 102*(1), 25–33.

Gurusami, S. (2017). Working for redemption: Formerly incarcerated Black women and punishment in the labor market. *Gender & Society, 31*(4), 433–456.

Haley, S. (2016). *No mercy here: Gender, punishment, and the making of Jim Crow modernity.* UNC Press Books.

Haney, L. (2013). Motherhood as punishment: The case of parenting in prison. *Signs: Journal of Women in Culture and Society, 39*(1), 105–130.

Hannah-Moffat, K. (2010). Sacrosanct or flawed: Risk, accountability and gender-responsive penal politics. *Current Issues in Criminal Justice, 22*(2), 193–215.

Harmon, M. G., & Boppre, B. (2018). Women of color and the war on crime: An explanation for the rise in Black female imprisonment. *Journal of Ethnicity in Criminal Justice, 16*(4), 309–332.

Hedderman, C., Gunby, C., & Shelton, N. (2011). What women want: The importance of qualitative approaches in evaluating work with women offenders. *Criminology & Criminal Justice, 11*(1), 3–19.

Hefner, M. K. (2018). Queering prison masculinity: Exploring the organization of gender and sexuality within men's prison. *Men and Masculinities, 21*(2), 230–253.

Holland, S., & Scourfield, J. B. (2000). Managing marginalised masculinities: Men and probation. *Journal of Gender Studies, 9*(2), 199–211.

Hughto, J. M. W., Clark, K. A., Altice, F. L., Reisner, S. L., Kershaw, T. S., & Pachankis, J. E. (2018). Creating, reinforcing, and resisting the gender binary: A qualitative study of transgender women's healthcare experiences in sex-segregated jails and prisons. *International Journal of Prisoner Health, 14*(2), 69–88.

Jarvis, B. (2005). The violence of images: Inside the prison TV drama Oz. In P. Mason (Ed.), *Captured by the media* (pp. 164–181). Willan.

Jenness, V., & Fenstermaker, S. (2014). Agnes goes to prison: Gender authenticity, transgender inmates in prisons for men, and pursuit of "the real deal." *Gender & Society, 28*(1), 5–31.

Jewkes, Y. (2005a). Creating a stir? Prisons, popular media and the power to reform. In P. Mason (Ed.), *Captured by the media* (pp. 147–163). Willan.

Jewkes, Y. (2005b). Men behind bars: "Doing" masculinity as an adaptation to imprisonment. *Men and Masculinities, 8*(1), 44–63.

Johnson, J. R. (2013). Cisgender privilege, intersectionality, and the criminalization of CeCe McDonald: Why intercultural communication needs transgender studies. *Journal of International and Intercultural Communication, 6*(2), 135–144.

Johnston, H. (2019). Imprisoned mothers in Victorian England, 1853–1900: Motherhood, identity and the convict prison. *Criminology & Criminal Justice, 19*(2), 215–231.

Kohler-Hausmann, J. (2017). *Getting tough: Welfare and imprisonment in 1970s America.* Princeton.

Lugones, M. (2007). Heterosexualism and the colonial/modern gender system. *Hypatia, 22*(1), 186–219.

Maguire, D. (2021). Vulnerable prisoner masculinities in an English prison. *Men and Masculinities, 24*(3), 501–518.

Malloch, M., & McIvor, G. (2013). Women, punishment and social justice. In M. Malloch & G. McIvor (Eds.), *Women, punishment and social justice: Human rights and penal practices* (pp. 3–12). Routledge.

Malloch, M.. McIvor, G., & Burgess, C. (2014). 'Holistic' community punishment and criminal justice interventions for women. *The Howard Journal of Criminal Justice, 53*(4), 395–410.

Matthews, E. S. (2015). The prison beauty pageant: Documenting female prisoners in Miss Gulag and La Corona. *Studies in Documentary Film, 9*(3), 220–234.

McCorkel, J. A. (2013). *Breaking women: Gender, race, and the new politics of imprisonment.* NYU Press.

McIntosh, T., & Workman, K. (2017). Māori and prison. In A. Deckert, R. Sarre, T. McIntosh, & K. Workman (Eds.), *The Palgrave handbook of Australian and New Zealand criminology, crime and justice* (pp. 725–735). Springer.

McNeill, F., & Beyens, K. (2013). Introduction: Studying mass supervision. In F. McNeill & K. Beyens (Eds.), *Offender supervision in Europe* (pp. 1–18). Springer.

Mescheryakov, V., & Wesolowsky, T. (2019). *"Welcome to hell": Life in a notorious women's prison.* Radio Free Europe.

Michalski, J. H. (2015). Status hierarchies and hegemonic masculinity: A general theory of prison violence. *The British Journal of Criminology, 57*(1), 40–60.

Millbank, J. (2004). It's about this: Lesbians, prison, desire. *Social & Legal Studies, 13*(2), 155–190.

Miller, R. J., & Stuart, F. (2017). Carceral citizenship: Race, rights and responsibility in the age of mass supervision. *Theoretical Criminology, 21*(4), 532–548.

Mirrlees, T., & Pedersen, I. (2016). Elysium as a critical dystopia. *International Journal of Media & Cultural Politics, 12*(3), 305–322.

Moran, D., Pallot, J., & Piacentini, L. (2009). Lipstick, lace, and longing: Constructions of femininity inside a Russian prison. *Environment and Planning D: Society and Space, 27*(4), 700–720.

Morse, S. J., & Wright, K. A. (2019). Imprisoned men: Masculinity variability and implications for correctional programming. *Corrections*, 1–23.

Murdocca, C. (2013). *To right historical wrongs: Race, gender, and sentencing in Canada*. UBC Press.

Nellis, M. (2012). Representations of British probation officers in film, television drama and novels 1948–2012. *British Journal of Community Justice, 10*(2), 5–23.

O'Sullivan, E., & O'Donnell, I. (2007). Coercive confinement in the Republic of Ireland: The waning of a culture of control. *Punishment & Society, 9*(1), 27–48.

Österman, L. (2018). *Penal cultures and female desistance*. Routledge.

Österman, L., & Masson, I. (2018). Restorative justice with female offenders: The neglected role of gender in restorative conferencing. *Feminist Criminology, 13*(1), 3–27.

Pallot, J., Piacentini, L., & Moran, D. (2012). *Gender, geography, and punishment: The experience of women in carceral Russia*. Oxford University Press.

Paton, D. (2004). *No bond but the law: Punishment, race, and gender in Jamaican state formation, 1780–1870*. Duke University Press.

Pemberton, S. (2013). Enforcing gender: The constitution of sex and gender in prison regimes. *Signs: Journal of Women in Culture and Society, 39*(1), 151–175.

Penal Reform International & Thailand Institute of Justice. (2020). *Global prison trends 2020*. Penal Reform International and Thailand Institute of Justice.

Phelps, M. S. (2020). Mass probation from micro to macro: Tracing the expansion and consequences of community supervision. *Annual Review of Criminology, 3*(1), 261–279.

Phillips, C. (2012). *The multicultural prison: Ethnicity, masculinity, and social relations among prisoners.* Oxford University Press.

Player, E. (2014). Women in the criminal justice system: The triumph of inertia. *Criminology & Criminal Justice, 14*(3), 276–297.

Ricciardelli, R. (2015). Establishing and asserting masculinity in Canadian penitentiaries. *Journal of Gender Studies, 24*(2), 170–191.

Richie, B. (2012). *Arrested justice: Black women, violence, and America's prison nation.* NYU Press.

Robinson, G. (2016). The Cinderella complex: Punishment, society and community sanctions. *Punishment & Society, 18*(1), 95–112.

Russell, T., Jeffries, S., Hayes, H., Thipphayamongkoludom, Y., & Chuenurah, C. (2020). A gender-comparative exploration of women's and men's pathways to prison in Thailand. *Australian & New Zealand Journal of Criminology, 53*(4), 536–562.

Rymhs, D. (2012). In this inverted garden: Masculinities in Canadian prison writing. *Journal of Gender Studies, 21*(1), 77–89.

Schwan, A. (2016). Postfeminism meets the women in prison genre: Privilege and spectatorship in Orange Is the New Black. *Television & New Media, 17*(6), 473–490.

Seal, L., & O'Neill, M. (2019). *Imaginative criminology: Of spaces past.* Bristol University Press.

Segrave, M., & Carlton, B. (2010). Women, trauma, criminalisation and imprisonment…. *Current Issues in Criminal Justice, 22*(2), 287–305.

Segrave, M., & Carlton, B. (2013). Introduction: Gendered transcarceral realities. In *Women exiting prison: Critical essays on gender, post-release support and survival* (pp. 1–12). Routledge.

Shabazz, R. (2015). *Spatializing blackness: Architectures of confinement and black masculinity in Chicago.* University of Illinois Press.

Sloan, J. A. (2016). *Masculinities and the adult male prison experience.* Palgrave.

Smith, P. J. (2018). Screenings: Behaving badly: Television's women in prison. *Film Quarterly, 71*(3), 72–76.

Søgaard, T. F., Kolind, T., Thylstrup, B., & Deuchar, R. (2016). Desistance and the micro-narrative construction of reformed masculinities in a Danish rehabilitation centre. *Criminology & Criminal Justice, 16*(1), 99–118.

Stubbs, J. (2020). Bringing racialised women and girls into view: An intersectional approach to punishment and incarceration. In W. Sandra, F.-G.

Kate, M. JaneMaree, & M. Jude (Eds.), *The Emerald handbook of feminism, criminology and social change* (pp. 295–316). Emerald Publishing Limited.

Sudbury, J. (2005). Introduction: Feminist critiques, transnational landscapes, abolitionist visions. In J. Sudbury (Ed.), *Global lockdown: Race, gender, and the prison-industrial complex* (pp. xi–xxviii). Routledge.

Terry, A. (2016). Surveying issues that arise in women's prisons: A content critique of Orange Is the New Black. *Sociology Compass, 10*(7), 553–566.

Thaggert, M. (2014). 12 years a slave: Jasper's Look. *American Literary History, 26*(2), 332–338.

Thomas, V. E. (2019). Gazing at "it": An intersectional analysis of transnormativity and Black womanhood in Orange Is the New Black. *Communication, Culture and Critique, 13*(4), 519–535.

Ugelvik, T. (2014). Paternal pains of imprisonment: Incarcerated fathers, ethnic minority masculinity and resistance narratives. *Punishment & Society, 16*(2), 152–168.

Weaver, B., & McNeill, F. (2010). Travelling hopefully: Desistance theory and probation practice. In J. Brayford, F. B. Cowe, & J. Deering (Eds.), *What else works? Creative work with offenders* (pp. 36–60). Willan.

Yousman, B. (2009). Inside Oz: Hyperviolence, race and class nightmares, and the engrossing spectacle of terror. *Communication and Critical/Cultural Studies, 6*(3), 265–284.

Zedner, L. (1991). Women, crime, and penal responses: A historical account. *Crime and Justice: A Review of Research, 14*, 307–362.

9

Extreme Punishment and Abolitionist Futures

This chapter retains the focus on gendered punishment and gendered governance discussed in the previous chapter, extending it to immigration detention, whole life prison sentences and the death penalty. Extreme punishment here conceptualises the blurring of the civil and the criminal, as in immigration detention, in ways that are undemocratic and create practices that lack accountability and oversight. It also encapsulates punishments that are especially harsh to endure, which are based in despair rather than hope, and which have permanent exclusion of individuals as their aim (Koenig & Reiter, 2015). Immigration detention acts as a precursor to deportation from a country. Whole life sentences and the death penalty entail removal from society, which is ultimately secured through death, whether that is the state inflicting death by execution or through death in prison. Extreme punishments have gendered impacts but also enact a tough masculinist approach to exercising state power and authority. As such, extreme punishment is a means to do masculinist politics (Kohler-Hausmann, 2017). The final part of the chapter counters the bleakness of extreme punishment with the hope of feminist and queer abolitionist futures.

L. Seal, *Gender, Crime and Justice*, https://doi.org/10.1007/978-3-030-87488-9_9

Immigration Detention

Detention of people seeking asylum or attempting to migrate is common practice around the world. Immigration detention centres are not officially a form of punishment; they are holding centres for people while decisions are made or prior to their removal from the country. However, in the context of 'crimmigration', the overlapping of criminal and immigration law and measures of social control, the treatment of asylum seekers and irregular migrants is punitive in its approach (Turnbull, 2017). Detention centres cannot prevent migration but have a symbolic function in representing governance and state power (Bosworth et al., 2016). Immigration detention centres resemble prisons in their architectural design and in features such as razor wire topped walls, use of handcuffing, solitary confinement and systems of surveillance (Bosworth & Slade, 2014; Griffiths, 2015; Rivas & Bull, 2018). In the United Kingdom, ex-prisons have been repurposed as Immigration Removal Centres (Bosworth & Slade, 2014). The same multinational companies that provide prison security also do so in detention centres (Rivas & Bull, 2018). Like prisons, immigration detention centres are gendered institutions; women and men are frequently housed separately (Bosworth & Slade, 2014). Even where this is not the case, norms of femininity and masculinity are part of the institutional regime.

Science fiction films *Children of Men* (2006) and *District 9* (2009) represent issues related to refugees, global migration and detention. In *District 9* (2009) an alien spaceship hovers above Johannesburg. The aliens, known as 'Prawns', live in a degraded refugee camp that segregates them from human society (Kountz, 2014). There are clear parallels with apartheid, the system of racial separation and terror that existed in South Africa in the second half of the twentieth century. However, as Joo (2015) argues, the setting is clearly post-apartheid South Africa and the Prawns are disparaged by white and Black South Africans. The status of the aliens as confined and reviled non-citizens is contextualised against a politics of securitisation and exclusion (Joo, 2015).

Set in 2027, *Children of Men* (2006) depicts the impending loss of humanity as there have been no human births for nearly twenty years. White British civil servant Theo helps pregnant illegal immigrant Kee, a

Black woman, to escape from Britain, where her illegal status puts her in danger. Sheltering illegal immigrants is a crime and immigrants are vilified for having infiltrated British society. Public service announcements warn of the threat immigrants pose and underline their status outside the law (Joo, 2015). As Joo (2015) highlights, the film shows the detention of immigrants as routine and incidental. Their detention is glimpsed fleetingly and is a constituent part of the film's dystopian backdrop.

Australian series *Stateless* (2020) explores the stories of four people in a detention centre—two detained people, a guard and the centre's manager. The programme is based on true stories and is a means to confront Australia's mandatory detention policies and practices of detention, including the role of bureaucracy in enforcing discipline. Notoriously, successive Australian governments detained asylum seekers in offshore camps in Papua New Guinea and Nauru, including the Manus Processing Centre. Manus was closed in 2017 but around 400 detainees refused to leave, instead running the camp themselves. Two Iranian men detained on Manus Island secretly filmed *Chauka, Please Tell us the Time* (2017) to document their experiences.

Asylum seekers and irregular migrants experience stigmatisation and scapegoating in their host countries for social ills such as crime and economic insecurity (Bosworth et al., 2016). The figure of the male asylum seeker or irregular migrant as criminal is an especially potent one. In the UK, 'foreign national offenders' are held in prisons specifically for foreign nationals, or special hubs within prisons (Kaufman, 2014). They face deportation if they serve more than 12 months cumulatively. Male asylum seekers experience racialised, gendered stereotypes that paint them as dangerous, terrorists and morally deviant (Griffiths, 2015). In the British Immigration Removal Centre where Griffiths (2015) conducted her research, men were subject to specific racist stereotypes such as Black men as hypersexual and Middle Eastern and Asian men as religious fundamentalists. Appeals for public sympathy for asylum seekers by NGOs rely on images of vulnerability, which men frequently do not fit. The experience of detention was infantilising as men could not make decisions for themselves and had to wait months or years for decisions on their cases. Family life, and concomitantly their identities as fathers, husbands and brothers, was curtailed.

The majority of people in immigration detention around the world are men (Rivas & Bull, 2018). Matos and Esposito's (2019) exploration of women's lived experiences of detention in Portugal identified detention centres as sites of struggle and resistance. Many of the women were from Brazil and Cape Verde, former Portuguese colonies. Racialised perceptions of Brazilian women of colour as highly sexed reflected colonial imaginaries of gender (Lugones, 2007). Trans detainees challenged staffs' notions of the gender binary—itself a colonial legacy—and the everyday order of the detention centre. Women are especially representative of national identity (Yuval-Davis, 1997). In the Athens Central Holding Centre in Greece, women detainees were viewed by staff as both 'failed' women and as emblematic of perceived faults pertaining to their national or ethnic groups (Bosworth et al., 2016).

Detention is an extreme environment, but detainees find ways to negotiate and navigate their identities and experiences. Women detained in Portugal made creative use of normative constructions of femininity, for example deploying a 'pregnancy as vulnerability' narrative to demand improved treatment (Esposito et al., 2020). In Athens, women sought to counter negative stereotypes held by staff through asserting their own narratives of migration, which emphasised attempts to find employment, or to seek safety (Bosworth et al., 2016). Struggles over detainees' need for respect and recognition also lead to conflict. Bosworth and Slade (2014) relate how, in a British Immigration Removal Centre, male detainees reacted to perceived slights from staff by attempting to assert dominant masculinity.

Last Resort (2000) is the story of Tanya, a Russian woman who travels to Britain with her young son to meet her British fiancé, who does not arrive. Although she and her son are not placed in detention, they are unable to leave Margate, the seaside town where she claimed asylum. The use of CCTV footage emphasises the permanent surveillance to which asylum seekers are subjected (Rydzewska, 2009). The gendered aspect of Tanya's experience is highlighted by the fact she has travelled with her son as well as her hope to marry a British man—the film plays on the Eastern European 'mail order bride' stereotype, although the portrayal of Tanya subverts this stereotype.

People who do not have their asylum claims upheld, or have criminal convictions, are deported to their country of origin. Golash-Boza (2016) draws a comparison between the growth of mass incarceration and mass deportation in the United States as examples of state repression. Both rely on a politics of fear centred on the racialised masculinity of Black and Latinx men to bolster practices of removing 'dangerous others' from society. During the Obama administration, 90% of deportees from the United States were men and 97% of them were originally from Latin America or the Caribbean.

Docudrama *The Infiltrators* (2019) dramatises the real life story of a group of undocumented young people in the United States who turned themselves in to the authorities in order to be sent to a detention centre. From there, they attempted to help undocumented people avoid deportation. These activists resist the need to hide and be invisible required of the undocumented, upon whom the American economy depends. Two filmmakers were embedded with agents from the US Customs and Enforcement Agency for two years to make the series *Immigration Nation* (2020), which depicts the agency's work upholding detention and deportation during the crackdown on immigration under President Trump. *The Deported* (2020) explores four different stories of people facing deportation during Trump's presidency, and also features interviews with officials who enacted American immigration policies.

Case study:

The Windrush Scandal—In April 2018, it emerged long-term residents of the UK, who were Commonwealth citizens from the Caribbean or the children of Commonwealth citizens, were being detained, threatened with deportation and deported due to lack of official documentation. This was despite the fact that before the Immigration Act 1971 came into force, Commonwealth citizens were entitled (and encouraged) to settle in the UK. Drama *Sitting in Limbo* (2020) portrays the experiences of Anthony Bryan, who had lived in the UK since 1965 when he was eight and was mistakenly identified as residing in the UK illegally in 2016. He lost his citizenship rights and was detained in an immigration removal centre before eventually winning his legal battle.

Whole Life Sentences

A notable aspect of mass incarceration is the expansion of very long and whole life prison sentences, which in the United States are not reserved for murder but attach to certain other crimes. These sentences can be understood as a form of extreme punishment, and their use raises questions of human rights and human dignity. Very long sentences, maximum security prisons and practices of solitary confinement perpetuate a masculinist approach to penality based on toughness. They derive legitimacy, at least in part, from the purported need to contain dangerous masculinity. For life sentenced male prisoners, the harshness of their punishment can cement their status as 'real men' who are superior in terms of masculinity to those convicted of more petty crimes (Jewkes, 2005). Similarly, Bandyopadhyay (2006: 189) quotes a participant who explained 'lifers' were regarded with a 'fearful respect' by other men. Length of the sentence was part of the hierarchy among prisoners, although not if their crimes were against women and children.

A gendered comparison of people serving long prison sentences from a young age in Britain found that women had higher severity scores than men in terms of their experiences (Crewe et al., 2017). Women were affected more severely by losing contact with family and friends, particularly their children, and more frequently experienced symptoms of trauma such as nightmares and flashbacks to their crimes. Consistent with what is known about women prisoners more generally, they also had more distressing life histories than the men. Loss of relationships with children, or the foreclosure of the chance to be a mother, was a painful aspect of extreme punishment for women serving life without parole in California (Vannier, 2016). The pre-prison lives of life sentenced women in Michigan, USA were characterised by abuse, poverty and neglect. They experienced their long sentences as a form of social death, exiling them from society (Lempert, 2016).

Women constitute under 4% of life sentenced prisoners around the world (Van Zyl Smit & Appleton, 2019). Some countries in the former Soviet Union, including Russia, prohibit life sentences for women but allow them for men, and there are other countries that do not apply them to pregnant women (Vannier, 2020). Gendered considerations, such as the special role of motherhood, women's prior experiences of abuse and the heavier psychological impact of life sentences inform this policy. While exempting women from life sentences reflects a gender responsive approach, Vannier (2020) argues there is a danger making women ineligible strengthens the continued use of life sentencing for men, preventing a wider human rights-based critique of this form of punishment.

Very long and whole life prison sentences are more 'thoughtless' than the most closely related form of extreme punishment, the death penalty and are comparatively culturally invisible. People consigned to spend the rest of their lives in prison are forgotten and 'ungrieved' (Girling, 2016). In recent years, these sentences have gained higher visibility through penal reformist and abolitionist campaigning. *Lost for Life* (2013) and *Teen Killers: Life Without Parole* (2014) examine people in the United States sentenced to LWOP for crimes they committed when under the age of eighteen. Via use of home movie footage, *Time* (2020) affectingly portrays the impact on his family of Robert Richardson's sixty year prison sentence for bank robbery. The home movies, shot over two decades by Sibil Richardson, Robert's wife, show their twin sons grow up and Sibil becoming a prison abolitionist and public speaker in her quest to free Robert. He was eventually freed through clemency in 2018 after nearly twenty years in prison.

The Death Penalty

Comparatively few women are on death row around the world, and even fewer are executed. An estimated 500 women globally are under sentence of death (Cornell Center on the Death Penalty Worldwide, 2018). This pattern was replicated historically. There is little empirical data about women and execution around the world; however, death sentenced women, particularly in the United States, are the subject of cultural fascination. Documentaries such as *Women on Death Row* (2017) and *Death Row's Women* (2020) feature interviews with death sentenced women in the United States. *Dead Women Walking* (2018) dramatises the stories of three women facing execution in their final days. It includes attention to how the death penalty affects their relatives and prison personnel, as well as the condemned women themselves.

Portrayals of femininity are particularly significant in relation to women and the death penalty. Constructions of femininity are crucial to demonstrating mitigating factors to avoid a death sentence or framing a case sympathetically to gain a commutation. If women can be 'rendered harmless' by meeting standards of appropriate womanhood, through mothering identities, for example, or as pathological and therefore not fully responsible, they are more likely to avoid the death penalty (Farr, 2000; Heberle, 1999). Familiar cultural stories about womanhood are integral to this process, mobilising discourses of respectability, motherhood and madness (Ballinger, 2000; Black, 2018).

Paternalism is, however, a double-edged sword. Women who cannot be 'rendered harmless' against common sense understandings of womanhood are more likely to be executed. In the United States, Black women have historically been over-represented among the small number of executed women, as have queer and lesbian women (Farr, 2000; Linders & Van Gundy-Yoder, 2008). Ballinger (2000) argues women who committed non-domestic murders in England and Wales 1900–1955 were proportionally more likely to be hanged than men who committed similar crimes. Masculinisation, whether because of intersections of sexuality, race and class and/or the nature of the murder, is significant in terms of making women more 'executable'. Femininity disrupts death penalty systems, highlighting their inherent masculinity and the bodily violence the state must enact to carry out execution. However, this disruption applies when women are deemed recognisably feminine, not in relation to all women who are sentenced to death (Grant, 2004; Howarth, 2002; Seal, 2010).

Case studies:

Aileen Wuornos and Wanda Jean Allen are compelling examples of women who were rendered executable due to their perceived failure to meet standards of normative femininity. Aileen Wuornos was executed in Florida in 2002. In the late 1980s she killed seven men she solicited to pay her for sex. She was in a relationship with a woman. Wuornos was portrayed as deviant and masculine, with a lack of attention given to her violent abusive upbringing and her mental health issues. Nick Broomfield's documentaries *Aileen Wuornos: The Selling of a Serial Killer* (1992) and *Aileen: Life and Death of a Serial Killer* (2003) examine her early life and inadequate legal representation. *Monster* (2003) highlights how, as a poor woman who lived on the margins socially and economically, Wuornos was reviled before she was convicted of murder. Wanda Jean Allen was executed in Oklahoma in 2001 for murdering her girlfriend in 1988. A Black and lesbian woman who was brain damaged after a traffic accident in childhood, Allen was portrayed in racist and homophobic terms by the prosecution during her trial and was inadequately represented by an inexperienced lawyer. *The Execution of Wanda Jean* (2002) relates Allen's story through extensive interview footage while she unsuccessfully attempted to gain clemency.

The death penalty is a deeply masculine punishment and symbolically affirms masculinist aspects of state punishment more generally, such as toughness and the demonstrable exercise of power and authority. Howarth (2002) argues the system of capital punishment demonstrates deep aspirations to masculinity, whether it is enacted upon, or carried out by, men or women. In this sense, the death penalty is a 'masculine sanctuary' as it requires classically masculine behaviour (Streib, 2002). The death penalty is usually carried out by men on men. Pro-death penalty arguments portray failure to deploy capital punishment as weak and effeminate, and a failure to uphold authority (Howarth, 2002; Seal, 2014; LaChance, 2016).

Case study:

Lisa Montgomery was executed in the United States by the federal government in 2021. She was the only woman on federal death row at that time. In 2004, she strangled a heavily pregnant woman to death and cut the baby from her victim's womb in order to kidnap the baby. Despite widespread concern that Montgomery was brain damaged, mentally ill and had experienced an extremely abusive childhood, she was executed during a spate of federal executions at the end of the Trump presidency. Between July 2020 and January 2021, there were thirteen federal executions. Prior to that, there had only been three since the 1960s (Death Penalty Information Center, 2021b). These executions can be understood as a show of toughness and masculinity, and as a political measure primarily aimed at garnering votes. Public discussion of Montgomery's case focussed on the injustice of her execution but also the propensity for the plight of a white woman to gain greater cultural attention than the plight of Black men.

The masculinity of capital punishment as a system is cleverly exposed by *Clemency* (2019), which depicts the increasing trauma experienced by Bernadine, a Black prison warden, as she must preside over an execution. Bernadine strives to preserve the dignity of condemned inmates but the impossibility of doing so is underlined by a botched execution of one man and doubts about the guilt of another. Bernadine is not a white man but that does not alter the masculinist nature of the death penalty and she is psychologically burdened by the demands of her position. In *Dead Man Walking* (1995) the masculinity of capital punishment is highlighted via the contrast between Matthew Poncelot, a violent man facing execution, and the nun Sister Helen Prejean who seeks to spiritually redeem him. It is possible to interpret this redemption narrative as justifying the death penalty because it enables Poncelot to admit responsibility for his actions and achieve a more acceptable masculine identity. However, *Dead Man Walking* also illuminates the death penalty as pitiless retribution—Poncelot undergoes a transformation through his meetings with Sister Prejean but must still be executed. As documentaries, *Into the Abyss* (2011) and *Life and Death Row* (2014–2018) provide excellent discussions of different aspects of the American capital punishment system, including the backgrounds and life experiences of men on death row.

Capital punishment systems produce multiple masculinities and delineate norms of masculine behaviour (Strange, 2003). Strange's (2003) analysis of men sentenced to death for femicide in New South Wales, 1880–1920 reveals those perceived as good husbands, or as mistreated by their wives, were more likely to receive mercy. However, if their actions seemed cold-hearted and calculated, they were likely to hang. Men of colour and 'foreigners' were also less likely to be able to avail themselves of mercy. Intersections of masculinity, race and class were significant to mercy decisions in capital cases in early to mid-twentieth-century England and Wales (Seal & Neale, 2020). Men of colour were frequently judged to be more emotional than white British men and to have a greater propensity for violence. Although this supposedly 'passionate' disposition could be deployed as an argument for mercy, such arguments were rarely successful, and men of colour were more likely than white men to be hanged for intimate murders (Seal & Neale, 2020).

In the United States, Black men make up a heavily disproportionate share of people on death row, and of executions. Black men constitute 41% of death row and have accounted for 34% of executions since 1976 (Death Penalty Information Center, 2021a). Black people make up 14% of the population (Tamir, 2021). *Just Mercy* (2019) is based on lawyer/activist Bryan Stevenson's memoir of the same title and focuses on how he established the Equal Justice Initiative as a young man recently out of Law School, and his fight to help get Walter McMillian, a wrongly convicted Black man, off death row in Alabama. The film contextualises the case in relation to the imbrication of racism and punishment, subtly evoking the spectres of slavery, segregation and lynching.

Case study:

Curtis Flowers was freed from prison in Mississippi in 2020 after being tried six times for the murders of four people at a furniture store in 1996. He was sentenced to death in four of these trials. Two of the verdicts were overturned due to racial bias in jury selection. Flowers's case is discussed in depth in the longform podcast, *In the Dark*, season 2 (2018–2020). Research undertaken for the podcast helped to get the charges against Flowers dropped. Over a period of 26 years, the District Attorney's Office had removed prospective Black jurors at a rate of 4.5 as many times as prospective white jurors (Yesko, 2020).

The racialised nature of the death penalty has historical parallels with lynching, which terrorised Black men and upheld the racial order of white dominance in late nineteenth and early twentieth-century America. Lynching was underpinned by a construction of Black masculinity as hypersexual, out of control and criminally violent, and a threat to white womanhood (Slatton, 2016). Racialised anxieties about the dangerousness of Black men echo in the capital punishment system of the late twentieth and early twenty-first centuries. In subordinating Black masculinity, the death penalty shores up the authority of white masculinity and symbolically reaffirms white supremacy (Howarth, 2002; LaChance, 2016).

In the episode 'Black Museum' (2017) of science fiction anthology series *Black Mirror*, Nish, a young Black woman, takes revenge on the proprietor of a crime-based tourist attraction in which visitors can replay the execution of her father Clayton Leigh by electrocuting his hologram. They can also buy a keyring that contains a bit of his consciousness as a souvenir. The spectacle of a Black man's pain is endlessly consumed for entertainment and vicarious thrills, recalling the postcards of lynching victims that circulated in the American South in the early twentieth-century. Even Leigh's afterlife has been colonised for profit (Bailey, 2020). The death penalty can be understood as the apotheosis of masculine power and authority as it is expressed and exercised through punishment. Although the use of capital punishment around the world has drastically declined in the twenty-first century it retains deep symbolic significance.

Feminist and Queer Abolitionist Futures

Anti-carceral feminism rejects state administered punishment, and criminal justice approaches more widely, as being part of the solution to gender and race oppression. Feminist abolitionism argues that the criminal justice system creates oppression rather than safety or protection. It cannot be relied on to end harms related to crime and violence as institutions such as policing and prisons perpetuate violence (Richie & Martensen, 2020). Richie and Martensen (2020) assert that prisons are not feminist; they do not reflect or achieve feminist principles. The prison system—and the wider criminal justice system—maintains the architecture of racism, which must be torn down to achieve social justice (Richie, 2015). The death penalty, although abolished in many countries and in decline in the United States, is a potent symbol and enactment of state violence, which reproduces and sustains inequalities of race and class in particular (Nagel, 2008).

Anti-carceral feminism originates from Black and women of colour feminisms, both intellectually and in terms of histories of activism (Richie, 2015; Thuma, 2019). Thuma (2019) traces the development of anti-carceral feminism from the resistance work of Black women's organisations in the 1970s. Anti-violence politics entailed critique of state violence, analysis of race, gender, class and sexuality as mutually constructed systems of power and coalition-based organising. Resistance to prisons and violent policing was an essential component of this politics and activism (Thuma, 2019). Feminist abolitionism connects the abolition of prison, policing and surveillance to the abolition of larger systems of oppression, with historical roots in movements for the abolition of slavery and to end colonial domination (Davis, 2003).

Queer abolitionism situates prison abolition as central to trans and queer liberation. Stanley (2015) argues gender is a volatile point of contact between bodies and the enactment of state violence. The prison and wider criminal justice system are produced by and reproduce gender normativity, which harms trans and queer people (Stanley, 2015). Prison is a gendering institution, but it is also, in its attempts to repress and outlaw sex and the expression of sexuality, a queer space (Stanley et al., 2012). Stanley et al. (2012) argue trans and queer people are historical outlaws, who have experienced this repression and outlawing beyond the prison and have nevertheless existed and built communities. Queer abolitionism opposes the violent imposition of racialised gender norms and like anti-carceral feminism sees inequalities of power as foundational to the existence of the criminal justice system (Stanley et al., 2012).

Carlton (2018) highlights that prison abolitionists are often opposed to prison reform as it arguably perpetuates the existence of prisons by making slight improvements to increase their legitimacy. She argues in waging anti-carceral campaigns, it is necessary to move beyond reform and abolition as a binary. The aim of anti-carceral feminism is to undermine the oppression that creates violence and injustice and that shapes patterns of criminalisation and systems of punishment. This larger aim sometimes entails reform work. Carlton (2018) discusses the 1993 'Save Fairlea' campaign in Victoria, Australia as a case study. Plans to close Fairlea, a women's prison, entailed the women being transferred to a high security men's prison, a worse outcome. Women inside the prison staged protests and vigils were held outside. The slogan 'We wish you weren't here but we don't want you to go' encapsulated the sentiment of the campaign. Activists were opposed to imprisonment but did not want imprisoned women to endure a harsher and less conducive regime than they already did.

Feminist and queer abolitionists argue alternatives to prison and to criminal justice approaches include better housing, healthcare, employment and education as well as community-based activist and intervention work. Organisations such as INCITE!, Critical Resistance and the Sylvia Rivera Law Project conceive of abolition as a long-term and wide-ranging political project. Richie (2015) describes prison abolition as an aspiration to work towards rather than something that can be achieved in the short term. Ben-Moshe (2018) addresses the main criticisms levelled at abolitionism: that it is too abstract, that it does not offer solutions and that it is utopian. She argues its utopianism and willingness not to know everything, to be open to the possibility of a different future, are strengths. Imagining a different world is at the heart of anti-carceral feminism and queer abolitionism (Stanley, 2015).

References

Bailey, M. (2020). A radical reckoning: A Black woman's racial revenge in Black Mirror's "Black Museum". *Feminist Media Studies*, 1–14.

Ballinger, A. (2000). *Dead woman walking: Executed women in England and Wales, 1900–55*. Ashgate.

Bandyopadhyay, M. (2006). Competing masculinities in a prison. *Men and Masculinities, 9*(2), 186–203.

Ben-Moshe, L. (2018). Dis-epistemologies of abolition. *Critical Criminology, 26*(3), 341–355.

Black, L. (2018). "On the other hand the accused is a woman…": Women and the death penalty in post-independence Ireland. *Law and History Review, 36*(1), 139–172.

Bosworth, M., Fili, A., & Pickering, S. (2016). Women's immigration detention in Greece: Gender, control and capacity. In M. J. Guia, R. Koulish, & V. Mitsiligas (Eds.),*Immigration detention, risk and human rights* (pp. 157–170). Springer.

Bosworth, M., & Slade, G. (2014). In search of recognition: Gender and staff–detainee relations in a British immigration removal centre. *Punishment & Society, 16*(2), 169–186.

Carlton, B. (2018). Penal reform, anti-carceral feminist campaigns and the politics of change in women's prisons, Victoria, Australia. *Punishment & Society, 20*(3), 283–307.

Crewe, B., Hulley, S., & Wright, S. (2017). The gendered pains of life imprisonment. *The British Journal of Criminology, 57*(6), 1359–1378.

Cornell Centre on the Death Penalty Worldwide (2018). *Judged for more than her crime.* Cornell University.

Davis, A. Y. (2003). *Are prisons obsolete?* Seven Stories Press.

Death Penalty Information Center. (2021a). *Facts about the death penalty.* https://documents.deathpenaltyinfo.org/pdf/FactSheet.pdf. Accessed 20 Sept 2021.

Death Penalty Information Center. (2021b). *Women.* https://deathpenaltyinfo.org/death-row/women. Accessed 20 Sept 2021.

Esposito, F., Matos, R., & Bosworth, M. (2020). Gender, vulnerability and everyday resistance in immigration detention: Women's experiences of confinement in a Portuguese detention facility. *International Journal for Crime, Justice and Social Democracy, 9*(3), 5–20.

Farr, K. A. (2000). Defeminizing and dehumanizing female murderers. *Women & Criminal Justice, 11*(1), 49–66.

Girling, E. (2016). Sites of crossing and death in punishment: The parallel lives, trade-offs and equivalencies of the death penalty and life without parole in the US. *The Howard Journal of Crime and Justice, 55*(3), 345–361.

Golash-Boza, T. (2016). The parallels between mass incarceration and mass deportation: An intersectional analysis of state repression. *Journal of World-Systems Research, 22*(2), 484–509.

Grant, C. (2004). *Crime and punishment in contemporary culture.* Routledge.

Griffiths, M. (2015). "Here, man is nothing!": Gender and policy in an asylum context. *Men and Masculinities, 18*(4), 468–488.

Heberle, R. (1999). Disciplining gender; or, are women getting away with murder? *Signs: Journal of Women in Culture and Society, 24*(4), 1103–1112.

Howarth, J. W. (2002). Executing white masculinities: Learning from Karla Faye Tucker. Wayne Morse center for law and politics symposium: The law and politics of the death penalty: Abolition, moratorium, or reform. *Oregon Law Review, 81*, 183.

Jewkes, Y. (2005). Men behind bars: "Doing" masculinity as an adaptation to imprisonment. *Men and Masculinities, 8*(1), 44–63.

Joo, H.-J.S. (2015). Reluctant heroes and petty tyrants: Reproducing race in the global war on terror in Children of Men and District 9. *Arizona Quarterly: A Journal of American Literature, Culture, and Theory, 71*(2), 61–86.

Kaufman, E. (2014). Gender at the border: Nationalism and the new logic of punishment. *Punishment & Society, 16*(2), 135–151.

Koenig, A., & Reiter, K. (2015). Introduction. In K. Reiter and A. Koenig (Eds.), *Extreme punishment: Comparative studies in detention, incarceration and solitary confinement* (pp. 1–13). Springer.

Kohler-Hausmann, J. (2017). *Getting tough: Welfare and imprisonment in 1970s America*. Princeton University Press.

Kountz, S. (2014). We come in peace: Immigration in post-Cold War science fiction film. *Foundation, 43*(119), 29–40.

LaChance, D. (2016). *Executing freedom: The cultural life of capital punishment in the United States*. University of Chicago Press.

Lempert, L. B. (2016). *Women doing life: Gender, punishment and the struggle for identity*. NYU Press.

Linders, A., & Van Gundy-Yoder, A. (2008). Gall, gallantry, and the gallows: Capital punishment and the social construction of gender, 1840–1920. *Gender & Society, 22*(3), 324–348.

Lugones, M. (2007). Heterosexualism and the colonial/modern gender system. *Hypatia, 22*(1), 186–219.

Matos, R., & Esposito, F. (2019). Women's experiences of border crossing: Gender, mobility and border control. *International Journal of Migration and Border Studies, 5*(4), 371–391.

Nagel, M. (2008). Abolishing the death penalty, abolishing prisons. In T. D. Dickinson, T. A. Becerra, & S. B. C. Lewis (Eds.), *Democracy works* (pp. 79–96). Routledge.

Richie, B. E. (2015). Reimagining the movement to end gender violence: Anti-racism, prison abolition, women of color feminisms, and other radical visions of justice converge reimagining the movement to end gender violence keynote transcript. *University of Miami Race & Social Justice Law Review, 5*, 257.

Richie, B. E., & Martensen, K. M. (2020). Resisting carcerality, embracing abolition: Implications for feminist social work practice. *Affilia, 35*(1), 12–16.

Rivas, L., & Bull, M. (2018). Gender and risk: An empirical examination of the experiences of women held in long-term immigration detention in Australia. *Refugee Survey Quarterly, 37*(3), 307–327.

Rydzewska, J. (2009). Beyond the nation state: 'New Europe' and discourses of British identity in Pawel Pawlikowski's last resort (2000). *Journal of Contemporary European Studies, 17*(1), 91–107.

Seal, L. (2010). *Women, murder and femininity: Gender representations of women who kill*. Palgrave.

Seal, L. (2014). *Capital punishment in twentieth-century Britain: Audience, justice, memory*. Routledge.

Seal, L., & Neale, A. (2020). 'In his passionate way': Emotion, race and gender in cases of partner murder in England and Wales, 1900–39. *The British Journal of Criminology, 60*(4), 811–829.

Slatton, B. C. (2016). The Black box: Constrained maneuvering of Black masculine identity. In B. C. Slatton & K. Spates (Eds.), *Hyper sexual, hyper masculine? Gender, race and sexuality in the identities of contemporary Black men* (pp. 33–44). Routledge.

Stanley, E. A. (2015). Fugitive flesh: Gender self-determination, queer abolition, and trans resistance. In E. A. Stanley & N. Smith (Eds.), *Captive genders: Trans embodiment and the prison industrial complex* (pp. 7–20). AK Press.

Stanley, E. A., Spade, D., & Queer, J. (2012). Queering prison abolition, now? *American Quarterly, 64*(1), 115–127.

Strange, C. (2003). Masculinities, intimate femicide and the death penalty in Australia, 1890–1920. *The British Journal of Criminology, 43*(2), 310–339.

Streib, V. L. (2002). Gendering the death penalty: Countering sex bias in a masculine sanctuary symposium: Addressing capital punishment through statutory reform. *Ohio State Law Journal, 63*, 433.

Tamir, C. (2021). *The growing diversity of Black America*. Pew Research Center. https://www.pewresearch.org/social-trends/2021/03/25/the-growing-divers ity-of-black-america/. Accessed 20 Sept 2021.

Thuma, E. L. (2019). *All our trials: Prisons, policing, and the feminist fight to end violence*. University of Illinois Press.

Turnbull, S. (2017). Immigration detention and punishment. In *Oxford research encyclopedia of criminology and criminal justice*. Oxford University Press.

van Zyl Smit, D., & Appleton, C. (2019). *Life imprisonment: A global human rights analysis*. Harvard University Press.

Vannier, M. (2016). Women serving life without the possibility of parole: The different meanings of death as punishment. *The Howard Journal of Crime and Justice, 55*(3), 328–344.

Vannier, M. (2020). Caught between a rock and a hard place—Human Rights, life imprisonment and gender stereotyping: A critical analysis of Khamtokhu and Aksenchik v. Russia (2017). In W. Sandra, F.-G. Kate, M. JaneMaree, & M. Jude (Eds.), *The Emerald handbook of feminism, criminology and social change* (pp. 271–287). Emerald.

Yesko, P. (2020). It's over: Charges against Curtis Flowers are dropped. *APM Reports*.

Yuval-Davis, N. (1997). Women, citizenship and difference. *Feminist Review, 57*(1), 4–27.

10

Conclusion

This book understands gender as an identity and a social practice and has explored different topics pertaining to gender, crime and justice from this perspective. Organisation by topic enables a thorough examination of the significance of gender to different aspects of crime, criminalisation, victimisation, punishment and justice. From interpersonal violence, to street crime, to corporate crime to imprisonment, analysis of gender is required in order to fully understand these topics. As this book has also argued, a gendered analysis must be intersectional as gender is constructed and shaped by other social categories such as race, class, age and sexuality. This concluding chapter considers what is next for taking forward research on gender, crime and justice.

Moving Beyond the Gender Binary

This book sought to include all genders in the discussion. Femininity and masculinity have not been addressed in separate chapters and do not in any case incorporate all gender identities. Criminological research

© The Author(s), under exclusive license to Springer Nature
Switzerland AG 2022
L. Seal, *Gender, Crime and Justice*,
https://doi.org/10.1007/978-3-030-87488-9_10

on the experiences of trans and non-binary people and of the significance of gender identities beyond the gender binary is growing but remains comparatively rare. In particular, non-binary people and non-binary identities are currently very under-represented in criminological research (Pickles, 2019). Moving beyond the gender binary in criminology is essential in order to comprehend the contemporary meanings and experiences of gender to crime, justice and punishment.

Studies that are about or include trans and gender non-conforming people are concentrated in particular areas, such as intimate violence, hate crime and imprisonment. There is much scope for research that extends to other criminological topics. Looking beyond the gender binary is important in terms of empirical research, but also for adequately theorising gender, crime and justice. Creating, reinforcing and regulating the gender binary is a key aspect of gendered social control and is therefore highly relevant to criminology. The well-established argument from feminist criminology that the absence of gendered analysis in work on crime, justice and punishment means there is only a partial analysis can be applied here. The absence of attention to the significance of the gender binary as a form of control in and of itself and to gender non-conformity means a partial gendered analysis.

The Gendering of Institutions and Systems

The importance of paying attention to how institutions and systems are gendered in their design and operation emerges from this book, as does the need to analyse gendered politics in relation to criminalisation and punishment. The gender binary is again relevant. As discussed in Chapter 8, the division of prisons into separate institutions for women and men is a key example of this. Chapters 7–9 examine how order and control are gendered masculine, which shapes both policing and punishment as institutions. The politics of order and control underpin the politics and practice of policing and punishment. Control and containment reflect a masculinist approach, which deepens with authoritarian strategies of gendered and racialised control.

Understanding gender, crime and justice requires not only researching and theorising gender at the micro and institutional levels, but also at the macro level. Chapter 6 examines the role of masculinised power in state and corporate crimes. As noted in Chapters 8 and 9, many examples of 'grand theorising' in criminology do not incorporate gender into their main arguments. There remains work to be done in order to adequately theorise the role of gendered and racialised hierarchies in the politics of order and control, and the development and operation of systems of policing and punishment. The masculinity of institutions and systems is a fruitful area for further developing the analysis of masculinity in criminology. Criminological research on masculinities is more frequently focused on the construction of masculine identities in relation to crime and punishment, rather than the impact of masculinist politics and economic systems.

Thinking Intersectionally

Intersectional feminism is key to fully comprehending how gender is constructed, understood and experienced. Intersections of gender with race, age and poverty are crucial to the analysis of criminalisation, victimisation and punishment. Chapters 2 and 3 draw on Collins (1998, 2017) to examine how violence binds different systems of hierarchy and domination together, the analysis of which makes power relations visible. Forms of intimate violence are deeply gendered and widely experienced by women and girls across the world, usually from intimate male partners and male relatives. However, gendered subordination is not the only cause of intimate violence and not all women and girls are equally at risk; race, class, dis/ability, citizenship status and gender non-conformity are all significant. Intimate violence takes place in LGBTQ relationships, which can be overlooked if intimate violence is conceptualised only as 'gender-based violence'.

There is a well-developed body of literature on intimate violence from an intersectional perspective. Intersectionality has not been as frequently incorporated into other criminological topics, including in studies specifically about gender. This book has drawn together a diverse range of studies about each topic in order to maintain an intersectional lens but intersectionality must be more thoroughly embedded in criminological analysis. Chapter 6 focused on crimes of the powerful, including corporate crime. This is an area in which there needs to be more gendered analysis and more use of intersectionality to fully assess the effect of different power relations to criminalisation, victimisation and punishment. Similarly, there is potential for more intersectional analyses of gender in relation to green crime to build on existing research from this perspective.

Intersectional analysis can further illuminate the significance of masculinity to criminological topics. Research from the United States emphasises how the figure of the 'dangerous Black man' has been central to perceptions of criminality and threat, and to racialised criminal justice policymaking and practice (Cassidy, 2013). The portrayal of the 'dangerous Black man' is intensely racialised but also heavily gendered. In criminology, the intersections between race and masculinity as they apply to criminalisation, victimisation and punishment require further analysis. Racism must be understood as gendered.

Gender and Decolonising Criminology

In recent years, criminology's bias towards research and theorising from the Global North has been criticised, as have the colonial roots of the discipline (Agozino, 2004; Carrington et al., 2016). From the perspective of Southern Criminology, Carrington et al. (2018) have argued it is essential to analyse the coloniality of gender, as well as differential experiences in local gender orders that are distinct from the gender orders of the Global North. Choak (2020) highlights the amnesia of British feminist criminology regarding colonialism—especially significant given Britain was the pre-eminent late nineteenth and early twentieth-century global colonial power. This book has touched on the coloniality of gender and includes examples of the relevance of gendered colonial legacies, for example in relation to imprisonment (Lugones, 2007). However, more research and theorising about the links between gender, colonialism, crime and punishment is needed in criminology as discipline.

The project of decolonising Northern criminology necessitates a gendered analysis but one that draws on intellectual work, concepts and theories from outside of the Global North (Blagg & Anthony, 2019; Dimou, 2021). This book includes examples of studies on gender and criminological topics from the Global South, but its orientation is within Western feminism and the majority of the research it discusses is from Northern researchers. Future texts that decolonise feminist criminology and focus on gender, crime and justice in the Global South will be indispensable.

Abolitionist Futures?

Debates about carceral feminism—a critical term that defines feminist approaches seeking gender justice through criminal justice, law enforcement or militarised solutions—are a thread running throughout the book and appear in relation to intimate and sexual violence, sex work, policing and punishment. Anti-carceral feminism argues criminal justice measures reinforce hierarchies of domination and systems of violence. They are not a solution to violence because they are in themselves forms of state violence. Chapter 9 discusses feminist and queer abolitionism, which seek to imagine a different world in which social problems are not resolved via recourse to confinement and coercive state power.

The best way to tackle gendered crime and harm is far from a settled question within feminist criminology. Through the lens of intersectional feminism, it is not possible to give wholehearted support for criminal justice and law enforcement interventions as measures well suited to achieving gender justice. People of all genders are harmed by these interventions, but especially racialised, Indigenous, poor, trans and gender non-conforming people. Whether feminist criminology should be abolitionist, advocate for reforming policing and punishment or, as Carlton (2018) suggests, mediate between these two approaches as part of the larger aim of ending gendered and racialised oppression are ongoing debates. Whether and how to work with the state in seeking to secure gender and racial justice is a longstanding and recurrent issue in feminist politics, scholarship and activism. Reflection on this bigger picture of gender, crime and justice must be taken forward in future research and teaching.

References

Agozino, B. (2004). Imperialism, crime and criminology: Towards the decolonisation of criminology. *Crime, Law and Social Change, 41*, 343–358.

Blagg, H., & Anthony, T. (2019). *Decolonising criminology*. Springer.

Carlton, B. (2018). Penal reform, anti-carceral feminist campaigns and the politics of change in women's prisons, Victoria, Australia. *Punishment & Society, 20*, 283–307

Carrington, K., Hogg, R., & Sozzo, M. (2016). Southern criminology. *The British Journal of Criminology, 56*, 1–20.

Carrington, K., Hogg, R., Scott, J., Sozzo, M., & Walters, R. (2018). *Southern Criminology*. Routledge.

Cassidy, L. (2013). *The myth of the dangerous Black man: The scandal of White complicity in US hyper-incarceration*. Springer.

Choak, C. (2020). British criminological amnesia: Making the case for a Black and postcolonial feminist criminology. *Decolonization of Criminology and Justice, 2*, 37–58.

Collins, P. H. (1998). The tie that binds: Race, gender and US violence. *Ethnic and Racial Studies, 21*, 917–938.

Collins, P. H. (2017). On violence, intersectionality and transversal politics. *Ethnic and Racial Studies, 40*, 1460–1473.

Dimou, E. (2021). Decolonizing Southern Criminology: What can the "decolonial option" tell us about challenging the modern/colonial foundations of criminology? *Critical Criminology*.

Lugones, M. (2007). Heterosexualism and the colonial/modern gender system. *Hypatia, 22*, 186–219.

Pickles, J. (2019). LGBT hate crime: Promoting a queer agenda for hate crime scholarship. *Journal of Hate Studies, 15*, 39–61.

Index

© The Editor(s) (if applicable) and The Author(s), under exclusive license to Springer Nature Switzerland AG 2022
L. Seal, *Gender, Crime and Justice*,
https://doi.org/10.1007/978-3-030-87488-9

Printed in Great Britain
by Amazon